DISCARDED

PORTRAITS AND BACKGROUNDS

PORTRAITS AND BACKGROUNDS

By
EVANGELINE WILBOUR BLASHFIELD

HROTSVITHA
APHRA BEHN
AÏSSÉ
ROSALBA CARRIERA

Essay Index Reprint Series

 BOOKS FOR LIBRARIES PRESS
FREEPORT, NEW YORK

Copyright © 1917 by Charles Scribner's Sons

Copyright © renewed 1945 by Grace Blashfield

Reprinted 1971 by arrangement with
Charles Scribner's Sons

INTERNATIONAL STANDARD BOOK NUMBER:
0-8369-2103-8

LIBRARY OF CONGRESS CATALOG CARD NUMBER:
73-134054

PRINTED IN THE UNITED STATES OF AMERICA

CONTENTS

	PAGE
HROTSVITHA	1
I. THE IRON CENTURY	3
II. THE STRONG VOICE OF GANDERSHEIM	8
III. THESPIS IN SANCTUARY	19
IV. BETWEEN TERENCE AND SAINT BENEDICT	35
V. GALLICANUS, AN ESSAY IN HISTORICAL DRAMA	43
VI. DULCITIUS, A FARCE	51
VII. CALLIMACHUS, A "TRIANGLE" PLAY	59
VIII. ABRAHAM AND PAPHNUTIUS, DRAMAS OF SENTIMENT	82
IX. SAPIENTIA, A TRAGEDY	106
X. THEOLOGY DRAMATIZED. THE MUSE AS DOCTOR	110
APHRA BEHN	113
I. THE MOST INGENIOUS ASTREA	115
II. THE EDUCATION OF AN AUTHOR	124
III. FROM GRAY TO GOLD	137
IV. THE ROUT OF COMUS	149
V. A WOMAN ABOUT TOWN	161
VI. A SECRET AGENT	172
VII. GRUB STREET OR PARNASSUS?	185
VIII. MISTRESS OF REVELS	194
IX. THE ROYAL SLAVE	236
X. ON THE SLOPES OF HELICON	259
XI. APHRA'S LAST ACT	272

CONTENTS

	PAGE
Aïssé	285
I. A COUNCIL OF TWO	287
II. A GREEK SLAVE	294
III. A KNIGHT OF MALTA	299
IV. AN IDYL OF THE REGENCY	306
V. AN ILLUMINATION	320
VI. A CONVERSION	358
VII. A RENUNCIATION	373
Rosalba Carriera	381
I. A DUKE'S PERPLEXITIES	383
II. ROSALBA CARRIERA	391
III. A PROCESSION OF PRINCES	404
IV. PARIS SOJOURN	436
V. THE COURT OF MODENA	453
VI. THE COURT OF VIENNA	462
VII. THE COURT OF ROSALBA	469

HROTSVITHA

"*Ame passionnée et esprit supérieur qui croyait imiter Térence et qui annonçait Racine.*"

—Philarète Chasles.

HROTSVITHA

I

"In the tenth century," said Stendhal, "every man wished for two things: first, not to be killed; next, to have a good leathern coat." Such limitation of desires implies hard conditions and a stunted development of the human plant. Difficult as it is to assign degrees to misery, in this aptly named "iron" age, when the first millennial period of Christianity was drawing to a close, mankind appeared to have attained the confines of its capacity for suffering, and to have entered the lowest infernal circle.

In the cell of the recluse, in the prayer of the ascetic, it was even whispered that the year ten hundred would see the annihilation of the globe. Limited as this belief was, and as powerless to influence action as it had been in the past, material causes for a failure of hope were many. The promise of the Church seemed falsified since its triumph; a decade of Christian centuries had almost passed away, and where in this blackest of the dark ages were the fruits of Christ's teaching to be found; the peace on earth, the purity of heart, the charity which is the greatest of all virtues?

4 PORTRAITS AND BACKGROUNDS

In England, harried by the Danish marauders? In the Orient, where Islam, after profaning all the holy places dear to the believer's heart, had become a redoubtable empire? In France, dismembered by the northern sea-thieves? In Spain, where the Infidel was not only master, but schoolmaster as well? In Germany, at bay between Norse pirates and the new terror from the East, the Huns, for so they were still called in affrighted memory of Attila's hordes? It is difficult to realize what potentialities of horror the name implied, for these scarcely human creatures, hissing an unknown tongue, possessing no laws of war, no respect for treaties, whirled over the empire like a cloud of locusts, innumerable, ubiquitous, devouring and exterminating with the ruthless, instinctive destructiveness of the famine-spurred insect. While the Teuton was deliberately preparing and arming for defense, they came, they ravaged, and vanished. "You may sooner catch the wind on the plain or the bird in the air," ran the old German proverb. From the shores of the North Sea to the southernmost point of Calabria, havoc and desolation followed in their trail.

If in this unhappy Europe, cowering under the triple scourge of the Norman, the Saracen, and the Hun, the kingdom of heaven was not to be sought in any material sense, the realm of the Church was not less distracted.

Rome presented a strange spectacle. Fortified churches housing mangonels and catapults; rival

HROTSVITHA 5

vicars of Christ intrenched respectively in Sant' Angelo and Santa Maria Maggiore, hurling stones and lighted tar-barrels against each other's adherents; defeated popes, eyeless, tongueless, noseless, paraded ignominiously through the Roman streets, though they form picturesque material for the historian, were a sorrow and a scandal to the devout. The contemplation of the softer sins of the supreme pontiffs was equally devoid of edification. The evicted head of Christendom appropriating the consecrated vessels and smuggling them off to Constantinople; St. Peter's chair become the couch of dissolute women who bestowed it at their pleasure on their lovers and children; the pope sunk to the position of gentleman-in-waiting to the emperor; successful papal candidates starving, poisoning, and strangling vanquished aspirants to the tiara; such were the sights which afflicted the pious, and added spiritual wretchedness to the evils of war, famine, and disease.

Penitent sinners, panic-stricken by that expectation of the last judgment which was the concomitant of plague and invasion in every century of the middle ages, sought safety by dowering monasteries, and making over their riches to the Church, inscribing the deeds of their donations with the still portentous though oft-repeated words, "the end of the world being at hand" (*appropinquante mundi termino*).

An iron century truly it seemed in which the clash

6 PORTRAITS AND BACKGROUNDS

of steel on steel was almost dulled by lamentations; a barren century, too despairing to create, too wretched to dream, hag-ridden by terror; blind even to the perennial magic of the external world, and seeing in the glories of sunset an awful vision of the avenging archangel furrowing the mantling clouds with blood-stained sword.

Thus it is too succinctly labelled by the student toiling through its grewsome annals. Had it no gentler, brighter side? Were the capacities for happiness and usefulness in the individual sterilized by this atmosphere of apprehension and despair? Art mirrored the surrounding darkness only, but the arts are products of a complicated and gradual evolution; they are deeply rooted in tradition, so dependent on their immediate ancestry that, until they have reached a high degree of technical perfection, they offer but an imperfect image of contemporaneous thought.

It is to literature, which in its simpler forms is merely a development of daily speech, it is to this comparatively familiar vehicle of expression that we turn for a more exact presentation of the temper of the epoch. As an exponent of the world-spirit, letters, the more habitual medium, have always distanced the arts. What message do the rude and scanty literary remains of the tenth century bear to us? A threnody, a prediction of oncoming woe? In Hun-harried Germany, for instance, when the poet-abbot of St. Gall, Ekkehard I, returned to his sacked cloister, desecrated by the heathen enemy, it would be natural to suppose that his poem would be a complaint, an appeal for vengeance, or a narrative of past suffering. On the contrary, his is a song of triumphant struggle, of young joy in life, as he celebrates the loves, the adventures, and the escape from the Huns of Waltharius and Hildgund, king's children sent as hostages to Attila's court.

Nor is this delight in existence imposed by the antique form. Epic in feeling though not in material, the Latin hexameters are wholly informed with the Teutonic spirit, which frequently discomposes the stately, borrowed toga. Here is no cloister-garden sheltered from the storm, but the wind-scourged forests of the young world.

These royal fugitives are high-hearted, meeting peril blithely, and are prudent as well, carrying away a handsome portion of Hunnish loot in their flight. Waltharius is the Northern lover; tender but practical, foreseeing about the commissariat, and almost frigidly respectful to his betrothed. Hildgund is a companion for heroes; intrepid, tranquil, and submissive, with the innocent heart of Gretchen under the broad breast of a walkyr. But where in this spirited, though crude narrative of Titanic fights, and weighty blows alternating with jests as ponderous, is there any stain of fear or gloom? On the contrary, it breathes a boisterous joy and resounds with heroic laughter. So much for one of the strong voices of the century, and for literature as an echo of contemporary feeling. Ekkehard, however, had been a soldier; he may still have felt in his veins the fine glow of the notable victory over the Huns to which he and his fellow-monks nobly contributed. The elation of triumph may have lent him a brief buoyancy of spirit. His work may not be typical, it may even be the exception that throws the prevailing spirit into even stronger relief. The convent may yield us what the monastery denied. The soprano voice is more poignant in lamentation, and the minor key, we are told, is that instinctively employed by women; perhaps the sorrow of the century found utterance through some wailing woman mourning for griefs not her own.

The only feminine voice which was heard above the din was that of a Benedictine nun. If in thought we penetrate to the cell of the poetess Hrotsvitha in the abbey of Gandersheim, do we at last discover the Pythia of the tenth century, the mouthpiece of its misery? No, for this cloistered maiden, with Terence open before her and her Virgil close at hand, is writing comedies for her sister nuns to act.

II

Though she cannot be utilized to buttress a theory, Hrotsvitha is a puzzling phenomenon well worth study. With the perversity of her sex, she flatly

HROTSVITHA

contradicts all our preconceived notions of the period she adorned. A nun of the strict Benedictine order, she sacrificed to Thalia and laid the thyrsus on the altar. A woman of the darkest of the dark ages, she pored over the Pagan poets, and knew her Terence as well as she did Boëthius, or the New Testament. A consecrated virgin, she did not shrink from depicting forceful scenes of passion. A recluse, her work betrays an intimate knowledge of the world and a tone of urbanity which indicates an advanced stage in the evolution of social life.

Her plays were the product of a professionally religious person, writing for a devout public and for pious actresses; they were dramatizations of well-known sacred legends, and they were composed with the avowed moral purpose of luring the nuns from the seductive study of the Latin love-comedies. Yet their spirit is not distinctly ecclesiastical, and nothing is more charming than the timid revelations of personality that the comedies betray; the high breeding of the lady; the woman's tenderness protesting against the sternness of the Law. If she called upon her auditors to repent, it was jubilantly rather than dolefully; if she preached, it was by the edifying example set by her characters, not only by didactic precept; she rarely scourged sinners, but preferred to convert them, and against evil-doers she directed the characteristically modern weapon, ridicule. Far from bewailing the vileness of earth or prophesying future ill, the infinite mercy of God was her constant theme. In an age of pious donations and fear-extorted endowments, she asserted more than once, before an audience of churchmen, that offerings of ill-gotten treasure were unpleasing to the Divinity. In short, an examination of her work (which dates from more than a hundred years before the battle of Hastings) gives the lie direct to the popular conception of the tenth century that had been duly docketed and pushed into a convenient pigeon-hole, marked "barbarous," and tacitly urges the narrower scrutiny of a period which has seemed swathed in darkness and gloom.

We have little knowledge of the life of the playwright who has brought us so near to the life of her time, not even the date of her birth or of her death. It is only from her dedicatory epistles that a few sparse biographical details can be gathered, and these are sufficiently vague to lend countenance to several ingenious theories and consequent controversies.

On her name which she herself in the unique MS. of Munich writes Hrotsvitha, some eighteen changes have been wrung from Seidel's fantastic "Helena of Rossow" to Gottshed's "White Rose." Her work has been confused with that of the English poetess Hilda Heresvida; she has been arbitrarily relegated to the ninth century, and made a contemporary of Pope Joan. It was reserved, however, for modern scholarship to deny her existence. Professor Aschbach, in what seems to the unlearned a playful mood, asserted that there never was any such person as Hrotsvitha; that Conrad Celtes, the Renaissance humanist who discovered her works, had, with the assistance of some twenty learned friends, written them, and had then forged this MS. in the Ratisbon monastery; that the secret, known to so many, had been devoutly kept; that Willibald Pirkheimer had composed his eulogy on the fictive author to help out the hoax; and that this elaborate deception had been planned and executed to justify the correspondence of Celtes with Pirkheimer's sister Caritas, a learned Franciscan nun!

Professor Aschbach's fanciful and ingenious treatise raised a controversial breeze that stirred the dust in many studies. The suggestions, however plausible, were unfortified by a single proof, or any fragment of positive evidence. The author has been contented to present conjecture in place of argument and to trust in his intuitions. He felt "a masculine spirit" in the work, and the style was too elegant, the Latin too good to be the product of a woman of the rustic tenth century. Like much unpondered, destructive criticism, these unsupported assumptions did not lack believers, and how readily a baseless theory is regarded as a proven fact was illustrated by Quérard's naïve acceptance of Aschbach's treatise in the "*Supercheries littéraires.*"

German erudition received it less kindly. Pens were drawn and ink spilt in defense of "*die älteste deutsche Dichterin.*" The consequences of much controversy were the critical scrutiny of the MS., which established its authenticity as a genuine document of the tenth century beyond a doubt; a meticulous examination of its language and style resulted in a general consensus of authorities that Hrotsvitha was a substantial personality that the most rigid inquiry could not dissipate, but on the contrary had solidly confirmed, and that no amount of spectacled research could resolve into air like that charming phantasm, Clotilde de Surville.

It is the authoress herself who supplies us with the rare data from which a faint outline of her biography may be traced. She informs us (with that obscurity of statement which usually envelops similar dates) that she came into the world long after the death of Otho the Illustrious, father of Henry the Fowler (912); and again in the preface to the legends she writes of herself as a little older than the daughter of Henry, Duke of Bavaria, Gerberga II. This Gerberga was consecrated abbess of Gandersheim in 959. As her parents were married in 938 and she was their eldest daughter, her birth may be approximately dated two years later (940). Hrotsvitha, then, was born probably between 930 and 935. The date of her death is more uncertain. She was alive and writing the history of her convent in Latin verse thirty-five

HROTSVITHA 13

years later, and if a chronicler of the bishops of Hildesheim is to be believed, she saw the beginning of the eleventh century.

Of her life in the world there is no record in her works save the inferences to be drawn from her familiarity with the usages of courtly society and her knowledge of the heart. In the province of the emotions, the girl who embraced the religious life at the age of twenty-three had little to learn, perhaps much to remember. Soon after Hrotsvitha entered the convent, Gerberga II became abbess of Gandersheim. This daughter of the Cæsars, who preferred the veil to the imperial crown, was true to the traditions of education which were a heritage from the great Charles, and to which the marriage of the Emperor Otho I with a Greek princess added a tincture of Hellenic culture.

It was under the new abbess's tuition and that of an accomplished nun, Rikkarde, that Hrotsvitha pursued the theological and literary studies which she had already begun in the world. In the religious houses under Benedictine rule a learned brother, the *Scholasticus*, directed the education of the monks; perhaps Rikkarde filled the same office in the community of Gandersheim, which was no refuge for idle women gabbling empty prayers and dreaming away the long, leaden afternoons, but a sanctuary of piety and erudition from its foundation. Its traditions were aristocratic, even imperial, its founder no less a personage than Ludolf, Duke of Saxony, grandnephew of Witikind. The site first chosen for the convent was Brunshausen, but it was soon transferred to the banks of the river Ganda, where the town of Gandersheim grew up around the abbey.

Ludolf did not live to see his work finished, but the gifts and personal supervision of his Frankish wife, Oda, were freely given to the establishment of the new religious house, whither she herself retired in 881, to seek the peace which, in that turbulent age, only the cloister could bestow. Her three daughters, Hathumoda, Gerberga, and Christina, became abbesses of Gandersheim, each in her turn. The period of their sway was a comparatively brief one; monastic life was unfavorable to the longevity of those who entered it in their springtime.

The literary history of the convent dates from the death of Hathumoda (874). It was then the custom at the funerals of illustrious or nobly born persons to recite or even to improvise a dramatic dialogue, in which eulogy was mingled with personal reminiscences of the dead. The *vocero* of the Corsicans, and the moving lamentation of the Coptic wailing women, whose melancholy office is to deepen the sorrow of the mourners, are modern survivals of these mediæval plaints. The abbess's brother Wichbert, Bishop of Hildesheim, who came to bury Hathumoda *and* to praise her, composed the funeral drama, in which, under the name of Agius, he filled the principal rôle. Fraternal love

HROTSVITHA

and tender memories of home and childhood find expression in this poem, which time has spared.

Hrotsvitha, fourth abbess of Gandersheim, succeeded to the last of the three sisters (903). This learned lady has often been mistaken for the more famous playwright of the same name; a pardonable confusion, since the abbess was also an author and continued the literary traditions of the convent. She excelled in rhetoric and logic, and though her treatise on the latter has not yet been discovered, modern criticism has assigned to her the "Lives of St. Willibald and St. Wunnibald." Her most noteworthy performance, though connected with a MS., was not in the realm of letters. By her skill in dialectics she managed to outargue the Devil and wrest from him a pact in which a shortsighted young man had signed away his soul, which incident, while proving the advantages accruing from the study of logic, redounded to the great honor of the abbey.

The convent was secularized in the beginning of the nineteenth century. Of its many buildings the fine Romanesque church alone remains. The rest of the cloister has probably furnished materials for the pretty, picturesque houses that line the narrow streets of Gandersheim, houses in whose walls are set bits of Byzantine and Romanesque ornament: disks, cords, and palms, relics of the heroic age of the sleepy little modern town. But though not a new building is to be seen in the long curve that leads from the convent church to St. George's, there is nothing left of Hrotsvitha's day but these fragments of sculptured stone. The Romanesque abbey-church founded by Ludolf and his Frankish wife Oda (853) is gaunt and bleak; its bare, pale-tinted interior is curiously enlivened by an elaborate eighteenth-century wooden tomb in white and gold of two great ladies who were abbesses here, remote successors of Hathumoda and Gerberga. To become one many quarterings were required, for the abbess of Gandersheim was also a prince, "Fürstäbtin," with the right to a seat in the Diet. Hence the inscriptions, escutcheons, and lists of honors and titles on tombal slabs in memory of these petticoated "prince-abbots" that read like pages from the *Almanach de Gotha*, and form the only decoration of the church walls. Evidently pride had become a cardinal virtue instead of a deadly sin when in an orgy of ostentation crown-bearing and weeping angels, flower-pots, family trees, tilting helmets, coats of arms, inscriptions in medallions, portraits in oval frames, cupids with skull and trumpet, gilded columns wreathed with green leaves were piled up in the boudoir-tomb of the abbesses Maria Elizabeth and her sister Christine. Coming to Gandersheim with the hope of discovering some trace of "the St.-Cyr of the middle ages," Hrotsvitha's convent, and of the learned princesses who ruled over it, and finding in their grim old church this frivolous *Régence* monument was one of the many surprises of travel.

But the gray church towers, the huddle of roofs around them, the dark folds of the wooded foothills of the Harz Mountains, the gentle dip of the valley, the cloister church of Brunshausen among the trees, the forest everywhere encroaching on town and meadow, is to-day much what it was when Hrotsvitha looked out from her convent window at the world she had renounced.

It was, however, more than half a century after the consecration of the abbess Hrotsvitha that her famous namesake began to surpass her teachers, the noble Gerberga and the wise Rikkarde, and to pursue a new method of self-expression. The dedications prefixed to her various works record the successive steps of her ascent of Parnassus. The preface to her first poems, the legends in verse, is the *apologia* of the novice. In the elegiac verses which precede the "History of the Nativity of the Blessed Virgin" she beseeches the divine Mother to loosen her tongue and quotes the example of Balaam's ass to whom God deigned to accord the gift of speech. The well-known modesty of young authors has seldom found a more felicitous comparison. She pleads for the reader's indulgence for her mistakes in prosody and syntax, and entreats you to bear with her, remembering the remoteness of the cloister, the weakness of her sex, and her age, still far from mature. She has no other aim in writing than to prevent the slender portion of genius which heaven bestowed on her from stagnating in her bosom and rusting there through her negligence. She desires "to force it, under the hammer of devotion, to emit a feeble sound in God's praise."

In the "Epistle to Certain Learned Persons," an introduction to the comedies, which followed the legends in verse, the tone is more assured. The writer here addresses a larger circle of erudite and eminent men. "Bowed down like a reed," as she vividly describes herself, her language nevertheless discloses a laudable desire to *remain* humble in the midst of plaudits, rather than the self-distrust and timidity of a tyro. Hrotsvitha has conquered success, she appeals to an enlightened public which supplies her with judicious criticism and stimulating eulogy; she has come into her own, and if in her later poem, the "*Panegyris Oddonum,*" the same tone of elaborate self-depreciation persists, it may be accepted as a convention. In Hrotsvitha's day a woman who handled a pen felt more obliged to apologize for her occupation than she who wielded a sword. In letters she still cowered behind the shield of her sex.

Hrotsvitha's last work, of which the original MS. has disappeared, is a poem, or rather a portion of a poem on the foundation of the convent of

Gandersheim. Both this and the "Panegyric of the Othos" afford precious data to the historian of the middle ages.

III

The comedies are, however, the most noteworthy of her productions. Not only are they the most personal in handling, the most abounding in human interest, but they possess a positive value for the student of manners, are enticingly suggestive to the psychologist, and form a unique document for the historian of the stage—a unique document, although the French humanist, Jean Prot, who prepared the MS. of *"Pamphilus De Amore"* for publication in the fifteenth century, called this anonymous Latin poem a comedy, and although some modern scholars have considered it a work of the tenth century. For as it could not be acted on any stage, even that of a *théâtre libre*, "Pamphilus" cannot be considered a play. The nature of the subject-matter prohibits dramatic representation. "Pamphilus" is also entirely Pagan in form and feeling; its characters—the lover, the maiden, the old woman—are part of the common stock of Greek and Latin poets; they are unbaptized and unregenerate heathen. The poem is a frank imitation of antique models, especially of Ovid's *"Amores,"* and of an idyl doubtfully attributed to Theocritus. Except in language, "Pamphilus" shows no trace of the century to which it has been ascribed.

In the long darkness which extended from the extinction of the classical drama to the rise of the mediæval miracle-play, Hrotsvitha's dramas present a single luminous point. Aided by the light of this spark of the sacred fire, snatched from the altar of Dionysos to illumine a Christian shrine, the new drama is revealed lying in the lap of the old, and the link between the comedy of Terence and the comedy of Shakespeare is recovered. Though it had no immediate following, Hrotsvitha's work is of the new, the modern epoch, for it shows the form the Latin drama assumes in Teutonic hands, and in the service of the new ideal.

It becomes narrative and didactic; it is no longer a comedy of movement and of manners like that of Plautus, nor of situations and poetic declamation like the work of Terence. It seeks to become ethical like the drama of Greece. It only succeeds in drawing morals and defining dogmas, but its *intention* is to teach a lesson. The Northern spirit has brooded over it until the old, light-hearted Latin play, whose mission was to divert and to amuse, turns Puritan, intones canticles, prays, and preaches—preaches always even in the house of Thais. Northern, too, is its jumble of the pathetic and the comic, of the fanciful, the grotesque, and the tragic; Dulcitius's sooty face moves us to mirth even while we fear for the persecuted maidens, and who can refrain from smiling at Julian's ironical application of the text: "Whosoever he be of you who forsaketh not all that he hath, he cannot be my disciple." Even scenes of martyrdom are relieved by touches of heavy-handed Teutonic humor, and a frolic spirit frisks through her dreariest digressions. It is the rough new wine of a younger race, of a more childlike faith, that Hrotsvitha pours into the old amphora, and the shapely vessel is fractured by the stir and ferment of the spirit within.

The narrative, as opposed to the purely dramatic form of the antique drama, was perforce imposed upon Hrotsvitha and the Elizabethan playwrights by the nature of their material. Dramatized legends and tales cannot present the swiftness of movement, the spontaneity of action, the prompt exposition of motive which the play originally conceived as a play possesses. In the acted legend, in the arranged *novella*, there are languors, hiatuses, violations of the unities, suspensions of interest which would try the patience of a Latin audience. Not so the more stolid Teuton or ruminant Anglo-Saxon. He wanted plenty of time, he expected to be edified as well as delighted; he liked to be sermonized. The very completeness of the antique play would have dissatisfied him, for it left his imagination unemployed. He had no love of art for art's sake, of beautiful words and delicate phrasing. He was intent on the thought conveyed by the diction, not on elegance of style. Later under the genial influence of the Pagan renaissance, significance was mated with beauty, but Hrotsvitha and her contemporaries considered art primarily as a vehicle for edification. Therefore she followed the monkish legends quite loyally, using the original dialogue whenever she could and only infringing upon their formal lines occasionally by some tender or delicate touch of feeling, some fiery outburst of passion that vivified and humanized her pious lay figures, either supernaturally holy and pure, or unnaturally vile and base.

It was not only her knowledge of the emotions that saved Hrotsvitha from servile imitation of her models, it was a feeling for essentials; a striving after a general effect that prompted her to select, to abridge, to develop, to concentrate her material as well as to add to it that indescribable quality which the wise Latins assigned to the feminine gender, grace.

The comedies are not liturgic in character; they are not Miracle-Plays or Mysteries. They have nothing in common with the religious drama of the middle ages, with such representations as "The Wise and Foolish Virgins," for instance, which is their contemporary. Compared to the "Massacre of the Innocents" with its chants and processions, Hrotsvitha's plays are secular, worldly affairs. They differ utterly from the performances, part pantomime, part pageant, part oratorio, a kind of religious opera, which were given in the churches at Easter and Christmas. In a word, Hrotsvitha's comedies are, in spite of their archaic subject-matter, comedies of manners. The scenes may be laid in the palace of Diocletian, or in the Nitrian desert, but the *dramatis personæ* are the author's contemporaries; their thoughts are those of Germans of the tenth century, and into them Hrotsvitha has breathed the soul of her age, their speech behind its antique mask is of her time; it is thus that her fellows argued, and preached and pleaded.

The scene between Tartufe and Elmire is not more alien to the spirit of antique comedy on the one hand, or to the form and intention of the "Mystery" on the other, than is the dialogue between Drusiana and Callimachus; the colloquy between Paphnutius and the abbess to whom he confides his penitent is a good example of an exchange of mediæval courtesies; the jargon with which Sapientia bejuggles the long-suffering Hadrian is the vernacular of the schoolmen of the tenth century of whom Paphnutius, when he flits from one proposition to another, like a verbal will-o'-the-wisp before his dazed disciples, is a well-drawn type. The characters are not abstractions, frigid personifications of virtues and vices, like the Fellowship and Good Deeds of "Everyman," but human beings, not subtly differentiated, it is true, but firmly and clearly drawn in the slight outlines furnished by tradition.

Callimachus, Dulcitius, Fortunatus, are the forerunners of the lovers, villains, and traitors of the

Elizabethan drama. Their like does not exist in the comedy of the ancients; we should search in vain for their counterparts among the cheats and rogues of Terence and Plautus. More modern still, further removed from the shy and helpless girls, the Pheleniums and Antiphilas, of the Latin plays, are the dauntless and argumentative maidens of Hrotsvitha. Compare the Mary and Thais of the Christian playwright with Terence's *hetairai*, the kind-hearted and sweet-tempered Chrysis and Bacchis. They are inhabitants of different moral planets. The former have souls to be saved, consciences to be awakened; their Pagan sisters have but soft hearts, inclined to love and pity. Their amiability is instinctive like that of some gentle animal, they are not oppressed by any sense of spiritual degradation; unhaunted by the consciousness of evil-doing, they feel no moral chasm between themselves and the innocent girls they befriend. It is not of such stuff that saints are made. The character of Drusiana shows as clearly the modifications the new faith brought to the old type. Her conception of duty is not more foreign to that of the Roman wife than are the modest evasions with which she repels her would-be lover's advances to the dignified frankness of the matron of antiquity. Slightly sketched as she is, Drusiana is more akin to Clarissa Harlowe than to the Alcmena or the Alcestis of classical drama.

Modern terms applied to Hrotsvitha's plays

possess of course only a relative value, and are perhaps misleading. Her *dramatis personæ* are treated much as the disciples of Giotto painted their figures: in flat tints, simply outlined. She is a "Primitive" artist and yet in writing of her work as in considering the productions of early Italian painters, one uses perforce the vocabulary which has grown out of a knowledge of perfected processes.

The action of the comedies is lively; the scenes change as constantly as on the English stage in the sixteenth century, and the unities are as blithely ignored; twenty years elapse between the second and third acts of "Abraham" for instance. The license of the Romantic drama was attained at one leap by Hrotsvitha who broke the leading strings of classical tradition at once, and in her first play.

The comedies were naturally written in Latin, which was then not only the tongue of the wise, but of the polite; it was the language of courts, ecclesiastical and secular; the slender bridge spanning a dark gulf of barbarism, by which the singer or the scholar attained the luminous, golden realm of old-world poetry and learning. The plays are written in prose because in the tenth century the verse of Terence was considered to be prose, but Hrotsvitha's prose, as Philarète Chasles has pointed out, is rhythmic and balanced, and when read with close attention a constant assonance is discovered in it, which divides the sentences sometimes into

two, again into three, unequal parts. The variety
and vivacity of the dialogue interrupt this regular
cadence, but as soon as the phrases acquire a certain degree of extension, the rhyme obstinately
reappears. This assonance is concealed by the
form of the sentences, but when they are properly
spaced it is obvious enough; for example, in this
citation from "Abraham," rearranged by Chasles:

Abraham

Hei mihi, o bone Jesu! Quid hoc monstri
Est quod hanc, quam tibi sponsam nutrivi,
Alienos amatores audio sequi?

Amicus

Hoc meretricibus antiquitus fuit in more,
Ut alieno delectarentur in amore?

Abraham

Affer mihi sonipedem delicatum
  Et militarem habitum,
Quo deposito tegmine religionis
  Ipsam adeam sub specie amatoris?

Chasles, convinced that Hrotsvitha had perfected for her own use the means of expression,
half classical, half barbarian, which she found ready
to hand, considers her as a precursor of the modern
poet, and Ebert finds in the habitual use of dimin-
utives and a certain caressing sweetness in the verse,
a winning betrayal of the writer's sex.

In any case the plays, whether written in free
verses of all kinds of feet, or in prose, sometimes

sonorous and cadenced, sometimes staccato and tripping, are not wanting in style or in terseness (a rare quality in the middle ages), probably due to loving study of the concise elegance of the seductive poet whom Hrotsvitha hoped to supersede. But though she might say of Terence as Dante did of Virgil:

"*Tu duca, tu maestro, e tu signore,*"

she was moved by the greater master; indeed her convent-garden is fragrant with many grafts from antique groves, and the spiritual spouse of Christ was a child of the Pagan poets as well.

Hrotsvitha did not herself call her dramas comedies. A later hand than hers (Magnan believes it to have been that of Conrad Celtes) wrote "*Prefatio in Comœdias*" over the introduction to the plays in the Munich MS. Readers of the Divine Comedy hardly need to be reminded that the term was an elastic and complicated one in the middle ages, and that it was more often applied to an epic narrative than to a dialogue. "A poetic tale beginning in horrors and ending in joy, and using lowly language, while tragedy commences tranquilly and ends in horror and uses lofty language"; thus Dante defines comedy in a letter to Can Grande.

The unique MS. of Hrotsvitha's works after remaining for centuries in the Benedictine monastery of St. Emmeran, at Ratisbon, was in 1803 brought to Munich and placed in the Royal Library where it still remains. The binding is of undressed brown leather; the ornaments and clasps have been torn from it; probably they were of intrinsic and artistic value, for in Hildesheim Hrotsvitha's bishop, Bernward, himself a painter and metal-worker, had founded a famous school of goldsmiths. The MS. is well written, though undecorated save by rubricated initial letters and small circular ornaments in red and black ink on the margins.

There is no spacing or paragraphing, no division of the plays into scenes, and the speeches of the different characters are indicated by an initial only after the name has been written out once. The titles of the comedies were added in script during the Renaissance at the tops of the pages, which have served as an autograph-album to generations of admirers. Conrad Celtes, whose notes in faded ink are elucidating and erudite, was the first of a series of authors who have marred the MS. with their effusions in prose and verse. Celtes, the poet laureate of Maximilian, was the discoverer of Hrotsvitha's writings (1492–3). He arranged and recommended them for publication to a society of humanists, the *Rheinische Sodalität*, which he had founded. This association was formed with the laudable purpose of demonstrating to an indifferent world, and especially to a sceptical Italy, that Germany was not a country of barbarians; that the seeds of classical culture had flowered there, and that books could be well printed by others than Aldus.

HROTSVITHA

The first edition of Hrotsvitha's works was published in 1501, in Nuremberg, and illustrated with engravings in the manner of Albrecht Dürer. It was probably owing to this spurt of national pride that the plays and poems were received with extravagant eulogies, and their author was styled "the tenth muse" and "the Christian Sappho" by Willibald Pirkheimer. A second edition which was merely a reprint augmented by biographical and philological notes by Schurzfleisch appeared in Wittenberg in 1717. It was not, however, until the middle of the nineteenth century that modern scholarship discovered Hrotsvitha. Since then many savants have added somewhat to the knowledge of the subject, and editions after the MS. have been published, accompanied by valuable commentaries. The bibliography of Hrotsvitha now fills a page. Naturally, German names are most numerous in the list, but Italian, Dutch, and English scholars are also represented, and France has contributed Charles Magnan, whose "*Théâtre de Hrotsvitha*," though published in 1845, has not been superseded. To Magnan's work most writers who have treated the subject subsequently are deeply indebted, and my own obligations to it are numberless.

Although Chasles states that the modern drama received its baptism in the chapter-house of Gandersheim, the question whether the comedies were merely recited or really acted has never been decisively answered. Magnan is convinced that their author had the stage in view while composing the plays. In support of his contention he cites the *didascalia* or directions to actors in the original, which were suppressed in the edition of Celtes; the apostrophes to the auditors which would have been meaningless in works intended for the study only; the compliments to the machinist, that true protagonist of mediæval drama, and the constant appeal to the eye in the arrangement of the scenes. Another consideration which may be urged in support of Magnan's conclusion is that the material of the comedies already existed in narrative form, admirably suited for reading aloud. Hrotsvitha, like all playwrights, "*prenait son bien où elle le trouvait*," and her goods were the legends of the saints which she had so often heard droned from the lectern while she sipped her fast-day soup. The process of turning a novel into a play is one with which we are familiar, and publishers of plays (if one may be permitted a modern instance) have no doubt as to which of the two literary forms proves the more attractive reading-matter. The stories of the saints of the desert, of miraculous conversions of persecuting Pagans, and the martyrdoms of virgin saints were pious *novelle* which cloistered folk, even those under the strict rule of St. Benedict, were allowed to read for edification, and coarse fare was sweetened and long hours of silence were shortened by these romances of the ascetic life. They formed a fund of material which it was as natural for the mediæval poet and painter to draw upon at his need as it was for the Pagan artist to invade the enchanted regions of fable. In a word, Hrotsvitha would hardly recast in a dramatic form for the purpose of having read aloud, tales which she was constantly hearing read.

Many critics have founded their scepticism in regard to the acting quality of the plays on the constant change of scene in them, the nature of the rôles, and the frequent representations of tortures and martyrdoms which they contain. The notion of consecrated maidens mumming as Pagan profligates, as painted courtesans, as Roman emperors, or even as venerable hermits, is a shock to modern sensibilities and a contradiction of our ideas of monastic rigor. The ages of faith were more easygoing. The road to Paradise was not then the bleak, straight path which a prim Reformation traced for the believer's feet; it was a broader avenue picturesquely diversified by "stations" of all kinds. Since the time when St. Ephrem set orthodox verses to the enticingly sweet Gnostic melodies, the Church, wisely deciding not to let the Devil have all the good tunes, had utilized æsthetic aids as bait for souls. The girl novice who tied a beard under her smooth chin, and bent her mild brows in a murderous scowl to personate the villain Fortunatus, or the Apostate Julian, was no more conscious of defying discipline or outraging the proprieties than were the sister nuns of Suor Plautilla Nelli when they equipped themselves in greaves and cuirass, or jerkin and hose to pose as models for the cloistered painter. Women devoted to Christ's service sang, wrote, illuminated missals, embroidered, made music; why should they not act as well? Was it not all for the glory of the faith and the convent? The illustrious names of Theodora and Pelagia were not without influence on the imagination. If one of the noblest reforms accomplished by the Church had been the emancipation of the female mime whom the Roman law had condemned to a life of slavery, the stage in its turn had given one empress and several popular saints to the Church. Why should not the drama, like the Pagan actress, when purified by holy water, become a minister to devotion?

It may be well also to remember that masculine costume had not become succinct and bifurcated in the tenth century. Long tunics almost covered the braccæ; only peasants and soldiers had cast aside the cumbrous grace of flowing robes; nobles and magistrates, as well as ecclesiastics, were gowned to the feet. The young nun who played Callimachus was no Rosalind preoccupied with what was to be done with her doublet and hose.

Nor was the difference between the form of the habit of the daughters of St. Benedict and that of the women of the world marked enough to alarm disciplinarians when the latter was assumed for an hour or two. The secular dress of the tenth century was a jealous guardian of its wearer's beauties. It rose to the throat, swept down to the hands, and covered the feet like the old *tunica talaris* from which it was derived. A mantle, the descendant of the *stola*, hung from the shoulders and was clasped on the breast; a wimple of finest linen was folded about the head and neck and fell like a long scarf over the left arm, and the hair, fastened with jewelled pins, was bound close to the head. Such a dress was austere enough to obtain the approval of the ascetic; it was sufficiently dignified in general lines to be magnificent when composed of costly materials. The MSS. of the tenth century reconstruct pictorially the *dramatis personæ* of Hrotsvitha.

From their own embroidery-frames, from the piled presses in the sacristy, the nuns could borrow the orfrays, and jewelled borders, the gorgeous webs of needlework for the stage emperor's chlamys, or Thais's tunic. The armory would supply an ample store of bright-scaled cuirasses and crested helmets for Gallicanus's soldiers, or the lances and parasol-shaped shields of Diocletian's guards.

Stage-setting was not more onerous than costuming when imagination was scene-painter. The unities were easily defied when by shifting a screen, or changing a tapestry, the docile spectators could be transplanted from court to camp, from camp to grove. A flutter of drapery, like the magic carpet of the "Thousand and One Nights," whirled them in a trice from one region to another. Centuries afterwards, in the Globe Theatre, "the Plaier when hee comes in, must ever begin with telling you where hee is, or else the tale will not be conceived. Now shall you have three Ladies walk to gather flowers and then wee must believe the stage to be a garden. By and by wee hear newes of shipwracke in the same place, then wee are to blame if we accept it not for a rocke; . . . while in the meane time two armies flie in, represented with four swords and bucklers, and then what hard heart will not receive it for a pitched field?" Hrotsvitha's audience, we may be sure, was not more hard-hearted than Jonson's or Marlowe's.

The most elaborate stage-setting is after all only a symbol. It is a convention even in our own realistic age, and we still constrain the spectator to meet the artist half-way. The question is only one of degree. The theatre of the middle ages made larger drafts on the imagination, which were promptly honored. Hrotsvitha's audience, which was required to accept a *bisellium* with its footstool, a bronze screen hung with rich fabrics, and a couple of novices bending under the unaccustomed weight of their armor, for a representation of a Byzantine *palatium* guarded by Pretorians, was no more conscious of a mental effort at pictorial realization than we are when looking at the painted mosaics and the *papier-mâché* sculptures of Sardou's palace of Theodora. The chapter-house audience was a mixed one: a prelate from Hildesheim in a place of honor near the abbess, a knight with his lady, and her women from the neighboring stronghold, perhaps a traveller or two, or a pilgrim with staff and cockle-shell fulfilling a vow, for to such every religious house gave kindly shelter. Seated on the rushes were the humbler folk: the convent serfs, the goose-girl, the shepherds, the grooms, and near the door the men-at-arms, the household troops that were no carpet-knights in lawless times of foreign invasion and parochial aggression.

Enough of paraphernalia and audience, the play is the thing after all, and the author herself speaks the prologue in her preface to the comedies.

IV

"There are many Catholics, and we are not ourselves quite free from reproach in this matter, who, tempted by the elegance of the language, prefer the vanity of the books of the Gentiles to the utility of the Holy Scriptures. There are others still who though attached to holy writ, and filled with scorn for other Pagan productions, frequently read the fictions of Terence and, beguiled by the charms of his diction, defile their souls with the knowledge of evil deeds. Therefore I, the strong voice [a pun on the name of Hrotsvitha] of Gandersheim have not refrained from imitating in my writings a poet that so many others permit themselves to read, in order to celebrate, in the measure of my slight capacity, the laudable chastity of Christian virgins, while employing the same form of composition which the ancients used to depict the shameless license of immodest women. One thing meantime embarrasses me, and often makes me blush, viz., the necessity, in a work of this kind, of employing my mind and my pen in portraying the lamentable madness of hearts given up to illicit love, and the deceitful sweetness of lovers' discourse. Nevertheless, if I had blushingly neglected these subjects, I should not have been able to fulfil my purpose, which was to represent the glorification of the innocent. In truth, the more seductive the sweetness of lovers' words, the more glorious is the triumph of the divine aid, and the greater the merit of those who conquer; above all, when you see the weakness of woman victorious, and the strength of man overcome, and covered with confusion.

"I do not doubt that some persons will object that my imperfect work, far from possessing the beauty and the grandeur of that which I have proposed to imitate, differs from it at all points. So be it. I agree with this criticism and I assert that no one can justly accuse me of trying to compare myself with those sublime geniuses who are so far above me. No, I am not so foolishly proud as to dare to liken myself to even the humblest followers of the ancient authors. I try only, though my capacity does not equal my desire, to use with humble devotion, for the glory of Him who bestowed it, the small portion of genius that His grace has allowed me. In truth I am not so much in love with myself that in order to avoid blame I should abstain from preaching, wherever I have the opportunity, the goodness of Christ, which unceasingly works miracles in the saints. If my pious work pleases I shall be rejoiced; if it delights no one by reason either of my incapacity, or of the faults of my rustic style, I shall still congratulate myself on what I have done; because, while in the other productions of my ignorance I versified heroic legends, here, in presenting a series of dramatic scenes, I have avoided rigorously the pernicious allurements of the Heathen."

To reconcile piety with pleasure, to unite edification to delectation, above all to celebrate the purity and fortitude of Christian saints, to show "the weakness of woman overcoming the strength of man," was the avowed purpose of Hrotsvitha, and we are obliged frequently to remind ourselves of the rectitude of her intentions in considering the situations she described for this praiseworthy end. Both art and ethics demanded an adequate presentation of evil in order that virtue might be properly relieved against a murky background. To cast a brilliant white light on the angel, the fiend should be strongly painted with no sparing of bitumen. The more enticing the lure, the greater the merit of its scorner. Panoplied in righteous intention, assured of the good faith of her auditors, the pious maiden led them into unseemly localities, and more than doubtful company. With the intrepidity of innocence she entered the house of Thais, the tavern of the *leno,* and spoke the language of the rake and the seducer.

But if the situations of her plays are sometimes offensive to propriety, her treatment of them is immaculate. The pure in heart who behold Divinity for that very reason are denied an equally distinct vision of the Devil and his works. They are incapable of visualizing vice. Some forms of evil remain to them words merely, abstract ideas which do not crystallize into images. The child lingers long in the heart of good women; much knowledge of the emotions can coexist in them with an almost cherubic candor, and capacity to seize and express the most delicate shades of sentiment is often unaccompanied by familiarity with the physical realities which are the obscure motors of feeling.

"There is an angel, Valerius, who walks unseen by my side," Hrotsvitha might say with St. Cecilia, for this celestial guardian, evoked by her own innocence of heart, is always with her. If at times he is as invisible to us as he was to Valerius, we may serenely trust that he is never far away. It is the sinner, not the sin, the repentance for evil done, not the representation of the culpable act, which Hrotsvitha invites us to contemplate. The past of Mary and of Thais is but briefly referred to, not lingered over or elaborated. The lawless passion of Callimachus, the brutal gallantry of Dulcitius are but short prologues to the real dramas of conversion and martyrdom which follow them. Vice is sparingly employed as a dramatic motive only, and is inferred rather than described; indeed, the playwright uses it under protest, much as Ruskin did the express-train from London to Oxford, as a means of rapid transit from sin to saintliness.

The legends on which the devout author based her plays were well chosen to display "the weakness of woman overcoming the strength of man." It was natural, almost inevitable that a daughter of the Church should turn to the lives of the saints for inspiration. They reflected the moral sentiment, and guided the imagination of the mediæval world. They were the exponents, under the form which most forcibly appealed to the popular fancy, of the new conception of human excellence which had succeeded to the antique model of virtue. From them the Christian derived the ethical stimulus which the Pagan found in the examples of his heroes and sages. Those who aspired to a devout life found in them patterns of sanctity, and counsels of perfection, a perfection which would be as unappreciated in a modern industrial republic as it would have been undervalued in a Greek oligarchy.

The moral canon varies, not only geographically, but chronologically, and each virtue may be said to have its day. Although the passions and affections are of no time, and have no limited habitat; although an ancient Roman, an Elizabethan, an American loves or hates alike with the same faculties, the same sensory and mental apparatus, the manifestations of these feelings are modified by outside pressure of divers kinds. For what does vary and impart local color to the ethical code of each epoch in history is the degree of approbation or reprehension accorded by public opinion to the different elements of human nature. Each civilization has its moral hierarchy, its special honor for certain virtues, and its special reprobation for certain vices; one age is indulgent to what the next anathematizes, and neglects the moral qualities which previously have been revered.

The amiable type of character which Christianity had elected to cultivate and glorify was more natural to woman than was the heroic ideal which Paganism venerated. The antique religion of virtue labored to ennoble the mind, to elevate the soul, and to harden the heart. It never sought to enter and possess the domain of emotion; it contented itself with striving to rule it from without, and an ethical code which neglected or suppressed the affections repelled tender and ardent souls.

Herein lay the defect of the Stoical philosophy, which sadly limited its potentialities for good. A system of morals which disdained such spiritual forces as love and hope; which bade the weak of will and intellect "be strong"; which distilled no balm for an aching heart; which contented itself with a temperate appeal to reason; which made of pride a vehicle of righteousness; which always addressed itself to the sentiment of human dignity, and which finely ignored compromise—such teaching attracted few female disciples.

Christianity, on the other hand, while it crippled woman socially (by its ascetic depreciation of marriage and domestic life) and fettered her legally (by the withdrawal of the rights which the later Roman law had accorded her), while it regarded her as the temptress of man, "the mother of human ills," had emancipated her spiritually. Religion gave her the citizenship of the city of God; it revealed to her that she had a soul which was her birthright, not something extraneous to be painfully acquired by following vain wisdom, and starving her heart, but a possession for which she was personally responsible to her Saviour who was also her Judge. And the means of saving her soul were within the scope of her natural capacities, for the saintly model of human perfection was more congenial to woman, more easily attained to than the Pagan exemplar had been; hence Christianity has given us a whole heavenful of women saints, while philosophy can show but a meagre array of female sages. Faith, belief in the unseen and the undemonstrated, chastity, humility were as prized by the church as they had been previously undervalued. Even woman's weaknesses were counted as signs of grace; excitable nerves, and "the gift of tears" were admired and envied.

Woman then had finally entered her kingdom. She was even more blessed in finding her King. Christianity had revealed an ideal to her which evoked the deepest tenderness and the most disinterested enthusiasm. No other conception of deity had ever touched the heart as did this incarnation of divine love, and what woman was not a lover of Christ? A new moral career was thus open to feminine capacity and the annals of the young Church witness the ardor with which it was embraced. It is this glorious company of saints, martyrs, and confessors, that Hrotsvitha borrows for her stage. With such material, in such hands, it is easy to predict the moral tone of her drama. The civic virtues, being of Pagan origin, were unpraised and unsung; the domestic virtues, as they arise from carnal ties, were unnoticed, and panegyric was naturally reserved for humility, faith, and obedience. Purity was of course the crown of them all, and pride the unpardonable sin. And yet there are not wanting betrayals of the author's personality, signs of revolt from the monastic code. "Paphnutius" contains an eloquent encomium on learning; there is more than one protest against the greed of the churchmen, and in "Callimachus" the saint, far too indulgent to the converted profligate, would persuade us that "*amor omnia vincit,*" even heaven's grace.

V

It may be assumed in considering the comedies that they were written in the order in which they appear in the MS. " Gallicanus," a relatively halting and patched-up performance, seems to justify the opinion that in it Hrotsvitha first essayed the buskin. The plot is a simple one borrowed from the "Acts of St. John and St. Paul" and an episode in the history of Gandersheim may have determined Hrotsvitha's choice of the *motif* of her maiden play.

Gerberga, daughter of the founders of the convent and wife of Count Bernhard of Saxony, constrained by an inward call to the devout life, left her husband, and fled to the holy retreat where her mother and sister had already found refuge from the cares and sorrows of the world. Bernhard, a rough soldier who did not share his wife's aspirations, and who felt that his claim upon her antedated that of heaven, followed her, and in spite of sanctuary would have possessed himself of what he considered his own again, if a hasty summons to arms had not called him to the head of his troops. Though he was evidently one of those who love honor more, he was sufficiently attached to his runaway wife to swear a solemn oath that at the first opportunity he would return to drag her from the altar. It was therefore to be expected that the hand of Providence would be against him in his campaign, and the news that his unregenerate heart had been pierced by an enemy's lance soon reached the sheepfold of which his widow assumed the pastoral staff.

The play of "Gallicanus" opens with a scene which was more than once enacted in the imperial palace at Constantinople, when a victorious mercenary, at the head of insubordinate troops, demanded a favor of his master which the helpless Emperor was unable to refuse. The hand of the Princess Placidia, sister of the imperial shadow Honorius, was probably sought much in the same fashion in which the general of Constantine asked for that of the Emperor's daughter Constantia before marching against the Scythians. Obliged to consent, Constantine goes to the Princess:

CONSTANTIA: Our lord the Emperor comes to us; he is unwontedly sad. I greatly wonder what he desires.
CONSTANTINE: Come here, Constantia, my daughter. I have a few words to say to you.
CONSTANTIA: Here am I, my lord; speak, what do you wish?
CONSTANTINE: My heart is troubled and I am oppressed by heavy sorrow.
CONSTANTIA: Just now when I saw you coming I noticed your sadness, and without knowing the cause of it, I became perturbed and sorrowful.
CONSTANTINE: It is on your account that I am distressed.
CONSTANTIA: On my account?
CONSTANTINE: On yours.
CONSTANTIA: You frighten me! what is it, my lord?
CONSTANTINE: I feared by telling you to afflict you.
CONSTANTIA: You will afflict me much more if you do not tell me.

CONSTANTINE: Gallicanus the general that a succession of victories has raised to the highest rank among the princes of my court, and whose help is often necessary to us for the defense of our country——
CONSTANTIA: Well, he——
CONSTANTINE: He wishes to marry you.
CONSTANTIA: Me?
CONSTANTINE: You, yourself.
CONSTANTIA: I would rather die.
CONSTANTINE: I knew it.
CONSTANTIA: Nor does it surprise you, for it was with your permission, with your consent, that I vowed my virginity to God.
CONSTANTINE: I remember.
CONSTANTIA: No torture will ever prevent me from keeping my oath inviolate.
CONSTANTINE: You are right, but your resolve plunges me into perplexity. If, as is my duty as a father, I permit you to carry out your resolution, then the republic will suffer, and not a little. If on the other hand, which God forbid (*quod absit*), I deny you your will, I subject myself to eternal tortures.
CONSTANTIA: If I despaired of the divine help, I most of all, I above all, would abandon myself to grief.
CONSTANTINE: True.
CONSTANTIA: But there is no place for sadness in a heart that trusts in the Lord's mercy.
CONSTANTINE: You speak well, my Constantia.
CONSTANTIA: If you deign to follow my advice I will show you a means of escape from this twofold danger.
CONSTANTINE: O, would that you might do so!
CONSTANTIA: Pretend to be willing to gratify the wishes of Gallicanus; and to make him believe that my will accords with yours, persuade him to leave with me, during his absence, his two daughters, Attica and Artemia, as an earnest of the love which will unite us, and on his side let him take with him my almoners, John and Paul.

CONSTANTINE: And what shall I do if he returns victorious?
CONSTANTIA: Before his return we must invoke the Father of All that he may divert the mind of Gallicanus from this design.
CONSTANTINE: O, my daughter, your soft words have so sweetened the bitter grief of your father that I feel no more uneasiness about this matter.
CONSTANTIA: Nor is it necessary.
CONSTANTINE: I go to Gallicanus and I will outwit him by this agreeable promise.
CONSTANTIA: Go in peace, my lord.

The soldier is dough in the hands of the equivocating Emperor. He cheerfully submits to the Princess's conditions; immediately confides his daughters to her, and courteously receives her almoners, "in order," as her father explains, "that he may become more familiar with her habits and character."

The scene of the battle with the Scythians was evidently suggested by the conversion of Constantine. It is more remarkable for vivacity of movement than for realistic illusion:

GALLICANUS: By Jupiter, O Tribunes, I behold the legions of an innumerable host; the different weapons are a horrible sight!
TRIBUNES: By Hercules! Here is the army.
GALLICANUS: Let us resist with courage and fight like men.
TRIBUNES: What is the use of fighting such a multitude?
GALLICANUS: What would you prefer to do?
TRIBUNES: Bow to the yoke.

GALLICANUS: Apollo preserve us!

TRIBUNES: By Pollux it must be done. See we are surrounded on every side, they are wounding us, they are exterminating us.

GALLICANUS: Alas! what will happen if the tribunes spurn my orders and betray us?

JOHN: Make a vow to God to become a Christian and thou shalt conquer.

GALLICANUS: I vow it and I will keep my vow.

THE ENEMY: Alas! King Bradan, fortune which showed us victory is playing with us. See our arms are becoming languid, our strength is growing exhausted, and our faint-heartedness forces us to lay down our arms.

BRADAN: I do not know what to say to you, the same ill that you bear now affects me. Nothing remains but to surrender to the Roman general?

THE ENEMY: Otherwise we shall not escape.

BRADAN: General Gallicanus, do not persist in destroying us, but spare our lives and dispose of us as your slaves.

GALLICANUS: Do not fear, do not tremble; give me hostages, acknowledge yourselves as subjects of the Emperor, and live happy in the peace of Rome.

BRADAN: You have only to settle the number and rank of the hostages as well as the weight of the tribute that you require.

GALLICANUS: Soldiers, lay down your arms, do not wound, do not kill any one; embrace as allies those whom we were fighting as enemies.

JOHN: How much more efficacious is a prayer than all human presumption.

GALLICANUS: True.

JOHN: What effective aid the divine mercy accords to him who recommends himself to God with humble devotion.

GALLICANUS: I perceive it clearly.

JOHN: But the vow man makes in peril must be kept when he is again in safety.

GALLICANUS: Yes, truly. Therefore I desire to be baptized as soon as possible, and to consecrate the rest of my life to God's service.

JOHN: That is but right.

Gallicanus returns in triumph to Rome, becomes a Christian in St. Peter's Church, and offering his love as an oblation to his divine Deliverer, he voluntarily renounces the hand of Constantia. Constantine, who has maintained a prudent reserve until quite assured of the general's change of heart, then confesses that not only Constantia but the two daughters of Gallicanus as well have taken a vow of chastity. This good news rejoices the lover and father, and accompanied by the Emperor he enters the Princess's apartment, where he announces his conversion to the overjoyed Princess, his desire to become the companion of the holy Hilarion, and after disposing of all his possessions to spend the rest of his life in praising God and succoring the poor.

The delighted Constantia replies:

May the Friend of virgin modesty, and the inspiration of all good resolutions; may He who made you renounce your evil design, and who has reserved me for Himself, deign as a recompense of our bodily separation to unite us some day in the joys of eternity.

GALLICANUS: So be it.

. . . .

CONSTANTINE: May the unique Being who is all powerful, permit you to accomplish your designs and to live according to His will. May He bring you to eternal

HROTSVITHA 49

felicity who reigns, and is glorified in the unity of the Trinity.

GALLICANUS: Amen.

So the comedy ends not with a marriage but with a renunciation of wedlock.

The second part of "Gallicanus" might be more appropriately entitled "The Martyrdom of John and Paul." An interval of twenty-five years separates its action from the first portion of the play. Magnan has observed that in the "*Acta Sanctorum*," which Hrotsvitha reverently followed, the two narratives were connected, and in the church celebrations they are divided only by the interval of a day. In the second part of the piece, the Saints, who were merely missionaries and teachers, become martyrs by the order of Julian the Apostate, and Gallicanus also dies for the faith. The two plays were therefore loosely bound together like the "Henry IV" and "Henry V" of Shakespeare.

In this second part the Emperor Julian the Apostate, nephew of the good Constantine, has the prominent rôle. This very honest and disinterested, though bungling and unintelligent, restorer of the old order, is (for the age) a well-drawn character. He is not a bloodthirsty despot, or a subtle fiend, but a learned fanatic, who has determined to reestablish the worship of the gods, and who at the same time is scrupulous in the choice of his agents, preferring mildness to violence, and desirous of retaining at his court the best among the Christians.

In the first scene, after ascribing the evils that assail the empire to the liberty of worship enjoyed since the time of Constantine, and the consequent ire of the neglected deities, he orders the soldiers to "take arms and despoil the Christians of their goods," meanwhile quoting to them the maxim of Jesus Christ, who said: "Whosoever he be of you who forsaketh not all that he hath, he cannot be my disciple."

The soldiers return to tell him that Gallicanus left his "castle" for Alexandria, where he has perished by the sword, but John and Paul still brave the new edict and distribute the riches of Constantia to the poor. Seized and dragged before the Emperor they refuse his offers of friendship, of a place in the palace, insult him, and after having been allowed ten days in which to reconsider their words, are carried off to prison.

In the scenes which follow, John and Paul suffer martyrdom, and the bodies are secretly buried, but the son of Terentianus, their judge, becomes possessed by a demon, and declares that his torments are caused by their prayers. This prodigy naturally effects the instant conversion of Terentianus; his baptism, and adoration of the holy martyrs restore his son to health and reason, and a troop of Christians arrive in time to announce that Julian has fallen a victim to the divine wrath. Thus all ends happily with the consecrated "Amen," the formula which in the religious plays of the middle ages succeeded to the "*Plaudite*" of Pagan comedies.

VI

In "Dulcitius" Hrotsvitha followed the legend less piously than in her first essay. The tragedy of the three holy virgins who suffered martyrdom under Diocletian (A. D. 290) is preceded by a farce: the grotesque misadventures of the love-smitten Dulcitius. The comic element which is kept in abeyance in the "*Acta Sanctorum*" is here exploited with zest, and with a keen appreciation of its mirth-provoking potentialities. In the three sisters, Hrotsvitha further developed the new idea of woman which she had palely foreshadowed in Constantia.

The first scene shows the usual examination of the Christians familiar to all readers of the "Lives of the Saints." The Emperor himself is grand inquisitor; it would diminish the importance of the martyrs to have this preliminary interrogation take place before any lesser dignitary.

Diocletian, touched by the youth and friendlessness of the girls, tries to propitiate them by compliments, offers of positions at court, and brilliant marriages:

DIOCLETIAN, AGAPE, CHIONE, IRENE, GUARDS

DIOCLETIAN: The distinction of your family, your high birth, the brilliancy of your beauty, lay on you the obligation to become united by the nuptial bond to the highest officials in my palace. My power will not be used against you if you will deny Christ and sacrifice to our gods.

AGAPE: You can spare yourself these cares, nor need you fatigue yourself with preparations for our weddings, for nothing could compel us to deny the name which we ought to confess, nor to soil our maiden purity.

DIOCLETIAN: Agape, what madness moves you?

AGAPE: What sign of madness do you find in me?

DIOCLETIAN: A considerable sign.

AGAPE: What one?

DIOCLETIAN: First, you renounce the observance of our ancient religion and follow the vain novelties of Christian superstition.

AGAPE: You calumniate the majesty of omnipotent God. It is dangerous.

DIOCLETIAN: For whom?

AGAPE: For you, and the republic you rule.

DIOCLETIAN: This girl raves. Take her away.

CHIONE: My sister does not rave; she justly blames your stupidity.

DIOCLETIAN: This second mænad is more violent than the first. Remove her also from my presence and let us question the third.

IRENE: You will find the third equally insubordinate and recalcitrant to your orders.

DIOCLETIAN: Irene, though thou art the least in age, become the first in dignity.

IRENE: Show me then how to become so.

DIOCLETIAN: Bow your head before the gods, and be for your sisters an example that will correct them and liberate them.

IRENE: Let those who wish to incur the anger of the Most High corrupt themselves by sacrificing to idols. I will not dishonor the head that has received the unction of the heavenly King by bowing it before vain semblances.

DIOCLETIAN: The worship of the gods, far from bringing shame, greatly honors those who practise it.

IRENE: Is there more shameful vileness, is there greater turpitude, than to give to slaves the homage one owes to masters?

DIOCLETIAN: I do not persuade you to honor slaves, but the gods of lords and princes.

IRENE: Is he not the slave of the first comer, the god that a workman sells like a piece of merchandise for a trifling sum?

DIOCLETIAN: Let tortures put an end to this presumptuous verbiage.

IRENE: Our wish, our most ardent desire, is to suffer torments for the love of Christ.

DIOCLETIAN: Load these obstinate women who resist our edicts, with chains, and confine them in a foul prison, where they will be questioned by the governor Dulcitius.

SCENE II

DULCITIUS, AGAPE, CHIONE, IRENE, *and* GUARDS

DULCITIUS: Soldiers, lead your prisoners this way.

GUARDS: Here are those you asked for.

DULCITIUS: Gods! What beautiful, what charming, what remarkable girls!

GUARDS: They are perfectly beautiful.

DULCITIUS: I am captivated by their charms.

GUARDS: That is easily believed.

DULCITIUS: I burn to persuade them to share my feelings.

GUARDS: It will be most difficult for you to prevail upon them to do so.

DULCITIUS: Why?

GUARDS: Because their faith is unshaken.

DULCITIUS: But if I persuade them by my blandishments?

GUARDS: They will despise them.

DULCITIUS: And if I terrify them with tortures?

GUARDS: They will scorn them.

DULCITIUS: What's to be done, then?

GUARDS: That is your affair.

DULCITIUS: Shut them up in the back kitchen next to the room where the cooking utensils are kept.
GUARDS: *Why* in that place?
DULCITIUS: So that I can visit them more frequently.
GUARDS: At your commands.

The next scene shows the intrepid Dulcitius attempting the triple seduction of all the sisters at once:

SCENE IV

AGAPE, CHIONE, IRENE

AGAPE: What is that noise at the outer door?
IRENE: It is the miserable Dulcitius coming in.
CHIONE: God protect us.
AGAPE: Amen.
CHIONE: What means this sound of pots and pans and kettles knocking together?
IRENE: You'll see. Come here, please, look through the cracks of the door.
AGAPE: What is it?
IRENE: See, this maniac has lost his reason; he thinks he is embracing us.
AGAPE: What is he doing?
IRENE: Now he tenderly presses the pots to his bosom; again he hugs the kettles and the frying-pans, and gives them loving kisses.
CHIONE: How ridiculous!
IRENE: Already his face, his hands, his clothing are so dirty and black that he looks exactly like an Ethiopian.
AGAPE: It is right that his body should appear as black as his possessed soul.
IRENE: Look, he is going away. Let us see what the soldiers who are waiting for him at the door will do when he goes out.

SCENE V

DULCITIUS, *the* GUARDS

GUARDS: Who is this demoniac, or rather this demon who is coming out? Let us fly.

DULCITIUS: Soldiers, whither are you fleeing? Stop, wait, attend me to my house with your torches.

GUARDS: It is the voice of our master, but it is the form of the devil. Do not stop, let us hurry our flight; this phantom desires to damn us.

DULCITIUS: I will hasten to the palace, to tell the Princes how I have been insulted.

SCENE VI

DULCITIUS, *the* PALACE GUARDS

DULCITIUS: Guards, let me enter the palace, I have a word for the Emperor's private ear.

PALACE GUARDS: What is this frightful and disgusting monster, covered with torn and blackened rags? Pound him and throw him down-stairs; he must not go in any further.

DULCITIUS: Woe, woe is me! What has happened? Am I not dressed in my richest clothes? Is not my person daintily neat? And nevertheless every one I speak to shows as much disgust at the sight of me as he would at the appearance of a horrible monster. I am going back to my wife. I will learn from her what has happened to me. But here she is; she runs to me with disordered hair, and all our household follow her in tears.

SCENE VII

DULCITIUS, *the wife of* DULCITIUS, *the* GUARDS

WIFE: Alas! Alas! my lord, from what evil are you suffering? You are distraught, Dulcitius. And you have become a laughing-stock to the Christians.

DULCITIUS: Now I understand it; I have been the plaything of their spells.

WIFE: What amazed me the most, what saddened me the most, was that you did not know that you were ill.

DULCITIUS: (*To the* GUARDS.) I order these girls to be exposed in the public square. Let their clothes be torn from them, that they may know in their turn what outrages we can inflict on them.

SCENE VIII

DULCITIUS *asleep in his tribunal, the* GUARDS

GUARDS: We tire ourselves in vain; our efforts are useless; the vesture of these maidens adheres to their bodies like their skin, and now our governor Dulcitius, himself, who pressed us to disrobe them, has gone to sleep, snores in his chair, and nothing can awaken him. Let us go to the Emperor and tell him what is happening here.

Here the farce ends, and is followed by the "passion" of the three sisters, for Diocletian, undismayed by the madness which fell upon Dulcitius, sends Sisinnius to replace him. Agape and Chione persist in their refusal to sacrifice, and are thrown into flames which play harmlessly about them. Finally, in answer to their prayers, death gently delivers them. Irene is then sent for that the sight of their dead bodies may terrify her into submission, but she, too, is avid of martyrdom. Threats of torture, of ignominy even, do not daunt her. "It is better that the body should be soiled by infamous treatment than that the soul should be stained by the worship of idols," she tells Sisinnius. "One is pronounced guilty only of the sins to which the will has consented," she says, as the guards carry her away to a shameful place. But "He whose providence governs the world" finds means to save her. Sisinnius's soldiers soon return to tell him the girl has been led to the top of a neighboring mountain by the two youths, "grave of aspect," "clothed in shining garments," whom he (Sisinnius) sent after them. Mystified and enraged, the baffled persecutor calls for his horse, and hurries off in pursuit of Irene and her celestial deliverers.

The following scene shows Sisinnius riding around the mountain, unable to advance or turn back, while Irene taunts him from its summit. The guards also are under a spell, and are oppressed with insurmountable lassitude.

SISINNIUS: Let one of my soldiers draw his bow, shoot an arrow, and transpierce this hateful witch.
IRENE: Blush, unhappy Sisinnius, blush, to find yourself shamefully vanquished, to have been unable to triumph save by force and arms over a weak little maiden.
SISINNIUS: I resign myself without much regret to such shame because I am sure that you are dying.
IRENE: It is for me a most great cause of rejoicing, and it should be a sorrow to you; for on account of your cruelty you will be damned in Tartarus [!], but I, on the contrary, shall receive the martyr's palm and the crown of virginity, and shall ascend the celestial throne of the Eternal King, to whom be honor and glory, world without end.

This is no feast for those who love delicacies. Purity is now a virtue so universally taken for granted, that there is something almost grotesque in the laudation of it. These holy maidens would be more abounding in it were they more reverently handled. From the Platonist Hypatia, Hrotsvitha might have learned that true modesty is not merely abstention from certain acts and thoughts; it is not restrained to conduct, it is an attitude of the soul which informs the whole personality, and emanates from it like an exquisite aroma. The nun's ideal is a more primitive one; her women guard their honor as a miser does his treasure, as a soldier does a magazine, quite as consciously and militantly. They lack sweetness, too, a still graver defect; one could wish them less bumptious before the conciliatory Emperor, more lamb-like with their persecutors. The same fault, lack of human interest, which removes the sufferings of the saints from the sphere of our sympathies, is found here. These girls are literally puppets in God's hand, they do not really live or suffer. One cry of sisterly tenderness, one touch of maidenly fear would melt this frigid perfection into warm life.

And yet it should be remembered that they stood in the presence of death, and that for them the torturer was the porter of Paradise; they were under the dominion of a fixed idea, uplifted by a transcendent enthusiasm. They were heroines in the true sense of the word; woman heroes called upon to endure; to put by all the softness and sweetness of life, committed to an unremitting exercise of the will. Their most potent appeal is in action. And these poor children singing in the darkness to sustain their courage, or peeping and laughing at Dulcitius's antics, do not entirely lack pathos or charm.

VII

If in "Gallicanus" Hrotsvitha sketched a model of heroic comedy, and in "Dulcitius" she essayed the farce, "Callimachus" is the prototype of the romantic love-drama. It is not a love-comedy like "The Andrian" or a love-tragedy like the "Hippolytus," but the forerunner of "Romeo and Juliet," to which it bears a curious resemblance. "Callimachus" also contains the germ of the modern novel, the struggle between sentiment and duty, the inner conflict between passion and honor. The hard-worked but ever vital *motif* of psychological fiction is suggestively indicated in this play, in which the triad of "Society" romances: the ardent and undisciplined lover, the unloved but noble husband, and the grievously tried but irreproachable wife make their début. Two other indispensable figures of the modern drama as well: the family friend (Friar Laurence, "*L'ami des Femmes,*" or the heavy father), the *deus ex machina* who reconciles, explains, saves, and the villain, who is born wicked and follows evil for the love of it, are also introduced for the first time in "Callimachus."

The *donnée* of the play was an entirely novel one, with which antiquity with all its combinations and deft handling of situations was unfamiliar. Love lawless, unbridled, meeting in its object a resistance as powerful as itself, and that resistance based on a sense of duty, not duty to another man, nor to a noble house, nor to an honorable name, but to an ideal of conduct, was a new thing which would have puzzled the auditors of Terence. Drusiana had no elder sisters in antiquity; she has many younger ones among the heroines of the Protestant Reformation.

The action of the play is in the past; the scene in Ephesus; the time, the first century. The Apocrypha, to which Hrotsvitha was already so deeply indebted, furnished the romantic legend, but the ideas and language are her own. It is perhaps stimulating to conjecture that the young nun whose saints and martyrs leave us cold, should in a succinct but forceful delineation of blind, delirious passion find the human touch which enforces conviction even when it does not evoke sympathy. For "Callimachus" is not only the most intense in feeling, it is perhaps, as an inevitable consequence, the most poetic in expression, of the plays. As it is also the most finished in form, and animated in movement, I have omitted a few lines only in translating it.

SCENE I

CALLIMACHUS *and his* FRIENDS

CALLIMACHUS: My friends, I should like to say a few words to you.

FRIENDS: Count on our conversation according to your pleasure.

CALLIMACHUS: I should prefer, if the proposition be not displeasing to you, to seek a shelter from the importunate.

FRIENDS: We are ready to do what is most comfortable for you.

CALLIMACHUS: Let us go to some more secret place, in order that no one may interrupt what I shall say.

FRIENDS: As you will.

SCENE II

CALLIMACHUS, *the* FRIENDS

CALLIMACHUS: For some time I have borne a deep grief that your counsels, I hope, will alleviate.

FRIENDS: It is right that a community of sympathy should cause all to feel what fortune brings of good or evil to each one of us.

CALLIMACHUS: O, would that you could share my suffering in pitying it.

FRIENDS: Tell us what thing afflicts you, and if it requires pity we will pity you; otherwise, we will make every effort to distract your mind from gloomy preoccupations.

CALLIMACHUS: I love.

FRIENDS: What?

CALLIMACHUS: A beautiful thing, a graceful thing.

FRIENDS: These attributes pertain neither to a single order of objects nor to all the objects of the same order. Hence we do not know from your answer what the particular being is which you love.

CALLIMACHUS: Woman.

FRIENDS: To say woman is to include them all.

CALLIMACHUS: Not all of them in general, but one in particular.

FRIENDS: What one says of a subject can only be understood of a definite subject. If then you wish us to know its attributes, first define the substance.

CALLIMACHUS: Drusiana.

FRIENDS: The wife of Prince Andronicus?

CALLIMACHUS: Herself.

FRIENDS: You rave, friend; she has been purified by baptism.

CALLIMACHUS: I care not for that if I can draw her on to love me.

FRIENDS: You cannot.

CALLIMACHUS: Why do you distrust me?

FRIENDS: Because you are seeking a difficult thing.

CALLIMACHUS: Am I the first who has sought such a thing, and do not many examples encourage me to dare it?

FRIENDS: Listen, brother; she for whom you burn follows the teaching of the Apostle St. John; for some time she has devoted herself entirely to God, so that nothing can recall her to the couch of her husband Andronicus, a zealous Christian; therefore still less will she consent to satisfy your vain wishes.

CALLIMACHUS: I asked consolation of you, and you inflict despair on me.

FRIENDS: He who dissembles deceives, and he who proffers flattery sells the truth.

CALLIMACHUS: Since you refuse me your aid, I shall seek Drusiana, and by my blandishments I will incline her heart to my love.

SCENE III

CALLIMACHUS, DRUSIANA

CALLIMACHUS: It is to you I speak, Drusiana, to you, my heart's love.

DRUSIANA: I ask with surprise, Callimachus, what you desire of me in speaking to me thus?

CALLIMACHUS: You are surprised?

DRUSIANA: Indeed.

CALLIMACHUS: First I would speak of my love.

DRUSIANA: What do you mean by your love?

CALLIMACHUS: I mean that I love you more than aught else.

DRUSIANA: What are the close bonds of blood, what are the ties formed by the law that move you to love me?

CALLIMACHUS: Your beauty.

DRUSIANA: My beauty?

CALLIMACHUS: Yes, assuredly.

DRUSIANA: What relation is there between my beauty and you?

CALLIMACHUS: Alas! there has been but little until to-day, but now I hope that there soon will be.

DRUSIANA: Go, go, vile procurer! I am ashamed to exchange words with you any longer, you who I feel are full of fiendish deceit.

CALLIMACHUS: My Drusiana, do not repulse a man who loves you, whose whole heart clings to you, but respond to his love.

DRUSIANA: Your beguiling words do not affect me, your loose desire disgusts me, and I utterly despise you.

CALLIMACHUS: Until now I have not yielded to anger because I thought that you blush to confess the delight that my tenderness arouses in you.

DRUSIANA: It excites in me nothing but indignation.

CALLIMACHUS: I believe that these sentiments will soon change.

DRUSIANA: Most certainly shall I not change.

CALLIMACHUS: Perhaps.

DRUSIANA: O, madman, frantic lover! Why do you deceive yourself? Why do you delude yourself with an empty hope? What reason, what insane fancy leads you to think that I will yield to your folly—I, who for so long have lived apart from my lawful husband?

CALLIMACHUS: I call gods and men to witness, Drusiana, if you do not yield, I shall never cease nor desist until I have entrapped you and made you captive.

SCENE IV

DRUSIANA, ANDRONICUS

DRUSIANA: (*Believing herself alone.*) Alas! Lord Jesus Christ! what availed it for me to have made a vow of chastity, since in spite of it my beauty has allured this madman. Lord, witness my fear, behold the pain I suffer. I know not what I ought to do. If I denounce the audacity of Callimachus, I shall cause civil discord; if I keep silence, I cannot, without thy aid, escape his diabolical machinations. Grant me rather, O, Christ, a speedy death in thee than that I should occasion the ruin of this young voluptuary. (*She dies.*)

ANDRONICUS: Ill-starred man that I am! Drusiana has just died suddenly. I fly to call St. John.

SCENE V

ANDRONICUS, JOHN

JOHN: Why do you sorrow so deeply, Andronicus? Why do your tears flow?

ANDRONICUS: Alas! Alas! my lord, my life has become tedious to me.

JOHN: From what do you suffer?

ANDRONICUS: Drusiana, your pupil——

JOHN: Has she left her human shell?

ANDRONICUS: Ah me, yes.

JOHN: It is most unfitting to shed tears at the death of those whose souls we believe to be enjoying heavenly repose.

ANDRONICUS: Though I do not doubt that her soul, as you assure me, is tasting eternal joys, and that her body, inaccessible to corruption, will rise again, nevertheless I am filled with sorrow that she herself, before me, should have called upon death to take her.

JOHN: Do you know her motive?

ANDRONICUS: I know it, and I will inform you of it when I am sufficiently recovered from my grief.

JOHN: Let us go and celebrate her obsequies worthily.

ANDRONICUS: There is near here a marble tomb in which we will place her body. To Fortunatus, one of our servants, I will confide the care of the sepulchre.

SCENE VI

CALLIMACHUS, FORTUNATUS

CALLIMACHUS: What will happen, Fortunatus, since even the death of Drusiana cannot deliver me from love?

FORTUNATUS: You are indeed miserable.

CALLIMACHUS: I perish unless your wit comes to my aid.

FORTUNATUS: How can I help you?

CALLIMACHUS: By letting me see her, even though she is dead.

FORTUNATUS: Her body, I think, is still intact because she was not consumed by a long illness, but carried off, as you know, by a short attack of fever.

CALLIMACHUS: How happy would I be if I could prove the truth of your words.

FORTUNATUS: If you will pay me handsomely I will show you her body.

CALLIMACHUS: Take first all that I have in hand, and be certain that you shall receive much more from me afterwards.

FORTUNATUS: Let us go.

CALLIMACHUS: It is not I who will linger.

SCENE VII

FORTUNATUS, CALLIMACHUS, DRUSIANA, *lying in her grave*

FORTUNATUS: Here is her body (*raising the winding-sheet*). Her face is not livid, her limbs are not wasted.

CALLIMACHUS: O, Drusiana! what heartfelt affection I devoted to you. How sincerely, from the very depths of my being, I loved you. (*He lifts her out of the coffin.*) And you always repulsed me, you always denied my wishes. . . . (*A great snake appears and glides towards them.*)

FORTUNATUS: O, O, a horrible serpent is rushing upon us.

CALLIMACHUS: Woe is me! Fortunatus, why did you tempt me? Why did you persuade me to commit this detestable sacrilege? See, you die by the serpent's bite, and I, through fear, expire with you!

SCENE VIII

JOHN, ANDRONICUS, *later* GOD

JOHN: Andronicus, let us go to the tomb of Drusiana, that by our prayers we may recommend her soul to Christ.

ANDRONICUS: It well becomes your holiness not to forget her who trusted in you. (GOD *appears.*)

JOHN: Behold the invisible God appears to us in a visible form under the semblance of a most beautiful youth.

ANDRONICUS: (*To the spectators.*) Tremble.

JOHN: Lord Jesus, why have you deigned to show yourself to your servants in this place?

GOD: It is for the resurrection of Drusiana and of that young man lying near her tomb that I appear to you, in order that my name may be glorified in them. (GOD *vanishes.*)

ANDRONICUS: With what swiftness He ascended to heaven.

JOHN: I do not quite comprehend the cause of all this.
ANDRONICUS: Let us hasten our steps; perhaps on our arrival we shall find the explanation of what you say you do not understand.

SCENE IX

JOHN, ANDRONICUS, *the three corpses of* DRUSIANA, FORTUNATUS, *and* CALLIMACHUS

JOHN: In the name of Christ, what miracle do I see here? Behold, the tomb is open, the body of Drusiana has been thrown out of its grave; beside it lie two bodies enlaced in the folds of a serpent.

ANDRONICUS: I divine what it means. During his life Callimachus loved Drusiana unlawfully. The affliction which it caused her threw her into a fever and she called upon death to take her.

JOHN: The love of chastity impelled her to this.

ANDRONICUS: After the death of her whom he loved, this madman, suffering at once from love and regret that he had been unable to commit the misdeed he contemplated, consumed his heart while he burned with still greater desire to look on her again.

JOHN: Miserable man!

ANDRONICUS: I have no doubt that he bribed this dishonest servant to furnish him an opportunity to do so.

JOHN: O, unexampled villainy!

ANDRONICUS: Thus both of them, I see, have been stricken by death.

JOHN: Nor is it an unjust punishment.

ANDRONICUS: What is most surprising in all this is that the voice of God announced the resurrection of him whose will was guilty rather than that of the man who was only an accomplice. It is perhaps because one enticed by the love of the flesh sinned ignorantly, while the other transgressed through love of evil only. . . . But now, blessed John, do what you were bidden to do.

Resuscitate Callimachus in order that we may untie this knot.

JOHN: I think that I should first invoke the name of Christ to banish the serpent, then I will resuscitate Callimachus.

ANDRONICUS: You are right; thus he will not be wounded anew by the serpent's bite.

JOHN: (*To the serpent.*) Away, away, cruel beast; henceforth he will serve Christ.

ANDRONICUS: Although the animal is without reason, at least its ear is not deaf; it heard your command.

JOHN: It obeyed not my power, but Christ's.

ANDRONICUS: It disappeared swifter than a word.

JOHN: Infinite God, whom no space can contain, being at once simple and incomprehensible, who alone art what thou art, who, uniting two dissimilar substances, hast from one and the other created man, and who, disuniting these two principles, hast separated that which formed one, command the vital breath to re-enter this body, that the sundered union may be re-established, and Callimachus may come to life, man as he was before, that thou mayst be glorified in thy creatures, thou who alone canst perform such miracles.

ANDRONICUS: Amen. Behold Callimachus breathes the vital air, but a stupor still benumbs him.

JOHN: Callimachus, rise in Christ's name. Whatever you have done, confess it; to whatever guilty temptations you have yielded, confess them, so that the truth may not be concealed from us.

(CALLIMACHUS *tells* JOHN *of his bribery of* FORTUNATUS, *the desecration of the grave, the apparition of the serpent, and continues:*)

CALLIMACHUS: There appeared to me a young man of terrible aspect. He covered the body reverently; from his radiant face beams of light shone upon the sepulchre, and at the same time a voice was heard saying: "Callimachus, die that thou mayst live." Having heard these words, I expired.

JOHN: An operation of celestial grace which does not delight in the perdition of the impious!

CALLIMACHUS: You have heard of my wretched fall. Deign to delay not in applying the remedy of your mercy.

JOHN: I will not delay.

CALLIMACHUS: For I am utterly confounded and contrite from the depths of my heart. I am troubled, I groan, I grieve over the dreadful sacrilege.

JOHN: Not without cause; so grave an offense requires the remedy of a heavy penance.

CALLIMACHUS: O, would that I could open to you the deepest recesses of my heart; you would see in them the bitterness of the grief that I endure and you would pity my sufferings.

JOHN: I rejoice in this suffering, for I feel that sorrow is salutary to you.

CALLIMACHUS: My past life disgusts me; guilty joys sicken me.

JOHN: Not wrongly.

CALLIMACHUS: I repent the sin I committed.

JOHN: Wisely.

CALLIMACHUS: I have so much distaste for what I have done that I cannot feel the love or pleasure of life if, through being reborn in Jesus Christ, I do not deserve to become better.

JOHN: I do not doubt that supernal grace will manifest itself in you.

CALLIMACHUS: Do not linger then, do not delay to raise up my soul, to lessen my sadness by your consolations, so that, aided by your counsels and by your guidance, from a gentile I shall become a Christian, from a libertine I shall become chaste, and that, having entered the true path under your leadership, I shall live according to the precepts of the divine law.

JOHN: Blessed be the only Son of God, who deigned to share our weakness and whose clemency, O, my son Callimachus, killed you, and in killing you gave you life.

Blessed be he who by this semblance of death has delivered his creature from the death of the soul. . . .

ANDRONICUS: And I, holy John. Do not delay to console me, for the conjugal love which I bear to Drusiana will not leave my soul in peace until I have seen her speedily resurrected also.

JOHN: Drusiana, arise in the Lord Jesus Christ.

DRUSIANA: Glory and honor to thee, O, Christ, who makest me to live again.

CALLIMACHUS: Thanks be rendered to him who saved you, O, my Drusiana, to him who accorded you a rebirth in joy, you who passed your last day in sorrow.

DRUSIANA: O, my venerable father, it would become your sanctity, if, after resuscitating Callimachus, who loved me with a sinful love, you should resuscitate also the slave who surrendered my dead body to him.

CALLIMACHUS: Apostle of Christ, do not believe that it is worthy of you to deliver from the bonds of death this betrayer, this evil-doer, who allured me, who seduced me, who tempted me to dare this impious desecration.

JOHN: You should not envy him the pardon of the divine mercy.

CALLIMACHUS: No, he who was the cause of his neighbor's fall is not worthy of resurrection.

JOHN: The law of our religion teaches us that man should forgive the trespasses of his fellow man if he wishes God to remit his own.

ANDRONICUS: That is just. . . .

CALLIMACHUS: Your remonstrances terrify me.

JOHN: Nevertheless, in order that I may not appear to deny your wishes, this man will not be resuscitated by me, but by Drusiana, who has the power, received from God.

DRUSIANA: Divine substance, who alone art immaterial and without form, thou who hast created and modelled man in thy image and who hast breathed into thy creature the breath of life, permit the material body of Fortunatus to recover its warmth and to become a living being, in order that our triple resuscitation may redound to thy praise, venerable Trinity.

JOHN: Amen!

DRUSIANA: Awake, Fortunatus, and by Christ's command break the fetters of death.

FORTUNATUS: Who takes my hand and raises me up? Whose voice bade me live again?

JOHN: Drusiana's.

FORTUNATUS: Is it Drusiana who resuscitated me?

JOHN: She herself.

FORTUNATUS: Did she not yield to a sudden death a few days ago?

JOHN: Yes, but she lives in Jesus Christ.

FORTUNATUS: And why has Callimachus this grave and modest air? Why does he not show his furious passion for Drusiana as usual?

JOHN: Because, renouncing his evil intention, he is transformed into a true disciple of Christ.

FORTUNATUS: No?

JOHN: It is so.

FORTUNATUS: Well, if, as you assure me, Drusiana resuscitated me and Callimachus believes in Christ, I reject life and freely choose death; for I had rather not live than continually see in them such an abundance of grace and virtue.

JOHN: O, amazing envy of the Fiend; O, malice of the serpent, who made our ancestors taste death and who is always lamenting over the glory of the just. This unhappy Fortunatus, completely filled with the bitterness of diabolical gall, resembles an evil tree that brings forth only bitter fruits. Let him then be cut off from the assembly of the just and cast out from the company of those who love the Lord; let him be thrown into the fire of eternal torture, to be tormented there without a single interval of coolness.

ANDRONICUS: Behold the serpent's bites are swelling; he turns again towards death; he dies more swiftly than I can speak.

JOHN: Let him who through hatred of others' happiness refused to live, die and become one of the inhabitants of hell.

ANDRONICUS: This is terrible.

JOHN: Nothing is more terrible than an envious man; no one is more wicked than a proud man.

ANDRONICUS: Both of them are wretched.

JOHN: One and the same man is always a prey to these two vices, because they always go together.

ANDRONICUS: Explain yourself more clearly.

JOHN: Yes, the proud man is envious, and the envious man is proud, because a mind gnawed by envy cannot bear to hear praise of another, and, desiring to abase those who surpass him in virtues, disdains to be placed below the most deserving and endeavors haughtily to be considered above his equals.

ANDRONICUS: Evidently.

JOHN: Thus the wretched man is cut to the heart and cannot bear the humiliation of recognizing that he is inferior to those in whom he sees the divine grace shining more brightly.

ANDRONICUS: I now, at last, understand why God did not count Fortunatus among those who would be recalled to life. It was because he was to die almost immediately.

JOHN: He deserved this double death, first for having desecrated a tomb that was confided to him, and then for pursuing with his hatred those who returned to life.

ANDRONICUS: The unhappy man has ceased to live.

JOHN: Let us retire and let the Fiend take back his son. We meantime will celebrate the wonderful conversion of Callimachus and this double resurrection. Let us pass the day joyfully, giving thanks to God, the equitable Judge, the penetrating Searcher of hearts, who, having subtly examined all things, and disposing of all things as is befitting, will justly distribute punishments and rewards to every man according to his deserts. To him alone honor, virtue, strength and victory; to him alone praise and rejoicing forever and ever. Amen.

HROTSVITHA 73

The opening scene of "Callimachus," as Cohn ("Shakespeare in Germany") has observed, offers a curious analogy to the dialogue of Romeo and Benvolio ("Romeo and Juliet," Act I, Scene I), wherein the pining lover piles *concetti* on *concetti*, paradox on paradox, and so obscures significance with a rapid succession of images as to cause wonder, not at his lady's disdain, but at his friend's patience. Callimachus's attempt at dialectical subtlety, his pedantic references to the doctrine of Universals, were no doubt characteristic of an exquisite of the tenth century. Every epoch possesses its own form of affectation in speech. What Euphuism was to the Elizabethan courtier, what Phébus was to the *habitués* of the Hôtel Rambouillet, the jargon of the schoolmen was to a man of fashion of the reign of the Othos.

Preciosity generally implies a limited area of culture in an ambient atmosphere of crudity, if not of barbarism. It is the refuge of a rather finical cultivation from ignorance, the defense of the esthete against the philistine. The shibboleth of scholasticism was the hall-mark of a polite education, above all of an ecclesiastical education; it pleased an audience of churchmen as Mercutio's and Jacques's fanciful discourse delighted an audience that loved poetry.

Nor does Callimachus abuse his metaphysics; he soon speaks "plain and to the purpose" and replies directly enough to the Job's comforters, the *amici*, who occupy the usual critical attitude of friends in council.

The scene which follows reads like a page from an eighteenth-century novel, and one might write Evelina or Pamela in place of Drusiana. The impudent young rake, and the innocent prude, who at first modestly opposes his reckless declaration with the pretext of misunderstanding it, and when its meaning becomes too gross to be blinked, repels him with an outburst of indignation, suggest a background in Bath or Tunbridge Wells. Callimachus, like Richardson's Lovelace, seems more the hunter than the lover; animated as much by the pride of conquest as by the hunger for possession, his passion when denied is instantly transformed into a desire to dominate, to impose his will on one who has presumed to resist him. Drusiana like Clarissa is fettered by her principles. She will not become a stumbling-block to Callimachus's spiritual welfare; she will not stir up discord by seeking protection from him; she dare not confide in her director St. John, she fears her headstrong suitor's revenge if she denounces him to Andronicus. She seems very helpless at first, enmeshed in the net of her own scruples. Her excessive anxiety to avoid disturbing the peace reminds one of Clarissa's perplexities. Nor is Drusiana, like Corneille's Pauline, armed against her heart; she finds no inner defense against a resolute lover.

"Whom can she trust who cannot trust herself?" Did she doubt her capacity for prolonged resistance to such ardent pleading? It would seem so since she asks no lesser refuge than death. Her weakness seeks asylum in the divine strength, and not in vain. According to the legend she is stricken with fever and dies within three days; the play naturally demanded swifter action and the miraculous nature of the celestial interference was made more manifest by her sudden death *en scène*.

Pagan plays had occasionally employed the proverbial *deus ex machina* to justify or deliver an innocent and persecuted heroine. It is Jove himself who vindicates Alcmena in "*Amphytrion*," and in the "*Aulularia*" the domestic Lar to reward the piety of Phædra provides her with a dowry and a husband. But in Pagan comedy no god had appeared to save the honor of his votaress, and the bashful, tongue-tied maids of Plautus and Terence are the mute victims of selfish and wilful boys. Helpless as flowers are they gathered and trodden under foot. Whence came the new force which sustained Irene and Drusiana? From the mental habit of regarding every act as a step towards heaven or hell. From a fixed faith in the paternity of God; belief in immortal justice as ever living and ever present, as a stronghold and a sanctuary. Drusiana calls on death naturally and confidingly because she is convinced with Rousseau's

Julie that "*qui s'endort dans le sein d'un père n'est pas en souci du réveil.*"

In Fortunatus the complaisant and venal slave or parasite of antique comedy became the modern villain, loving wickedness not as a means to an end, but platonically for itself. Tranio and Pseudolus cheat and lie and steal quite as often for their masters as for themselves, and were generally employed as were the Scapins and Mascarilles of Molière, to do the dirty work of their betters. The poor Latin scamps with their shifts and tricks, their dolorous jests about crosses and stripes, are distinctly human and excite pity rather than reprehension. They are pliant tools fashioned by the slave system, and are not responsible for their diverting misdeeds. Fortunatus on the contrary is a freeman; he possesses a will and a purpose, and elects to do evil. The motive for his hatred of virtue is obscure, like that of Iago; his delight in wrong-doing is not apish but devilish; he is not the mischief-maker but the villain; like "the Fiend his father," he delights in the fall of sinners, and dies of spite surely, for his own venom must have rendered him immune to the serpent's bite, at beholding the felicity of those he has tempted and injured.

The apparition of Christ under the form of a beautiful adolescent proves Hrotsvitha nearer the art of Byzantium than that of the middle ages, and that the repulsive notion of the ugliness of Jesus was not yet prevalent among the devout. Memories of the youthful Saviour on early Christian sarcophagi, of the beardless Lord of the mosaics, doubtless lingered long among the cultured who imported their art and learning from Constantinople, the Athens of the early middle ages. Descents and ascensions of celestial beings, and angel-freighted clouds, complicated mechanism of all sorts were commonplaces of mediæval stage-craft; the robust imagination of the spectators suffered no shock at the sight of the windlass which raised or lowered these supernal visions, and the master machinist probably found no more difficulty in managing the serpent than the modern electrician does in manœuvring Fafner.

To the serpent's victim, Callimachus, Hrotsvitha and her editors have shown a rather inexplicable indulgence. This hot-blooded and impetuous suitor becomes such a craven when in peril, such a sneak as a penitent, and such an egotist as a convert that those who hail in him the prototype of the modern lover, "the exponent of a sentiment unknown to antiquity," regard him, as well as an important branch of classical literature, with curiously partial eyes. Hrotsvitha follows the pious legend in showing far greater compassion for the sins of the flesh than for those of the spirit. The lover who erred through excess of passion is pardoned and saved, the unfaithful servant who transgressed through avarice is damned; but Fortunatus is not only avaricious, he is malevolent as well, a tempter of his fellow-man, acting the fiend's part, and is punished for his general perversity rather than for any particular offense. Indulgence towards the misdeeds that sprang from an illicit attachment foreshadows the sentiment of the later middle ages as crystallized in the decrees of the courts of love. Perhaps the reason of this clemency to the frailty of the heart may be sought in the nature of Christianity itself. A faith that had discovered and exploited the realm of emotion which Pagan ethics and religion had ignored and neglected, possessed far more hold on a man of strong feelings than on one of a colder constitution or a more calculating disposition. The capacity for loving, for complete surrender of self to the inrush of a great emotion was a rare gift of temperament, which grace often transmuted into a desire for things heavenly. Those who loved much had taken the first step on the path of abnegation. The belief that a force which expands the bonds of egotism possesses an element of the divine may be traced all through the middle ages in sharp opposition to the standard of asceticism. That Hrotsvitha was affected by this unformulated conviction is not surprising; what is personal in her delineation of a desperate, unhappy love is the language she lends to Callimachus; fiery words of impassioned tenderness, agonized cries from a flaming heart which bear the unmistakable accent of sincerity, and read like a self-betrayal. ("*Drusiana, præcordialis amor."* "*O Drusiana, Drusiana, quo affectu cordis te colui, qua sinceritate delectionis te viscera tenus amplexatus fui!*")

It is unfortunate that in portraying a lover Hrotsvitha did not follow Terence more closely. Even if she found no model for Callimachus in those suave and urbane pages, she might have borrowed her master's stylus to describe "the deceitful sweetness of lovers' converse," for Terence's young gentlemen, though they occasionally behave like ruffians, speak like poets and dreamers. Something of the tenderness of the "*Hecyra*," the devotion of the "*Andria*," or the passion of the "*Heautontimorumenos*" would have lent charm to "Callimachus," and increased sympathy for Drusiana. Moreover, Terence's undisciplined, often brutal, lovers are willing, nay, most desirous to suffer the consequences of their misdeeds. They assume the sole responsibility of their acts. The whole action of the play is generally dependent on a wrong done some unprotected girl, and the effort to repair it. If these Pagans love without reverence they love warmly and faithfully; if they lack delicacy they are rich in affection; if it is through faith and humility and the immolation of self that passion proves its divine right to dominion over the soul, the Antiphilas and Pamphiluses of the Latin poet need no further justification. Their standard of probity in love matters is far higher than that of many of Shakespeare's gentlemen. The dower-hunting Bassanio and Petruchio, the base Bertram, the heartless Claudio, the treacherous Proteus would have failed to win from Terence's audience the applause and sympathy which the Renaissance public accorded them.

In the Roman's code man as the stronger animal, the active agent, the more highly developed being, was solely responsible in such infractions of social law as rise from aberrations of the affections. Young girls were mere chattels, inert dolls, passive in the grasp of strong hands. And yet from a study of the fates and fortunes of these meek maidens Hrotsvitha might have learned that there is more than one way of "overcoming the strength of man," even of enlisting that strength in the willing service of weakness. "Yielding I conquer" might have been the device of the poor girls who through submission and unwavering faith in the men they loved acquired a certain pathos and dignity. They are but silhouettes; we know nothing of them save their love and their sorrows, and yet they appeal more potently to our sympathies than do the polemical and invincible heroines of the Christian playwright.

Naturally in making such comparisons one discounts the immense difference between a delicate and polished work of art and the half-barbarous, pedantic production of a tyro; Hrotsvitha is struggling awkwardly to express a new ideal in an unfamiliar medium; Terence is handling with consummate ease and skill a rich heritage of fixed types of character and of conventional situations.

The sudden conversion, the change of heart which was one of the moral phenomena of Christianity was an invaluable though often abused factor in the production of dramatic situations, and the disentangling of an involved plot. Penitence, grace, redemption have afforded fresh material to the playwright. The Pagan stage and novel had already exploited supernatural intervention in human affairs but in a strictly material sense. The Greek romancers leaned heavily on supernal interference and aid, in the action and *dénouement* of their stories. Eros, Pan, and the Nymphs guarded Daphnis and Chloe; Artemis counselled and justified Leucippe, and Isis rescued her erring votary after a series of stirring adventures. The Pagan miracle was external; it had no effect on character; it did not imply (save in the case of Lucius in the "Golden Ass") the moral regeneration of the person saved, or benefited by it; the Christian miracle, on the other hand (at least before it was employed mechanically and trivially), signified either the conversion or the sanctification of its object, and the beneficiary was spiritually enriched, or delivered. The divine optimism of Christianity was nowhere more beautifully manifested than in this attitude of constant expectation of the operation of grace, this implied salvation of the apparently lost and abandoned.

The study of modern problems; the evolution of

character; the long, stumbling ascent to higher moral levels; the uncertain conquest over temperament and inclination, which form the elements of the present psychological drama, are with difficulty adapted to the requirements of the stage; but the spiritual drama of the past, the inner illumination, the sudden, marvellous efflorescence of the soul were admirably fitted for theatrical representation. Shakespeare's most idyllic comedy would have ended less blithely without the repentance of the usurping Frederick and the conversion of Oliver. It is only the gradual invasion of the world of fancy by the scientific spirit which has finally relegated the sudden reformation of the wicked to the rubbish heap of cast-off dramatic devices.

VIII

In no other play is the inherent quality of optimism as admirably demonstrated as in "Abraham." The material is simple enough, derived from the "Acts of Abraham and Mary" ascribed to St. Ephraim the Hermit and Deacon who lived at Edessa in the fourth century. Other authorities attribute it to an Ephraim who was the contemporary of St. Abraham, and who is one of the characters in the play. In any case the best text of this charming tale is found to-day in Rosweyde's "*Vitæ Patrum.*"

Mary, the orphaned niece and ward of Abraham, a pious recluse, is persuaded by him to renounce the world and become a hermit at the age of eight. After twenty ascetic years of solitude in the desert Mary escaped from her cell and fled with a vicious priest to a neighboring town. Soon abandoned by her lover, in despair she became a courtesan. Abraham, when he learns of her flight, goes like a good shepherd to seek and save this strayed lamb. He finally finds Mary in an inn at Assos, disguises himself in the slouched hat and military cloak of a soldier and visits her there. After supper, when the host has left them, Abraham throws off his disguise, and Mary, overcome with shame and terror, falls at his feet. His prayers and exhortations persuade her to renounce her evil life, and to return to her deserted cell. The reformation of lost women by Christian enthusiasts who assumed the dress and manners of libertines in order to gain access to them, formed a vivid episode in the lives of several saints: Serapion, Vitalius, and Paphnutius, but Hrotsvitha's treatment of such spiritual conquest far surpasses in pathos and tenderness all similar scenes. In it human love and the sacred tie of blood are factors equal in force to the divine compassion of the sinless for the sinning. The gentle pleading of a loving kinsman moves the erring girl more than the terrors of the law. The thought of Abraham's broken vows —broken for her—of his patient, weary quest; of the self-effacing affection which had drawn the saintly old man over many leagues of desert, and into the vilest company, bows her before him in an agony of remorse and tenderness. Abraham is no Roman father, jealous of the family honor; he does not hint at the exercise of authority; even his reproaches are full of love; he addresses himself to the heart of his niece; nor does the ascetic's horror of carnal frailty cause him to shrink from her, or to fail in kindly offices. By his tender pleading he vanquishes her shame, her remorse, her despair. To the penitent he is no longer the head of her house, or her spiritual director, he becomes an incarnation of redeeming love in its most winning form: that of the good shepherd. Touched by the human affection that has sought her out to save her, her faith in the divine love for the repentant sinner is quickened. This extremely delicate situation is rendered with exquisite tact by Hrotsvitha. The past sinfulness of Mary is an obscure prologue, her return to virtue is the motive proffered for contemplation. In more recent literature, Erasmus in his "Colloquies," and the Elizabethan poet and dramatist Dekker, have exploited the same motive, exhibiting far less moral delicacy in their manipulation of it, adding, indeed, a touch of cynicism, a Rabelaisian suggestion, which contrast unfavorably with the nun's maidenly reticence. Charles Reade, in "The Cloister and the Hearth," borrowed this episode, with never a word of thanks to Sister Hrotsvitha.

In Scene II of "Abraham" Mary accepts lightheartedly the grim fate that Abraham has chosen for her, forgetting, like Fra Lippo's Aunt Lapaccia, that

> "You should not take a fellow eight years old
> And make him swear to never kiss the girls."

ABRAHAM: O, my adopted daughter! O, part of my soul! Mary, yield to my paternal advice, and to the salutary counsels of my companion Ephraim; try to imitate by your chastity the patroness of virginity whom you already resemble in name.

EPHRAIM: It is not fitting, my daughter, that you, who by the mystery of your name, are raised above the world near Mary, the mother of God, in the midst of the fixed stars, should remain inferior in virtue among the meanest characters of the earth.

MARY: I do not know the mystery of my name, therefore I cannot understand the meaning of the circumlocutions which you use.

EPHRAIM: Mary means star of the sea, around which the world turns and the peoples are called.

MARY: Why do they call her star of the sea?

EPHRAIM: Because it never sets and always lights the way to seafarers.

MARY: And how can it be that I, such a weak creature, formed of clay, can attain to the merit which illumines the mystery of my name?

EPHRAIM: You can do so by a virginal purity of body, and a complete holiness of spirit.

MARY: It is a great honor for a mortal being to equal the splendors of the stars.

EPHRAIM: Yes, if you remain virginal and undefiled you will become the equal of the angels of God. When you shall have cast off your coarse, corporal envelope, surrounded by their cohort floating through the air, soaring through the clouds, traversing the whole circle of the zodiac, you will not stop until you reach the arms of the Virgin's Son, on his mother's radiant throne.

MARY: Whoever is incapable of appreciating such joy lives like an ass, therefore I despise earthly happiness and I give myself up in order to be worthy to enjoy such consummate felicity.

EPHRAIM: In truth we find in the heart of this child an old man's maturity of mind.

ABRAHAM: It is to divine grace that she owes it.

EPHRAIM: One cannot deny it.

ABRAHAM: But though she is guided by grace, nevertheless it is not fitting that, at so tender an age, she should be left to her own will.

EPHRAIM: That is true.

ABRAHAM: Near my hermitage I will build her a cell with a narrow door, through the window of which I will repeat to her, during my frequent visits, the psalms and the other parts of the divine law.

EPHRAIM: Well said.

MARY: Ephraim, my father, I submit to your guidance.

EPHRAIM: May the heavenly bridegroom, to whose love you have devoted yourself in your tender age, protect you, my daughter, against all the snares of the Evil One.

In Scene V Abraham in disguise has arrived at the tavern where Mary, now a notorious courtesan, is living.

ABRAHAM: Health, mine host.

HOST: Who salutes me? *Salve*, my guest.

ABRAHAM: Have you a place for a traveller who wishes to spend the night at your house?

HOST: Yes, of course, no one is denied at our humble hostelry.

ABRAHAM: I owe you much for this gracious welcome, but I have a greater service to ask of you.

HOST: Demand what you desire, and you will surely obtain it.

ABRAHAM: Accept this trifling gift which I offer you and so arrange matters that the very beautiful girl who I know lives here shall be at our table.

HOST: Why do you wish to see her?

ABRAHAM: Because I wish to enjoy the acquaintance of this woman whose beauty I have so often heard praised.

HOST: Those who vaunt her charms lie not, for by the loveliness of her countenance she eclipses all other women.

ABRAHAM: Hence I am consumed with love for her.

HOST: I am astounded that you, old and decrepit as you are, can sigh for a young woman.

ABRAHAM: It is most true that I came here only to see her.

HOST: Come forward, Mary, and show your beauty to this neophyte.

MARY: Here I am.

ABRAHAM: (*Aside.*) With what constancy, with what firmness of mind must I not arm myself when I see, with the painted face of a courtesan, her whom I reared in the solitude of my hermitage. But it is not yet time that my countenance should reveal what is passing in my heart. I restrain, like a man, the tears that are ready to burst forth, and I will hide with a feigned gayety the deep bitterness of my grief.

HOST: Fortunate Mary, rejoice, for not only the young men of your own age, as is natural, but old men as well seek you in crowds to show their love for you.

MARY: Those who love me receive from me an equal love in return.

ABRAHAM: Come here, Mary, and kiss me.

MARY: Not only will I give you sweet kisses, but I will even gently clasp your aged neck in my arms.

ABRAHAM: By all means.

MARY: What do I smell? What is the strange scent that I inhale? This fragrance recalls that of my former abstinence.

ABRAHAM: (*Aside.*) Now must I dissemble, now must I frolic like a boy, for fear my gravity may betray me and shame may compel her to leave me.

MARY: Woe to me, unhappy one! From what have I fallen away, and into what an abyss of perdition am I plunged.

ABRAHAM: This place where a crowd of merrymakers assemble is not a fit one for lamentations.

HOST: Lady Mary, why do you sigh? Why do you shed tears? Have not you lived here for two years and have I ever heard you complain? Never before have your words been as sad as to-day.

MARY: O, would to God I had died three years ago— I should not then have fallen into this evil life.

ABRAHAM: I did not come to weep over your sins with you, but to share your love.

MARY: A slight twinge of compunction saddened me, hence my words; but come let us sup and enjoy ourselves, for, as you have reminded me, this is not the time to weep for my sins.

ABRAHAM: We have supped generously, we have drunk copiously, thanks to your liberal hospitality, oh, worthy host. Allow me to leave the table and to go to bed to restore my weary body with sweet repose.

HOST: As you will.

MARY: Rise, my lord, rise. I will accompany you to your room.

ABRAHAM: I desire it; nothing could have made me leave this place without you.

ABRAHAM: Push the bolts carefully, so that no one can enter.

MARY: Do not trouble yourself. I have ordered that no one may have easy access to us.

ABRAHAM: (*Aside.*) It is now time to take off the hat which hides my face and to show her who I am. (*Aloud.*) O, my adopted daughter, O, part of my soul, Mary, do you recognize in me the old man who brought you up with the tenderness of a father and who betrothed you to the only Son of the heavenly King?

MARY: Alas for me! It is my father and my master Abraham who speaks to me. (*She is stupefied with fear.*)

ABRAHAM: What has happened to thee, my daughter?

MARY: A great misfortune.

ABRAHAM: Who deceived thee? Who seduced thee?

MARY: He who overthrew our first parents.

ABRAHAM: Where is the angelic life thou didst lead on earth?

MARY: Utterly lost.

ABRAHAM: Where is thy virginal purity? Where is thy admirable chastity?

MARY: Lost.

ABRAHAM: If thou dost not re-enter the way of salvation, what reward canst thou hope to receive for thy fasts, thy vigils, when falling from the height of heaven thou art drowned in the abysses of hell?

MARY: Alas!

ABRAHAM: Why didst thou despise me? Why hast thou abandoned me? Why didst thou not tell me of thy fall? Aided by my dear Ephraim, I would have done penance for thy fault.

MARY: After I fell into sin, soiled as I was, I no longer dared to approach your holiness.

ABRAHAM: Whoever was exempt from sin except the Son of the Virgin?

MARY: No one.

ABRAHAM: It is human to sin, it is devilish to continue to sin. Not he who falls should be blamed, but he who does not rise again at once.

MARY: Unhappy wretch that I am!

ABRAHAM: Why art thou overcome? Why dost

thou remain motionless lying on the ground? Stand up and listen to what I say to thee.

MARY: I am terror-stricken. I cannot bear the weight of your paternal rebuke.

ABRAHAM: Think, my daughter, of my tenderness for thee and cease to fear.

MARY: I cannot.

ABRAHAM: Was it not for thee that I left the desert and renounced the observance of discipline? Was it not for thee that I, a professed eremite, became the boon companion of debauchees? I, who for so many years have been vowed to silence, have I not bandied light jests in order not to be recognized? Why with bent head dost thou look downward? Why dost thou disdain to answer me?

MARY: The consciousness of my guilt overwhelms me. I dare not raise my eyes to heaven nor mingle my words with yours.

ABRAHAM: Do not distrust heaven, my daughter; do not despair; rise out of this abyss of desperation and put your hope in God.

MARY: The enormity of my sins has plunged me in the deepest despair.

ABRAHAM: Thy sins are great, but the divine grace is greater than all created things. Banish then this sadness and profit by the short time that remains to thee for repentance.

MARY: If I had the slightest hope of meriting forgiveness, I should not fail to give myself up to penitence.

ABRAHAM: Let the toil which I have borne for thee move thee to pity, my daughter; cast aside this fatal discouragement, which is more wicked than any sin, for he who despairs of God's mercy to evil-doers commits an unpardonable transgression. As truly as the spark that darts from the pebble cannot fire the sea, the bitterness of our sins cannot alter the sweetness of the divine clemency.

MARY: I do not deny the greatness of the supreme

goodness, but when I consider the magnitude of my offense, I fear that no penitence can suffice to expiate it.

ABRAHAM: I take your iniquity on myself; only return to the place you have left and resume the life that you abandoned.

MARY: I shall never oppose one of your wishes and I obey your commands with respect.

ABRAHAM: I see now that I have found my daughter again, her to whom I was a father. Now indeed are you dearer to me than aught else.

MARY: I possess some gold and several costly garments. I will dispose of them as your authority dictates.

ABRAHAM: What you have acquired by sin, you must abandon with sin.

MARY: I thought that I would distribute them among the poor or offer them to the altar.

ABRAHAM: The wage of sin is not an agreeable offering to God.

MARY: Then I will trouble myself no more about it.

ABRAHAM: Dawn is whitening the sky; it is growing light. Let us go.

MARY: It is you, beloved father, who should precede, like the good shepherd, the sheep that you have found, and I, following you, will walk in your footsteps.

ABRAHAM: No, not thus. I will go on foot and you shall ride my horse, so that the roughness of the road may not bruise the soles of your tender feet.

MARY: O, how can I praise you worthily? What gratitude can repay so much goodness? Far from forcing me to repent through terror, you gently lead me to penitence by the tenderest exhortations.

ABRAHAM: I ask nothing of you but to remain faithful to the Lord during the rest of your life.

MARY: I will follow God with all my will, with all my strength; and if I lack the strength, at least I shall never lack the desire.

ABRAHAM: You must now serve God with that ardor with which you followed the vanities of the world.

MARY: I will ask God that through your virtue His will may be done in me.

ABRAHAM: Let us hasten to return.

MARY: Yes, let us hasten; the least delay is painful to me.

ABRAHAM: With what celerity we have surmounted the difficulties of this hard journey.

MARY: Devotion makes all things easy.

ABRAHAM: Here is your deserted cell.

MARY: Ah, me! it was the witness and the confidant of my sin. I dare not enter it.

ABRAHAM: You are right. It is better to flee from a place where the enemy has triumphed.

MARY: And where do you order me to do my penance?

ABRAHAM: Enter this inner cell, in order that the old serpent may not again find an opportunity to deceive you.

MARY: Unresisting, I submit to your commands.

ABRAHAM: I will now find Ephraim, my companion, that he who alone wept with me for your loss may now rejoice with me that you are found.

—*Scenes VI-VIII.*

The play ends with a scene between the two hermits in which Abraham recounts to Ephraim the conversion and repentance of Mary. Dramatically an anticlimax, and practically commonplace, this *coda* was required to assure the spectators that the sympathizing confidant was kept fully informed of the progress of events; there was nothing elliptical or inferential about an old comedy.

That "Abraham" was the most successful of Hrotsvitha's dramas may perhaps be surmised from the repetition of its motive in "Paphnutius," which lacks, however, the effusion and pathos of the earlier play, and which is propped up by a display of learning that rings hollow on a modern ear. What the scientific jargon of a Dumas *fils*, or the medical technicalities of an Ibsen are to a modern audience, was this terminology of new-born scholasticism to mediæval auditors. It would be unjust to call it pedantry; with the unconsciousness of a child exhibiting its toys or its pets, Hrotsvitha ranges in smooth lines the spoils of her studies, which lack significance to a secular age. The argument, taken from the story of an unknown Greek writer of the fourth century, ran on lines already familiar through "Abraham" to Hrotsvitha's public. In Paris the attention of the learned and the lettered was drawn to the legend of Thais by M. Anatole France's novel, and Massenet's opera. Through them we are familiar with the plot, the situations, and the characters of Hrotsvitha's play of "Paphnutius." M. France has, by reversing the modern process, made a novel of the nun's drama with very few changes, the only notable one, the transformation of St. Paphnutius, holy hermit, into an erotomaniac. It seems curious that a lover and writer of history like M. France should feel justified in smirching the reputation of an irreproachable saint, to whom many churches and monasteries are dedicated, and whose intercession is daily sought by thousands of Eastern Christians. M. France would have hesitated to take away the character of a French saint, or one nearer home. But St. Paphnutius is an Egyptian, therefore like "Punch's" collier he has no hesitation in "'eaving 'arf a brick at a stranger." Nor has M. France acknowledged his debt, his great debt, to Hrotsvitha. How great it is may be judged from a comparison of the situations and characters in his "*Thaïs*" with the original play. Of course, the master of French prose has, in form, enormously bettered what he borrowed, and by his polished style has developed a rude and naïve poem into a finished work of art. But the pure and delicate aroma of the original has been lost in the process. Sister Hrotsvitha is sincerely devout, and handles her material reverently and modestly. Sin, vice, penitence, are terribly real to her, hence, there is a conviction, a fervor in her primitive painting akin to that of the Pre-Raphaelite masters that is always convincing, sometimes moving.

The popularity of M. France's novel, which may be regarded either as a rude trampling of an exquisite flower of asceticism under satyr's hoofs, or as a powerful delineation of the tardy awakening of passion in an intense and concentrated nature, aroused public interest in M. Albert Gayet's discovery of the tomb and body of a holy woman named Thais in the Christian necropolis of Antinoë in Lower Egypt. Although the archæologist has publicly made his declaration of unfaith: "I have no document that permits me to identify Thais of Antinoë with the Thais of history; on the other hand, I have none authorizing me to deny the possibility of such identification." Although the costume of Thais is not that of a recluse, yet the position of the tomb which was found in the midst of the cemetery, surrounded by sepulchres of the fourth century; the inscription on its wall, "Here reposes the blessed Thais," and the articles found with the body favor the hypothesis that in the Musée Guimet lies the blackened husk of the bewitching mime who inflamed the youth of Alexandria, listened to the preaching of Paphnutius, burned her treasures, and followed the hermit into the Thebaid to save her soul. Those who would play the devil's advocate and unsaint this poor shell argue that the dress, the coquettish wreath-like hood, borrowed from the roguish Tanagrian Loves, the rich-toned draperies that warm the eye like the tints of sun-soaked nectarines, is that of a child of the world, provoking rather than repelling glances. To this objection M. Gayet replies that saints who passed their lives in sordid rags were often buried in rich clothing and hoarded their festal garments to enter the Presence bravely; quoting the words of St. Macarius of Thebais, who when summoned before the governor of Antinoë was advised by his disciples to change his tattered tunic for a more decent habit and who answered: "I am keeping my new robe to appear before my Saviour." In a remote Nitrian convent the adventurous traveller is shown to-day the body of the "Holy Maximus," son of the

Emperor Valentinian, clothed in purple and gold tissue, the costume of an imperial prince, though Maximus who fled the court and became a monk, wore during his lifetime the coarse brown garb of his fellows.

The richness and beauty of a secular dress prove nothing against the asceticism or sanctity of the wearer. That of Thais may have been the "glorious habit" of pious legend which every Christian tried to provide for his triumph in death over the sorrows and snares of life; it may have been the garments which the penitent wore when she received the favor of heaven through St. Paphnutius, and bade farewell to the theatre and her mourning lovers. There is no *mundus muliebris* buried with this Thais; no mirror, no jars of nard or stibium, no lute or embroidery-frame; hers is the funeral baggage of the eremite. The chaplet, the cross, still recalling in form the *ankh* of the Egyptians, found by the side of the body; the rose of Jericho, symbol of resurrection, held between the skeleton fingers; the basket and goblet case of woven palm fibres to contain the Sacrament which the Oriental Christians buried with the dead; the palm branches, martyrs' attributes in which she lies as in a nest of verdure, all testify to the exceptional holiness of the "blessed Thais" of Antinoë, and impart to her sepulchre a distinctly religious character, differentiating it from the other tombs of the same necropolis. In any case, without attaching undue importance to it,

HROTSVITHA

the "find" of M. Gayet lends vitality to the legend of the courtesan-saint, and provides costume and properties for the winning figure of the repentant actress.

The first scene of Paphnutius passes in the Theban desert in the laura of the holy man whom his disciples find pensive and abstracted. To their inquiries as to the cause of his anxiety he replies with mystifying subtleties: dissertations on the major and minor worlds, the nature of man, the laws of harmony, the sciences of the "quadrivium, and music celestial, human and instrumental." Pythagoras, Boëthius, Martinus Capella, contribute in turn to the edification of the spectators, and the somewhat reluctant admiration of the disciples, who, after having audibly regretted the flood of erudition which they have brought upon their own heads, protest against further inundation.

DISCIPLES: We have no taste for philosophical discussion. Our intelligence cannot grasp the subtlety of your arguments. . . . [*The master apologizes modestly.*]

PAPHNUTIUS: I saw, without myself being seated at the banquet of science, a tiny drop fall from the cup of the sages. I gathered it up and wished to share it with you.

The DISCIPLES *reply, perhaps with satiric intention*

DISCIPLES: We thank your goodness but the saying of the Apostle alarms us: "But God has chosen the foolish things of the world to confound the wise: (*Nam stulta mundi elegit Deus, ut confunderet sophistica*)."

PAPHNUTIUS: Wise or simple deserve to be put to confusion before the Lord if they do evil. . . . It is not all the learning that it is possible to possess that offends God, but the unjust pride of the learned.

DISCIPLES: True.

PAPHNUTIUS: In what manner can knowledge be more properly and worthily employed than in the praise of Him who has himself created all that can be known and who provides us at once with knowledge and the means of understanding it.

DISCIPLES: In nothing more perfectly.

PAPHNUTIUS: The more thoroughly man understands by what admirable laws God has regulated the number, the proportion, and the harmony of all things, the more he burns with love for Him.

Here the learned nun speaks through Paphnutius's lips, she, who "whenever she could collect some threads, or bits torn from the ancient mantle of philosophy, took care to weave them into the fibre of her book," as she did not forget to warn her hearers in her "Epistle to Certain Wise Persons."

The disciples, a trifle dashed by the master's knowledge, again inquire the reason of Paphnutius's melancholy, and he confesses that the thought of Thais, of the ruin she has caused, the souls she has lost, saddens him, and at the same time inspires him with the desire to convert her. The docile disciples approve his design and promise him the aid of their orisons. The old recluse goes to Alexandria, and in the guise of a lover, like Abraham, he obtains an interview with Thais. She is an amiable, soft-natured creature, already a Christian though an erring one, and therefore easily accessible to the fear of hell. Paphnutius shows her none of the deep tenderness which sweetened Abraham's reproaches, there is no bond of kinship and affection between these two. He threatens and denounces; she shudders and weeps. Her terrors sweep her to his feet, her hope of forgiveness renders her a lax doll in his hands; she bids farewell to her admirers, piles up her riches, easily collected in the days of chattel property, in a pyramid of vanities, and follows her mentor to a community of holy women. The abbess comes to meet them, already warned, as Thais, who was a lover of Virgil, suggests by "Rumor whose course is stayed by no delay," and a pretty exchange of ecclesiastical compliments follows in Scene VII.

PAPHNUTIUS: A happy meeting, illustrious abbess. I was seeking you.

ABBESS: You are welcome, venerable Father Paphnutius. Blessed be your coming, beloved of the Lord.

PAPHNUTIUS: May the grace of the Creator pour out upon you the beatitude of His eternal benediction.

ABBESS: From whence comes to me this happiness: that your holiness deigns to visit my humble house?

PAPHNUTIUS: I require your help in my immediate need.

ABBESS: You have only to let me know by one word what you want of me, and I shall hasten to obey you and gratify your desire, according to my power.

PAPHNUTIUS: I bring you a half-dead goat that I have taken from the teeth of the wolf: I beg you to bestow on her your merciful cure for her healing until she shall have changed her rough goat's hide for the soft fleece of a sheep.

ABBESS: Explain yourself more clearly.

PAPHNUTIUS: This woman that you see before you has led the life of a courtesan.
ABBESS: How deplorable.
PAPHNUTIUS: She abandoned herself utterly to wantonness.
ABBESS: She lost her soul.
PAPHNUTIUS: Finally, through my exhortations, Christ co-operating with me, she now feels nothing but horror for the vanities that beguiled her and has resolved to live chastely.
ABBESS: Thanks be to the author of this conversion!
PAPHNUTIUS: The diseases of the soul, like those of the body, are cured by the use of contraries. Therefore this sinner sequestrated from worldly distractions should be shut up alone in a small cell where she can at her leisure meditate on her transgressions.
ABBESS: Nothing could be better.
PAPHNUTIUS: Will you order a cell to be prepared immediately?
ABBESS: It will soon be ready.
PAPHNUTIUS: It should have neither entrance nor exit; only a narrow window, through which she may receive a little food which you will have sparingly given her at certain days and hours.
ABBESS: I fear that the delicacy of this woman accustomed to luxury will be unable to bear such rigor.
PAPHNUTIUS: Do not be troubled; for great transgressions we must have recourse to desperate remedies.

. . . .

ABBESS: The cell which you asked for is ready.
PAPHNUTIUS: Good. Enter, Thais, this tiny dwelling where you can weep for your sins.
THAIS: O, how narrow, how dark, and how uncomfortable is this cell for a tender woman!
PAPHNUTIUS: Why do you loathe this little cell? Why do you tremble with horror in entering it? Untamed you have wandered at your own will until to-day, now you must submit to restraint in solitude.

THAIS: A soul accustomed to luxury easily turns towards its past life. . . .

PAPHNUTIUS: Fear the tortures of eternal punishment, do not be afraid of passing annoyances.

THAIS: My weakness obliges me to fear them.

PAPHNUTIUS: You should expiate by loathsome discomforts the luxury and guilty enjoyments of your past life. . . . You should pray not with words but with tears; not by the plaintive sound of your voice, but by the cry of your repentant heart.

THAIS: If I am not permitted to pray to God in words how can I hope for forgiveness?

PAPHNUTIUS: The more perfect your humility is the more quickly you will be pardoned. Say only "Thou who madest me, have mercy on me."

THAIS: I have great need of mercy that I may not be conquered in this doubtful combat.

PAPHNUTIUS: Fight manfully and you will gain a happy triumph.

THAIS: Your task is to pray for me that I may obtain the palm of victory.

PAPHNUTIUS: Your recommendation is superfluous.

THAIS: I hope so.

PAPHNUTIUS: It is time for me to take my way back to my dear hermitage, and to visit my beloved disciples. Venerable abbess, I confide this prisoner to your solicitude and to your charity. I beg you to supply her with necessities, to show a little indulgence to her frail body, and abundantly refresh her spirit by your salutary admonitions.

ABBESS: Be without anxiety. I shall have for her the care and tenderness of a mother.

PAPHNUTIUS: I go.

ABBESS: Depart in peace.

Paphnutius, it will be observed, is far more severe in his treatment of the sinner in his colloquy with her than in his recommendations to the abbess. His pity for the softly nurtured woman is delicately indicated even while he imposes mortifications on her.

In this scene which is filled with painful suggestions, Hrotsvitha unconsciously lifted a trap-door beneath which the terrible subterranean world of the convent yawned in darkness. For monastic life presented a dual aspect: above, the treasure-filled chapel, the library, the sunny cloisters, gracious courtesies, bounteous charities, humane studies; below, the noisome horror of the *in pace*, the wet, chill vaults where the rebellious or erring nun was walled up. No hut in Egypt built on the dry sand, with the desert winds blowing about it, could be compared with these narrow stone chambers, sometimes below the sea-level, which Hrotsvitha had in mind, and which were accepted as a necessity of conventual discipline; witness that fetid cell, cramped as a grave, in which Barbara Ubryk was found buried alive in the middle of the nineteenth century.

Paphnutius returns to his disciples, and three years later when he desires news of Thais, after the indirect manner of saints, instead of sending a messenger to the abbess, he visits a still more famous cenobite Antony, hoping for a vision or a miracle to inform him of the state of his penitent's soul. He is not disappointed, for soon afterwards, Paul, a young disciple of Antony's, receives news *via* heaven of the penitent.

ANTONY: Already the evangelical promise is fulfilled in us.

PAPHNUTIUS: What promise?

ANTONY: That which assures us that in uniting our prayers we can obtain anything from Jesus Christ.

PAPHNUTIUS: What has happened?

ANTONY: My disciple Paul has had a vision.

PAPHNUTIUS: Call him.

ANTONY: Paul, come here and tell Paphnutius what you have seen.

PAUL: I saw in heaven a magnificent couch hung with white draperies; around it stood, like sentinels, four young virgins shining with light. While admiring this festal splendor, I said to myself: "Such honor belongs only to my father and my master Antony."

ANTONY: I do not consider myself worthy of such happiness.

PAUL: Hardly had this reflection occurred to me, when a divine voice thundered: "It is not for Antony, as you hoped, but for Thais, the courtesan, that this triumph is reserved."

PAPHNUTIUS: Praise be to the sweetness of thy mercy, O Christ, only son of God, who hast deigned to accord this consolation to my sorrow.

ANTONY: Let us praise the Lord, who is worthy of our praises.

PAPHNUTIUS: I am going to visit my captive.

ANTONY: The time has come to make her hope for pardon, and to console her with the promise of eternal beatitude.

PAPHNUTIUS: Thais, my adopted daughter, open your window that I may see you.

THAIS: Who speaks to me?

PAPHNUTIUS: Paphnutius, your father.

THAIS: Whence comes so great a happiness to me? Why do you desire to meet me, a sinner?

PAPHNUTIUS: Though for three years I have been

absent in the body, I have nevertheless felt constant solicitude for your salvation.

THAIS: I do not doubt it.

PAPHNUTIUS: Tell me the story of your converted life and of your repentance.

THAIS: I can tell you only that I have done nothing worthy of the Lord.

PAPHNUTIUS: Who would be justified if God took account of all our iniquities?

THAIS: If, meantime, you wish to know what I have done, I have in thought gathered up the multitude of my sins; I have not ceased from contemplating them and turning them over in my mind. And the fear of hell was never absent one moment from the eyes of my heart.

PAPHNUTIUS: Because you have punished yourself by repentance you have deserved forgiveness.

THAIS: Would it were so.

PAPHNUTIUS: The time has come for you to put away fear and to begin to hope for eternal life, for your penance is acceptable to God.

THAIS: Let all the angels praise His mercy, for He has not despised the humility of a contrite heart.

PAPHNUTIUS: Persist in the fear of God and be firm in His love, for when fifteen days have passed away you will cast off your human slough, and with the aid of the divine grace you will depart to dwell in the stars.

THAIS: O, may I escape the torments of hell, or at least be burned by milder flames; for I cannot obtain eternal felicity by my own merits.

PAPHNUTIUS: Grace, the free gift of God, weighs not the merit of man, for if it were accorded only to merit, it could not be called grace.

THAIS: Let the harmony of the heavens, let the plants of the earth, let all manner of beasts, let even the depths of the waters unite in praise of Him who not only bears with sinners, but who generally lavishes unwon rewards on those who repent.

HROTSVITHA 105

PAPHNUTIUS: He has through all eternity preferred mercy to punishment.

THAIS: Do not leave me, my venerable father. Remain near me to console me at the hour when my body wastes away.

PAPHNUTIUS: No, I will not leave you, I will not depart until your soul rises in triumph to heaven and I have given your body to the grave.

THAIS: I am beginning to die.

PAPHNUTIUS: Now is the time to pray.

THAIS: Thou who madest me, have pity on me, and permit the soul that Thou breathedst into me to return to Thee in bliss.

PAPHNUTIUS: Thou uncreated truly immaterial being, who, a simple essence, hath formed of different parts man who unlike Thee is not that which is (eternal), let the elements of which this human creature is composed return without hinderance to the principle of their origin: that the soul which came from heaven may have its share of celestial joy, and that the body may find a peaceful bed in the bosom of the earth from whence it came until that day when this dust shall be reunited, and the spark of life shall kindle in these limbs, and this same Thais shall rise again a perfect human creature as before to take her place among the spotless sheep of the Lord, and to enter into the joys of eternity. O, Thou who alone art what Thou art, who reignest in the unity of the Trinity, and who are perpetually glorified century after century.

—*Scenes XI–XII–XIII.*

A noble prayer, a trifle lacking in unction, the flight of it somewhat clogged by anxiety for theological correctness. It would never do to let a loophole for heretics appear in the utterance of so venerable a father, and the doctrines of the resurrection of the body and the divine essence must be clearly stated lest the Searcher of Hearts should make any mistake about the orthodoxy of his votary. A fine sonorous prayer, with stately music in the ample phrases of the original Latin, and yet how much more vital, more poignant, I may even add intelligent, is the simple petition: "O, Thou who madest me, have mercy on me," an appeal to the Infinite Comprehension, which prefigures the spiritual attitude of Goethe, the *"comprendre c'est pardonner"* of Madame de Staël, and voicing the sentiment of a secular age, foreshadows the direction which such devout aspiration as subsists to-day will follow: *"Qui plasmasti me, miserere mei!"*

IX

"*Sapientia*" betrays a lack of spontaneity, the tone is more sombre, unrelieved by any gleam of humor or hint of playfulness; in form it is Janus-like, reverting to an earlier type of drama, the tragedy of antiquity, and forestalling the Mystery, though the allegory is yet in abeyance to a feeling for life and nature. In spite of the grand character of Sapientia, the old patrician speeding her daughters to martyrdom with brave words, and dying of grief on their tomb, which recalls the august figures of Greek tragedy, there is a failure of inspiration, of invention, in the play. Sapientia's learned quibbling with the Emperor is an echo of Paphnutius's hair-splitting; her snubbing of the patient monarch recalls the impertinences of Irene; the scene of martyrdom is a repetition of that in "Dulcitius"; in fine, Hrotsvitha's muse begins to show fatigue, and formalism fetters originality.

The plot of "*Sapientia*" was borrowed from the Greek legend of "Faith, Hope, and Charity, Daughters of Sophia." A noble Christian lady comes to Rome to dedicate her three daughters to Christ's service; she is apprehended by the prefect Antiochus and led before the Emperor Hadrian. In spite of his amiable endeavors to save them, Sapientia and her girls persist in denying the gods and in reviling the Emperor. The girls after submitting to atrocious tortures which they do not feel, and working many miracles and prodigies, are decapitated, and the three bodies are given back to their mother.

The last scene, which recalls the burial rites of Greek tragedy and the pious chorus of libation-pourers, shows Sapientia and her friends, Roman matrons, carrying the bodies of the three daughters to the sepulchre.

SAPIENTIA: Come, illustrious Matrons, and bury with me the bodies of my daughters.
MATRONS: We will pour perfumes on these delicate bodies and render them funeral honors.
SAPIENTIA: Great is the goodness, admirable is the compassion that you show to me and to my dead.
MATRONS: We do devotedly whatever can alleviate your sorrow.

SAPIENTIA: I know it.
MATRONS: What place have you chosen for their tomb?
SAPIENTIA: A place three miles from Rome, if it is not too far for you.
MATRONS: No, indeed, we wish to follow you to the place you have chosen.
SAPIENTIA: Here is the place.
MATRONS: It is a suitable one for their remains.
SAPIENTIA: O earth, I confide to thee these tender flowers of my body, preserve them in thy bosom formed of like matter until the day of resurrection when I hope they will bloom again in glory. And meantime do Thou, O Christ, fill their souls with celestial splendors, and give peace and repose to their bones.
MATRONS: Amen.
SAPIENTIA: I thank your humanity for the consolation you gave me after the death of my children.
MATRONS: Shall we remain with you?
SAPIENTIA: No.
MATRONS: Why not?
SAPIENTIA: For fear that the kindness you have shown may injure you. Is it not enough to have watched three nights with me? Depart in peace and go back to your homes in safety.
MATRONS: Will you not return to Rome with us?
SAPIENTIA: Not at all.
MATRONS: What have you decided to do?
SAPIENTIA: To remain here to see if my prayers will be granted.
MATRONS: What have you asked for? What do you desire?
SAPIENTIA: Only to die in Jesus Christ as soon as I have finished my prayer.
MATRONS: Our duty is then to wait until we have laid you also in the grave.
SAPIENTIA: As you will. Adonai, Emmanuel, thou who before the beginning of time wast engendered by the

All Father and who in time wast born of a virgin, thou whose two natures miraculously form one Christ, without the diversity of these natures dividing the unity of thy person, or the unity of thy person confusing the diversity of these natures; O Christ, let the amiable serenity of the angels and the sweet harmony of the stars praise thee. May the knowledge of all that can be known, and all that is formed of the matter of the elements praise thee, for thou only with the Father and the Holy Spirit art an immortal substance. By the will of the Father and the co-operation of the Holy Spirit thou hast not disdained to become human, mortal as man, immortal as God.

And that no man who believes should perish, and that all, on the contrary, may enjoy eternal life, thou hast not scorned to taste death like one of us, and to return again to life. Perfect God, very man, I remember thou hast promised that all those who for thy name's sake will renounce the enjoyment of earthly things, and prefer thee to the love of fleshly ties, will be rewarded an hundredfold and will receive the gift of eternal life. Encouraged by this promise, I have done what thou hast commanded, and I have lost without complaint the children to whom I gave birth. Delay not, then, O Christ, faithfully to fulfil thy promise, that soon delivered from corporeal shackles, I shall have the joy of seeing my daughters received into heaven, they whom I unhesitatingly sacrificed to thee, hoping that while they follow thee, O Lamb of the Virgin, singing the new canticle, I shall have the bliss of hearing them and of beholding their glory; ever trusting that though I cannot sing like them the hymn of virginity, I may at least be worthy to praise thee continually with them, O, thou who art not the Father but who art of the same nature, who with the Father and the Holy Spirit art the only Lord of the universe and the unique ruler of the upper, middle, and lower worlds, who reignest and governest through the infinite duration of time.

MATRONS: Receive her, Lord, in your bosom. Amen.
—*Scene IX.*

X

Though Hrotsvitha's handling of them is traditional, her characters are planned on fine, large lines. In the conflict between desire and duty, she manifests her knowledge of the heart, and the struggle between spiritual aspiration and the moral supineness induced by habitual sin is deeply felt and adequately expressed. But it is only when she breaks from the duress of tradition, when she abandons herself to the guidance of temperament, that Hrotsvitha is an exponent of human nature. It is, thanks to her portrayal of the emotions, that men are not altogether passive media in her stage-world, that her miracles of grace, sudden departures from the guiding principles of her characters, do not arrest their evolution and destroy the illusion of reality. Callimachus is still selfish, Gallicanus easily tempted, after their conversions. The introduction of supernatural agencies disturbs the operation of natural forces, but not more radically than do emotional crises, of which they were symbols.

Does the overworld of spirits with its marvels obscure and confuse the vision of the earth world? Does Hrotsvitha's thraldom to convention, to the theological necessities of her plays, render her false to the facts of human nature? No, not to the kind of human nature that she elected to represent. The efflorescence of character under the stress of events is not an unrolled scroll to her, because she imputes its sudden flowering to a stress of feeling. She does not exhibit the growth of personality as effected by contact with life but as influenced by a special spiritual experience, and her *dramatis personæ* do not move in accordance with natural law, but by the operation of what she would have called a higher law. Human nature is not a fixed quantity, its incalculable potentialities, its transformations are recognized by even a scientific age. With Hrotsvitha the introduction of supernatural agencies was a figurative expression of the precipitate action of spiritual forces. To her auditors the spectacle of the Hand of Providence occasionally pulling the wires that move the mortal puppets did not dissipate dramatic interest any more than the Greek idea of destiny deprived antique tragedy of human interest. The heroes of the "Iliad," the heroines of "The Trojan Women" are the playthings of warring deities, but do they lack vitality? Primitive man thinks in images; the Greeks did not believe that Ulysses was not wise unless Athene was at his elbow, but that Athene aided him *because* he was wise. True, moral growth is from within, and in spiritual contests a man's fiercest foes are those of his own bosom, but does not Hrotsvitha delicately indicate this inner struggle by a few significant phrases? Her visions and apparitions are conventions like our electrical stage-lighting, or the *coup de foudre* of a modern love drama. It was not her celestial machinery that arrested Hrotsvitha's art, it was the weight of tradition, the iron rule of St. Benedict; cloistered it became sterile; but, like the rose of Jericho which apparently dry and lifeless blooms again with a little kindly care, her comedies were revived in the genial Renaissance.

What was Hrotsvitha's contribution to the drama? Its conversion to Christianity: extension of interest, employment of fresh material, expression of a new ideal by new means. True, she was hunting old trails, but she found strange flowers in them, vistas of unfamiliar realms, novel *motifs*, the appeal to the heart, the potent mainspring of human action, hope, which the stoic called a slave, the Christian a cardinal virtue. What does it matter if the miracles of hope and love are symbolized by prodigies and visions? Their essentials are eternal and are still in operation.

APHRA BEHN

TO THE ADMIRED ASTRÆA

"... Some Hands write some things well and elsewhere lame,
But on all Themes your Power is the same;
Of Buskin and of Sock you know the Pace,
And tread in both with equal Skill and Grace:
But when you write of Love, Astræa, then,
Love dips arrows, where you wet your Pen,
Such charming Lines did never Paper grace,
Soft as your Sex, and smooth as Beauty's Face."
—Sir Charles Cotton.

APHRA BEHN

I

THOUGH reverence for the past is far from characteristic of our age, in one respect our veneration for it surpasses that of our forebears. The piety that forbids us to restore the broken antique statue is a modern sentiment. Formerly collectors and art lovers mended marbles and patched up pictures as freely and naturally as we now repair damaged and aged humanity, and no more counted it a sin to piece out a god's broken nose than we do to replace a lost tooth. Arms and the woman seemed more attractive to these admirers of an ensemble, than shattered stumps. It was as sincere a love of beauty, the love of a general effect that supplied these missing members to the Medicean Venus, as that which devoutly respects the mutilation of the Melian goddess. Nor was restoration confined to the plastic arts. Many examples have familiarized us with the repairing of marbles and canvases; less well known, perhaps, are instances of the same free handling applied to history and biography, which, however, were then considered arts.

The biographer, especially, unhampered by vassalage to data, treated his material in an artistic spirit rather than by scientific method. His aim was to present a well-rounded ensemble. He seldom applied the solvent of analysis to his subject. Destructive criticism was not yet born, and investigation proceeded only along certain conventional lines. There was no lack of minute and profound scholarship, but it was not applied to biography, which was eminently constructive. If exact knowledge was lacking, conjecture made shift to replace it; if data were few, fancy was abundant, and an ample narrative style cloaked the meagreness or distortion of the facts in the case. This preoccupation with form, with the decorative presentation of subject, is evident in many vivid and noble literary portraits, but often outlines were blurred, and character weakened by generalization, lack of precision, and in some cases by lavish application of *couleur de rose*. The biographies of contemporaries were frequently an apologia or a panegyric, an offering of affection, or an unabashed bid for a handful of guineas. Even among the high-minded no effort was made to examine impartially or judge impersonally. Scrupulous Mistress Hutchinson may be pardoned her special pleading in her husband's memoirs, but most of her contemporaries were quite as biassed with less excuse. If there were passages in the life of hero or heroine that for their credit should be veiled, the biographer had no more hesitation in so doing than had Homer in summoning a discreet cloud at critical moments. Unpleasant or derogatory detail was eluded or vaguely referred to in general terms. Ruthless realism was rare in portraiture.

The seventeenth century, brutal in many ways, in others showed more respect of persons than the twentieth. The author, as well as the painter of portraits, enveloped his subject with soft shadows, drowned his background in a rich penumbra, and eliminated detail at will. The X-rays and the spot-light, the scalpel and the microscope were not among the biographer's tools. He was ill supplied with documents, for archives were not accessible to the investigator, even had he desired to consult them. The indexing and criticism of sources, the result of scientific methods applied to research, was unknown. Modern curiosity which scans washing bills, analyses boluses, and performs autopsies on bodies that it has never seen, in its unappeased hunger for data, is foiled by the reticence of the old biographer.

A notable example of this tantalizing reserve is the "History of the Life and Memoirs of the Ingenious Mrs. Behn," which precedes Gildon's edition of her novels. This biographical sketch of the first Englishwoman who earned a living by her pen, was written by "One of the Fair Sex," and an admirer of the author. As might be expected, it is an unstinted eulogy of its subject. It may be that we are told all that it is most desirable for us to know about the lady, but we are not told what most we desire to know. That intimate acquaintance with the private life, and personal opinions of those who divert it, which the inquisitive public demands to-day, and which is apparently so easily acquired, is absent. "One of the Fair Sex" was no press agent, and was sadly deficient in the knack of working up her material into a "story." Of Mrs. Behn's education, of her début as novelist or playwright, of her sponsors in literature, there is never a word. Nor is there any record of her sales, even those of her "best seller," or of her earnings generally. The determining episodes of her career; her interviews with Charles II, her secret service in Holland, her marriage with the elusive Mr. Behn, are very succinctly treated. Her friendships with famous wits and men of letters, her relations with Betterton, Nell Gwyn and the noted players of her comedies, her professional and social life in London remain unchronicled. Here is no confidential chat about authors, none of their own unbosomings that swell the bulk of the Sunday newspapers; the "Fair" friend is admiring, but reticent.

Yet this slight sketch in rose color stimulates interest; behind its elisions and reserves it suggests an engaging and exceptional personality. Would it be worth while to know more of the "ingenious Mrs. Behn"? Can these faint outlines be strengthened? Can sufficient material be gathered from public documents, from private letters, from the references of contemporaries, from personal allusions and reminiscences in the author's own works to round out the barely indicated contours? Side-lights are often illuminating. A better acquaintance with the actors of her plays, the poets who wrote her prologues, the patrons who received, and (it is to be hoped) paid for her dedications, might reflect some light on the pale portrait of the preface to which history provides a varied and picturesque background.

But why should we desire a more definite picture of Mrs. Behn? Why raise her ghost? Why resurrect another author now when so many write and so few read? Because she was not only the inventor of the novel with a purpose, and the first advocate of "a cause" in fiction, but also the first Englishwoman who made a livelihood by writing. She was the pathfinder for the long succession of professional women who have hunted the trail she blazed. Her career, therefore, could it be "reconstructed," might offer points of interest to her successors. How a woman humbly born, poor, and not overwell educated, acquired through talent and industry a position and a competence in the London of the Restoration, arouses curiosity. Not only what she did, but why she did it, her manner of working, her tone, her technic, her choice of subject provoke further questions. Her astonishing versatility puzzles and piques. How could a singer so gifted, capable of writing such poems as

"Love in fantastic triumph sat,"

turn out such pages of doggerel, *vers de société* as artificial as shell grottos? How could the generous and tender woman who first pleaded the cause of the slave, pen the indecencies that have smirched her name, and obscured her talent?

Which was the true Aphra? The *précieuse of* "The Lovers' Watch," which the habitués of the Hôtel Rambouillet read with approval, or the playwright of "Sir Patient Fancy"? Her lightning changes of rôle are bewildering. She did not become a penitent like Rochester, who tried to atone for sins he no longer had a mind to by turning his experienced hand to devotional poetry. The versatility of Mrs. Behn was always with her. Never did woman clap in turn the masks of antique drama over her débonair, brown face with more surprising rapidity. Her industry was as great as her versatility; she was at once a poet, a novelist, a playwright, and a translator of La Rochefoucauld and Fontenelle. To-day it is by her plays only that she is known; the evil that she wrote lives after her, the good is interred with her bones. Pope's line, "The stage how loosely doth Astræa tread," is the only reference familiar to us to a woman who in the age of Dryden was considered worthy of a place in the Poets' Corner of Westminster Abbey.

The looseness of Astræa's tread has been deplored with reason ever since the inevitable reaction against the license of the Restoration set in. Walter Scott's grand aunt (almost as well known to posterity as his famous little button) marked Mrs. Behn's works with a danger-signal to a generation of readers. "Take back your bonnie Mrs. Behn," said the old lady, who had wished to reread the books that had been a joy of her girlhood, and to whom Sir Walter had sent them sealed and marked "confidential," "and if you will take my advice put her in the fire. . . . But is it not a very odd thing that I, an old woman of eighty and upwards sitting alone, should feel myself ashamed to read a book which sixty years ago I have heard read aloud for the amusement of large circles, consisting of the first and most creditable society in London?"

Subsequent writers have unhesitatingly adopted the grand aunt's views. Mrs. Behn has been the subject of much posthumous rebuke; reprehension, however elegantly phrased, is not enlightening, and post-mortem chastisement of sinners is dull reading. What interests is *why* Astræa trod the stage loosely? *Why* a woman of her varied attainments, of such wide reading, of such generous feeling, should be such a hardened offender in her plays piques curiosity, and tempts us to pick her memory out of the scrap-heap and wipe the dust off her other books, for her dramas were only part of her work.

A "restored" Mrs. Behn can hardly resemble the real woman very closely, no doubt, but it is perhaps possible that the lines of the dim portrait of her friend's preface may be strengthened and freshened. Not that an array of carefully collected facts, however deftly mortised together, can bestow vitality on a subject. In that quality the critical, "documented," sketch is often as wanting as the generalized fancy picture. The latter at least approaches the ideal of the period, the type of character which was admired and imitated. It shows us what was considered desirable and therefore brings us in touch with the folk who so considered it. The biographer's preliminary collation of data supplies only the framework of his study like the armature on which the sculptor builds up his statue. The exact knowledge afforded by the editing and indexing of authorities that have placed at the student's disposal, ready to his hand, material that was formerly inaccessible, is but a small part of the biographer's equipment.

To realize the motive power of spent forces, the stimuli of outworn beliefs, is becoming increasingly rare, for as intellectual tolerance advances, imagination declines. The royalist sentiments of Mrs. Behn's cavaliers ring hollow in modern ears. Their Puritan foes' ardent interest in infant baptism, and kindred subjects, excited only the gentle amusement in Matthew Arnold that his own spirited animadversions on "marriage with a deceased wife's sister" arouse to-day. And yet without sympathetic imagination the most diligent compiler of facts, the wariest scrutinizer of sources is but an annalist. The biographer's task has grown easier and more arduous at once! It demands not only erudition, cultivation, knowledge of the world and of character, but the precious faculty of discriminating appreciation as well. Historical specialization only gives us a neatly labelled and well-arranged collection of specimens. On the other hand resurrection of the past though far more difficult than dissection of it, is more often attempted, and attempted carelessly and hastily. But neither specialized knowledge nor lively fancy can replace saturation with the general history of a period, an extended acquaintance with its arts and letters, familiarity with its habits of life and thought, and a sympathetic understanding of its ideals and beliefs; these alone supply the atmosphere, the vital air without which the portrait is as lifeless as though it were painted in a closed retort. Only the gifted few can unite these qualifications, but the humblest worker in this rich field can endeavor to keep in touch with the spirit and temper of an age by not ignoring contemporary documents, which should be considered cautiously, not contemptuously, in the historical spirit rather than in that of destructive criticism. It is prudent, therefore, not to abandon Aphra's unknown biographer, though leaving her when stubborn facts divide us, differing with her occasionally, seeking the light of modern research though it cast but a glimmer on the path through dark places, and inviting counsel at crossroads where sometimes Aphra herself, and her friends, may furnish a clew. To-day Mr. Montague Summers provides the best modern *carte du pays.* His recent publication, "The Works of Mrs. Aphra Behn" (1915), enriched with notes and some new material from original documents, is the only complete and authoritative edition of her writings, and one on which any future study of the subject must be based.

II

"My intimate acquaintance with the admirable Astræa" (thus the Fair Unknown) "gave me naturally a very great Esteem for her; for it both freed me from that Folly of my Sex, of envying or slighting Excellencies I could not obtain, and inspired me with a noble Fire to celebrate that Woman, who was an Honour and Glory to our Sex: . . . She was a Gentlewoman by Birth, of a Good Family in the City of Canterbury in Kent; her Father's Name was Johnson, whose Relation to the Lord Willoughby—" Here already must a halt be called, for Mr. Summers has recently discovered that Aphra's family name was Amis or Amies, and a contemporary, a poetess and an admirer of Aphra, flatly contradicts the statement that Amies was related to Lord Willoughby. The contradiction remained unknown, buried in the manuscript, and for two hundred years Aphra's memory was gilded with the shadow of a coronet. But in 1884, a folio volume containing the poems of Anne, Countess of Winchelsea, copied in 1695, under her supervision, with notes and corrections in her own hand, was bought by Mr. Edmund Gosse. In one of the poems in this collection called "The Circuit of Apollo," the god of poetry, a confirmed democrat, prone to touching plebeian lips with the divine fire, is described gazing sorrowfully on Aphra's birthplace.

> "And standing where sadly he now might descry
> From the banks of the Stowre the desolate Wye,
> He lamented for Behn o'er the place of her birth,
> He said among Women was not on the earth
> Her superiour in fancy, or language or witt
> Yett owned that a little too loosly she writt."

The countess after laying this branch of laurel on Aphra's grave very properly put the upstart in her place, and demolished her pretensions to gentility in the following note appended to the second of these lines: "Mrs. Behn was Daughter to a Barber who lived formerly in Wye, a little market town (now much decayed), in Kent. Though the account of her life before her Works pretends otherwise, Some Persons now alive do testify upon their knowledge that to be her Original."

Aphra Behn had been dead only six years when this note was written; her novels preceded by the anonymous friend's preface were published in 1696, the next year. The countess's testimony was that of a contemporary. Which account of Mrs. Behn's lineage was the true one? Both witnesses were ladies, both poetesses, therefore equally reliable.

Mr. Gosse, seeking light on this vexed question, wrote to the clergyman of Wye, who discovered in the parochial register of his church that "Ayfara,* the daughter, and Peter, the son of John and Amy Amis," were baptized at Wye on July 10, 1640. John Amis's profession is not mentioned; there is no evidence to support the countess's assertion or to prove that he was not a distant connection of Lord Francis Willoughby, of Parham; noble families were many-branched, and sometimes smothered in offshoots, or Amis may have been merely a *protégé;* the word relation is rather ambiguous, and sufficiently elastic to admit of several interpretations.

Canterbury, the nearest town of any importance to her birthplace, was probably where Ayfara (or Afra, finally Aphra) went to school, or picked up what education she possessed. Wye would be unusually favored if it boasted even a dame school. Very likely in her talks with her admiring biographer Aphra's memories turned more tenderly to the beautiful cathedral town with its romantic associations than to humble, little Wye, which was a far less picturesque background for a poetess.

Picturesqueness not only in Wye, but in England

---

*Ayfara's name, rare in England, was that of a beautiful Pagan actress who became a Christian saint. In the midst of a brilliant dramatic career she was suddenly converted by a holy anchorite, and retired to a hermitage in the desert to do penance for her sins. A strange celestial patron for an English baby, but a propitious one for a future playwright. Astræa was Aphra's *nom de guerre* by which she is known to blame. The *Astrée* of La Calprénède's famous romance was a learned shepherdess.

generally, was anathema in the sober-suited years of Aphra's birth and childhood. 1640 was a grim birth-year for an amiable hedonist, and England was as turbulent as the fierce Pagan world into which Aphra's name-saint was born. Charles I was losing ground in his duel with the people. Scotland in arms against prelacy, had, forcing the Tyne, already crossed the border, and from Newcastle was defying her King. Strafford, summoned in haste from Ireland, was raising recruits to crush "Scotch treason," but they deserted, profaned churches, and murdered their superior officers whom they suspected of "papistry." Even in camp discipline was defied. Laud, no better loved than Strafford, was mobbed at Lambeth, and the high commission sitting at St. Paul's rose and fled before the wrath of the people. The Parliament called "Short" for an obvious reason was summoned, and, as it announced that "the redress of grievances must ever precede the grant of moneys," the King angrily dissolved it after three weeks' sitting. "Things must go worse before they go better," was the optimistic comment of a patriot member.

Puritanism, a new moral force, was rapidly undermining the ancient order. People long divided by opinions and beliefs were brought together by the strong tie of a common love, and the still stronger tie of a common hatred: the love of liberty, the hatred of despotism. The King, wanting money, lacking troops, again summoned the

Houses, "So great a defection in the kingdom has not been known in the memory of man" (Northumberland). The misgovernment of the past fourteen years, the revival of obsolete prerogatives, illegal customs, the fines and confiscations, the ingenious devices of the court lawyers to fill the Royal Exchequer, had alienated one class after another, and provoked wide-spread discontent. Every new exaction was a fresh provocation to revolt. With the good tidings of the meeting of a new Parliament hope returned to men who had been mulcted and jailed, the Puritan emigration to the Plantation in Massachusetts was suddenly and completely arrested. "The change made all men stay in England" (Winthrop), where a Somerset squire, the member from Tavistock whom the Royalists later dubbed "King Pym," was riding through the miry roads, bringing home to his electors' minds the supreme importance of the issue of the coming conflict.

Pamphlets burst into leaf, the first flowering of those thirty thousand that appeared before the Restoration. All England studied politics, and every thinking man evolved a private theory of government. Prynne and his fellow pamphleteers, shorn of ears, but not of hope and courage, made a "progress" through London on a laurel-strewn path, and many other civic processions, bands of farmers and trades-folk, followed. Each member of the new Parliament brought with him from borough or county a petition of grievances, and forty committees were at hard labor examining and reporting on them. At every sitting some form of tyranny was abrogated.

In 1640, several notable additions were made to the Lower House. Edward Hyde, afterwards Earl of Clarendon, entered the Commons and tasted the fierce delights of Parliamentary strife. About the same time Sir Philip Warwick, coming one morning into the House, "perceived a gentleman speaking whom he knew not," in a cloth suit, ill-made by a country tailor, with plain and not very clean linen. "His countenance was swollen and reddish, his voice sharp and untunable, and his eloquence full of fervor." Sir Philip was told that this slovenly, red-nosed person was the member for Cambridge, Oliver Cromwell.

In 1640, however, with all her political preoccupations, England was still a green nest of songsters. The music of the Elizabethans was still sweet in men's ears. The nasal chant of Sergeant Moretext and Zephaniah Break-the-chains-of-Satan could not drown those resonant echoes. Not a quarter of a century had passed since Shakespeare became immortal (1616), Ben Jonson had gone "to sing high and aloof" only three years before (1637). Dekker and Ford had published their last plays in 1636, and in 1639 Herbert and Vaughn and Crashaw, not yet strayed from the fold, were making devotion lovely. In 1640 John Milton, the scrivener's son, just returned from the grand tour, already author of the "Masque," at Ludlow Castle opened a school for boys where the rod was not spared. In the same year Herrick in his Devonshire vicarage was watching the morris-dancers, and maying with Corinna, Waller was coquetting with Puritans, and plotting with Royalists, Andrew Marvell was an *attaché* of the English embassy at Constantinople, Sedley was but a year old, Dorset only three, while Suckling, who lived just long enough to be Aphra's contemporary, was writing his ballad of "The Wedding." Lovelace was laboriously composing his play of "The Soldier," which we have forgotten, and dashing off the lovely verses to Lucasta that we remember. Meanwhile Davenant, Aphra's patron, was seeing the last of the plays before the theatre was closed for many years.

In 1640 Wycherly was born, when Etherege, the founder of the new school of comedy to which Aphra and Wycherly belonged, was four years old. In 1640, Samuel Pepys had spent eight summers in what, even then, perhaps, he found a noteworthy world; in the same year young Mr. Evelyn, just turned twenty, took up his residence in the Middle Temple in a handsome apartment up four pair of stairs. In 1640 John Bunyan, still sunk in sin, at twelve years old, was (not without qualms) ringing church-bells, swearing like a cavalier, and playing hockey and tip-cat. No record has reached us of the youthful errors of another John, who counted nine years in 1640, the son of the Puritan Dryden, a stanch Committee man. But the Muse of history who is most popular when she turns gossip, mentions that another boy who refused to take physic, and was deeply attached to "a billet of wood," was, in this same year, specially guarded by his governor against "all lewd and suspected persons who shall presume to haunt near the abode where the Prince may happen to be." Pity that such guardianship could not have been prolonged through Charles II's maturity.

With all the singing birds it was a serious-minded world, this of Aphra's childhood. As she grew older life lost color year by year. All pleasures save spiritual ones were frowned upon. The mediæval church festivals, the merrymakings of the people fostered by the temper of the Renaissance were considered heathen, which they were, and iniquitous, which they were not always. Even the Royalists were obliged outwardly to respect Puritan restrictions; Aphra may have eaten a forbidden mince pie or so in private, may have played the lute or the virginals at her fireside, but as Parliament closed the theatres and whipped the mummers at the cart's tail, she could not see a play or a pageant; even a puppet-show was anathema in regenerated England, "Hamlet" and "Mr. Punch" were under the same ban. The most poetic revel of the year, going-a-Maying, was sinful; Herrick's slender youths and maidens dressed in green, the spring's livery, returning at sunset with baskets piled with cowslips, were as the crew of Comus in the eyes of the godly. Dancing in rounds was as criminal as gaming, singing of part-songs and madrigals was an abomination, making of verses, vanity. Bears, not only those Pride and his company of soldiers officially delivered, but ordinary, uncommemorated bears, enjoyed immunity from torment. The watch patrolled unbeaten, highwaymen's receipts fell off; cock-throwing and bull-baiting were made legal offenses, and the furred and feathered creatures of field and forest lived for a time unharmed. But if dastardly forms of cruelty, if gaming and swearing were fined and punished, many innocent amusements were interdicted, and even children were disciplined for playing games, or wrestling. The sweet observances of the older faith, the diversions that made Sunday a feast-day were outlawed, the church-bells were muzzled, and the organs silenced.

The eye was disciplined. Belial's sons, the cavaliers, and Jezebel's daughters laced their linen, and curled their hair, therefore the godly eschewed such practices. Cropped hair, plain bands, and sad-colored habits testified to the outer man's conformity with the inner man's ideal. Many portraits of the period, especially those of women and children, illustrate the new severity of taste; the ladies are pensive, often grave; their graceful draperies are simple, they have few jewels, save Cornelia's; banished are the lap-dogs and the lutes. Some devout women like Mr. Evelyn's friend Mary Godolphin, "would be drawn in a lugubrious posture, sitting upon a tombstone, adorned with a sculptured urn." Even the children's portraits have a prim and pinched air, a world removed from the natural and beautiful seriousness of childhood.

The conviction of the unrighteousness of human happiness which no thoughtful person who had even passed by Puritanism could entirely escape, was universal among the finest minds of Puritan and churchman alike. The price of the manly virtues of Puritanism, and, perhaps, the inevitable price of its chaste living, sobriety, rigid discipline of the will, and capacity for high and sustained enthusiasm, was a blunting of æsthetic perceptions, a contraction of human sympathy, a lack of geniality and humor, and often overweening self-esteem. Self-contained, self-reliant, and self-sufficient was the typical Puritan, even the noblest of them. That "learned but otherwise highly objectionable child," Lucy Apsley, tells us: "play among other children I despised, and when I was forced to entertain such as came to visit me, I tired them with more grave instructions than their mothers, and plucked all their babies to pieces, and kept all the children in such awe that they were glad when I entertained myself with elder company." Milton the ideal Puritan, with his exquisite sensitiveness to beauty, his enjoyment of the pageantry of life, writes of himself: "Always a certain reservedness of nature, an honest haughtiness, and self-esteem kept me still above those low descents of mind," viz.: vulgar dissipation and coarse pleasures. Again he says: "If ever God instilled an intense love of moral beauty into the mind of any man, he instilled it into mine." Such intense love of moral beauty, however, sometimes came dangerously near to dislike and contempt for the vulgar, and cramped the mind as well as the sympathies. In pious women this inflexibility of temper and shrinkage of kindliness was as prevalent. Mistress Wallingford, whom her son in his "Diary" described as a model of burgher virtue, and most tender and affectionate in her own circle, *"while loving all that were godly, much misliked the wicked and profane"!*

It was among such limitations, and under such influences that Aphra in her father's Royalist household was bred. How was she educated? How did she acquire her knowledge of French, her acquaintance with history and literature? Neither she nor her biographer answers this question. The education of girls in Aphra's walk of life was strictly utilitarian. "To read, write, and cast accounts in a small way," was a sufficient equipment, anything more they would never have occasion for, "and the mind should not be burdened with needless application." A light hand at puff-paste was more esteemed than an ear for music or a knowledge of tongues. Of course, the country girl was more versed in certain branches of learning than the town-bred lady, and was generally "an accomplished artist in whipt Sillabubs, and Almond Butter, of great Cunning in Cheese-cakes, even initiated into the mysteries of *Aqua Mirabilis*, and Snayl water." Indeed the typical country maid, like the modern German Fräulein of the conservative type, spent her time, "Not in reading novels of Fights and Battels, of Dwarfs and Giants: but in writing out receipts for Broths, Possets, Caudles and Surfeit Waters."

What the embroidery-frame was to the loom, the simple closet, or the still-room, was to the kitchen. A flavor of mystery and sweet herbs still lingers about it, the good housewife was still near enough to the mediæval *châtelaine* to be something of a leech, and was an efficient substitute for the country doctor. There amid roses and lavender, camomile and motherwort, the Lady Bountiful, like a benevolent Medea, brewed diet drinks, distilled sweet waters, compounded balsams and beauty-washes. The austerity of these pursuits was softened, at least in higher social circles, by lighter accomplishments: "the Needle, Dancing, and the French tongue, a little Musick on the Harpsichord or Spinet." Pepys during the great fire of London noticed that when the household goods of the burned-out city folk were loaded on the lighters for safety, every third boat carried a pair of virginals. Vocal music was cultivated also, even by village maidens. Dancing in Royalist households, particularly in those of gentlefolk, was an integral part of education, and dancing was still Greek in its comprehensive significance: it included deportment, carriage, "a particular behaviour at the tea-table," the technic of the fan, and the etiquette of the snuff-box. Ruskin's scheme of education for girls: sewing, cooking, and dancing, was that of Aphra's contemporaries.

Here was a pitiful falling away from the high standards of Tudor times, the humane studies of the ladies of Elizabeth's court. Still the idea that knowledge, initiative, and independence of judgment were inimical not only to the welfare of the individual woman unfortunate enough to possess them, but to society in general, had not received the universal sanction accorded it under the Georges, and there were ladies who even in their tender years were recalcitrant to this system of practical education, and reverted to the more virile accomplishments of their forebears of the Renaissance. The Countess of Winchelsea, Aphra's contemporary, admits that she neglected the domestic arts, and to devote herself to the muses, declined to

"in fading silks compose,
Faintly the inimitable rose,
Fill up an ill-drawn bird, or paint on glass
The Sov'reign's blurred and indistinguished face,
The threatening angel and the speaking ass:"

Lucy Apsley, who afterwards became the wife of Colonel Hutchinson, when she was but seven years old had "eight tutors in languages, music, dancing, writing and needle-work, but," she confesses: "my genius was quite averse from all but my book. As for music and dancing I profited very little in them, and would never practice my lute or harpsichords, but when my masters were with me; and for my needle, I absolutely hated it."

Was the lowly born Aphra one of these "revolting daughters" who preferred study to puff-paste, and writing verses to stitching Biblical scenes? Presumably, for from her tenderest years she was a poet and "even in the first Bud of Infancy, discovered such early hopes of her riper years that she was equally her Parents' Joy and Fears: for they too often mistrust the Loss of a Child, whose Wit and Understanding outstrip its Years, as too great a Blessing to be long enjoyed . . . besides the Vivacity and Wit of her Conversation, at the first Use almost of Reason in Discourse, she would write the prettiest, soft, engaging Verses in the World."

III

While Aphra was still a callow songster the background of her life was suddenly shifted. Her father "whose Relation to the Lord Willoughby, drew him, for the advantageous Post of Lieutenant-General of many Isles, besides the Continent of *Surinam*, from his quiet Retreat at *Canterbury* to run the hazardous Voyage of the *West Indies*.

With him he took his chief Riches, his Wife and Children; and in that Number Afra, his promising Darling, our future *Heroine* and admired Astræa."

John Amis, the barber, Lord Lieutenant! A barber, and a barber of poor, little run-down Wye intrusted with the government of thirty-six islands and "the Continent of Surinam" to boot! Even the "Arabian Nights," wherein barbers are greatly honored, offers no parallel elevation. Either the Countess of Winchelsea was mistaken or Aphra endowed her father with the position and powers of some better-born or more fortunate kinsman. At all events the Amis family sailed for Surinam or British Guiana under the protection of Lord Willoughby when Aphra was a poetess *en herbe*.

If we did not know that formerly ladies began their profession of heart-breaking very early in life, and that woman was considered in her prime at the age of fifteen, her biographer's statement would seem surprising. "She accompanied her Parents in their long Voyage to *Surinam*, leaving behind her the Sighs and Tears of all her Friends, and breaking Hearts of her Lovers. Her Father lived not to see that Land flowing with Milk and Honey, that Paradise which she so admirably describes in *Oroonoko:* [the novel] where you may also find what adventures happened to her in that Country."

Aphra's father died on the outward voyage: his daughter briefly mentions his death in "Oroonoko": "My stay was to be short in that Country: [Surinam] because my Father dy'd at Sea, and never arrived to possess the Honour designed him (which was Lieutenant-General of six and thirty Islands beside the Continent of Surinam) nor the Advantages he hoped to reap by them: So that tho' we were obliged to continue on our Voyage we did not intend to stay upon the Place."

Not long afterwards "the Lord, her Father's Friend, perished in a Hurricane," but the widow, Amy Amis, and her children (Aphra mentions one brother, possibly Peter, and a sister), were well received at the settlement on the Surinam River, and "the best House in it, called St. John's Hill, was presented me," wrote Aphra.

Surinam, to-day Dutch Guiana, was a new English possession, and a hotly contested one when Aphra and her mother took possession of this charming villa. Although the Dutch had long (1580) been familiar with the coast of Guiana, and in 1614 the States of Holland granted to any Dutch citizen four years' monopoly of any harbor or trading-place which he might discover in that region, it was an Englishman, whose name is still preserved by Marshal Creek, who made the first settlement there in 1630. English colonization had been attempted on the Surinam River, but in 1652 the colonists returned to Paramaribo. In 1662, ten years later, Charles II handed over the whole colony to Lord Willoughby, but in 1666 the English settlement was taken by storm by the Zealanders under Krijssen, and after the Peace of Breda, in 1667, the Dutch were recognized finally as masters of the country, in spite of the protest of the Willoughbys, who considered their rights infringed.

It is puzzling, almost impossible, to fix the date of Aphra's sojourn in Surinam. She may have left England in 1655, or perhaps a little later. At this time relatives and protégés of Lord Willoughby's would be *personæ gratæ* in the young colony, though his government was not securely established, and the colonists were in constant expectation of a foray from their encroaching Dutch neighbors, an attack by the native savages, or a rising among their own negro slaves.

They were very insufficiently prepared to meet any of these emergencies. Their militia, six hundred strong, which was ordered out to quell the revolt of the slaves under Oroonoko, might have marched out of "Hudibras." They were armed "with cruel Whips they call Cat with Nine Tails, some had useless rusty Guns for Shew; others old Basket Hilts, whose Blades had never seen the Light in this Age, and others had long Staffs and Clubs." "The Men of Fashion," however, Aphra adds reassuringly, were not among these troops; they were in covert revolt against the Deputy Governor, Byam, who was in command of the Colony. His unpopularity with the planters was amply deserved, and Aphra considered him, and was justified in so doing, if her account of his actions is true, "a Fellow whose Character is not fit to be mentioned with the worst of the Slaves." His counsel was composed of "Rogues and Runagades, that have abandoned their own Countries, for Rapine, Murders, Thefts and Villanies . . . and had no sort of Principles to make them worthy the Name of Man, but at the very Council Table would contradict and fight with one another, and swear so bloodily that it was terrible to hear and see 'em. Some of them were afterwards hanged when the Dutch took possession of the Place, others sent off in Chains."

In fact, Surinam possessed the usual quantum of broken men and desperadoes common in most new lands. The planters very naturally held aloof from this official circle, and from Parham House, the seat of the government, "because they did not love the Lord Governor," and still less Byam and his crew. Among these planters Aphra and her family found friends; especially entitled to honorable mention was a Mr. Trefrey, a young Cornish gentleman: "a Man of great Wit, and fine learning, and was carried into those Parts by the Lord-Governor to manage all his Affairs; he occupied Parham House, and was in no way subject to Byam. Indeed Byam's jurisdiction did not extend to the Lord-Governor's Plantation of Parham, where Trefrey was vizier, and which was a Sanctuary as much exempt from the Law as White Hall." Colonel Martin was another friend ("brother to Harry Martin, the great Oliverian"), who from "the

Fineness of his Parts, bore a great sway over the Hearts of all the Colony. . . . A Man of great Gallantry, Wit and Goodness, and whom I have celebrated in a Character of my new Comedy ["The Widow Ranter"] by his own Name, in Memory of so brave a Man," Aphra wrote years later.

With these notable exceptions humanity was vile indeed in the earthly Eden where every prospect pleased a susceptible and beauty-loving girl. Perhaps the patina with which Time gilds the memories of past joys adds its glow to the warmth of Aphra's descriptions, but the charm of the tropics has been so often felt by colder temperaments than hers, that her youthful intoxication needs no explanation. The local color may have dazzled her young eyes, but her descriptions suggest the camera rather than the pencil; the jewel-like color, the abounding life, the blinding lights and purple-velvet shadows, though they at first enthralled the simply bred girl, did not lessen her habit of careful observation, or her English love of exact detail.

Psyche when she awoke, in the dream-palace of the enchanted valley, could hardly have been more enraptured than Aphra with the dwelling awaiting her after the actual suffering and confinement of the long sea voyage. "It stood on a vast Rock of white Marble at the Foot of which the River ran a vast Depth down, the little Waves still dashing and Washing the Foot of this Rock, made the softest Murmurs and Purlings in the World; and the

opposite Bank was adorned with vast quantities of
different Flowers eternally blowing, and every Day
and Hour new, fenc'd behind 'em with lofty Trees
of a thousand rare Forms and Colours, that the
Prospect was the most ravishing that Fancy can
create. On the edge of this white Rock, toward
the River, was a Walk, in the Grove, of Orange and
Lemon-Trees, about half of the Length of the Mall
here, whose flowery and fruit-bearing Branches met
at the Top, and hindered the Sun whose Rays are
very fierce there, from ent'ring a Beam into the
Grove: and the cool Air that came from the River,
made it not only fit to entertain People in, at all
the hottest Hours of the Day, but refreshed the
sweet Blossoms, and made it always sweet and
charming."

Was ever a fledgling songster more sweetly nested?
What an incitement to a poet was this novel, pro-
fuse beauty, this teeming richness of life. What
stimuli to awakening senses were these "noble
aromatics," these golden fruits, and gem-like flowers.
All the common needs and uses of every-day life
were beautified by the bounty of Nature. In place
of the scanty coals and tallow dips of little damp,
poverty-stricken Wye, there was cedar for the
common firing, and flambeaux of such rich balms
and gums that they diffused sweetness and light
at once. The grove and garden of St. John's Hill
were not exceptions; the whole country was a
plaisance. Aphra, years afterwards when time and

experience had softened the vividness of first impressions, reflects sadly that: "Certainly had his late Majesty, of sacred Memory, but seen and known, what a vast and charming World he had been Master of in that Continent, he would never have parted so easily with it to the *Dutch.*" [See Pepys's *Diary*, 8 Sept., 1667.] "'Tis a Continent, whose vast Extent was never yet known, and may contain more noble Earth than all the Universe beside; if, they say, it reaches from East to West one way as far as *China*, and another to *Peru.*"

It is to be hoped that Aphra's descriptions were more exact than her notions of geography. She saw Surinam as a land of perpetual spring, a glowing vision of beauty, a feast of fragrancies. There were flowers everywhere, in the deep valley-meadows, in the rich twilight of the mighty trees which were themselves so many giant nosegays; flowers overhung the banks of the river and dropped into the foam of the breakers to meet the water-flowers below them. Living blossoms darted and floated through the sweet air, "little paraketoes, great parrots, and muckaws"; rainbow-hued birds, butterflies, and insects in fairy coats of jewelled mail. The sky was a huge arch of undimmed light, the sea a vast precious stone, glancing like a dove's neck in the shallows, burning blue like a peacock's breast in the depths, opaline in the rock-pools, or wine-dark under the shadows of passing clouds. The blossoms of these radiant southern waters shone like submerged gems, the fish were armored in gold and silver scales, or housed in shells of rose and pearl. Strange fruits glowed on the great trees that shaded these delicate coasts, strange beasts wandered in the forests: the armadillo in his white harness, "the Marmoset having Face and Hands like a human Creature's," the black jaguar, and "prodigious Snakes some three score yards in length"!

The natives of this land of enchantments went as bravely as the birds and butterflies in wreaths and little habits woven from feathers, "whose Tinctures are inconceivable." Aphra compared these aborigines to the Adams and Eves of an earthly paradise and forestalled the eighteenth-century view of the noble savage. The Indians were easily conciliated and were on friendly terms with the planters, who used more diplomacy in their treatment of them than is the general habit of English colonists. A strong desire to see the natives at home impelled Aphra to collect an exploring party to visit some Indian villages. After eight days' journey on the river they came in sight of one, and decided that as the native tribes were at feud with one another it would be wise for the white members of the party to go alone to the village, leaving the others in hiding until a kind reception was assured them. Aphra, her "Woman, a Maid of good Courage," and her brother went on to the huts, where they were greeted with a loud cry "that frighted us at first," Aphra admits, but it seems "it was of Wonder and Amazement." She modestly explains that the admiration and surprise her party aroused were not due so much to their persons as their clothes. A description of the costumes they had chosen for exploring the wilderness follows, and still excites surprise in breasts less savage: "They (the natives) were all naked, we were dressed so as is most commode for the hot Countries very glittering and rich, so that we appeared extremely fine; my own Hair was cut short, and I had a Taffety Cap, with black Feathers on my Head, my Brother was in a Stuff-Suit, with silver Loops and Buttons, and abundance of green Ribbon. . . . By Degrees they [the Indians] grew more bold and . . . touched us, laying their Hands upon all the Features of our Faces . . . taking up one Petticoat, then wondering to see Another, admiring our Shoes, and Stockings but more our Garters, which we gave 'em, and they ty'ed about their Legs, being laced with Silver Lace at the Ends [*sic*] for they much esteem any shining Things."

The other members of the party were called and reassured, the huts were visited, a feast was spread, and the medicine-man interviewed. Finally, the explorers were presented to the great captains, who had been at a council when the foreigners arrived, and this visit "begat so good an understanding between the *Indians* and the *English*, that there were no more Fears, nor Heart-burnings during our Stay, but we had a perfect, open, and free Trade with them."

Aphra's amusements were as perilous as her journeys; searching for "young *Tygers* in their Dens" was one of them. This beast is *not* a native of Dutch Guiana, but before the eyebrow of scepticism is raised we may remember that the jaguar is a very efficient understudy for the tiger. These sporting and exploring expeditions of Aphra and her friends were generally directed and planned by Oroonoko, an African slave of Mr. Trefrey's, who had been a chieftain in his own country, and whose tragic story was afterwards often told, and finally written by Aphra, his champion and confidante.

The story of "Oroonoko," which contains Aphra's own portrait painted with fine unconsciousness, arouses as much admiration for its author as for its ill-starred hero. Swinburne characterized it with unwonted terseness as "one feverish and impassioned protest against cruelty and tyranny." It is the first arraignment of slavery, the first literary exposure of its shames and crimes. To have seen them so clearly, to have felt them so deeply, honors Aphra's head and heart. Only a tender as well as an ardent nature could be so fiercely indignant at injustice, and so compassionate to its victims. Oppression of the weak fires Aphra's blood, but her pity is never outrun by wrath, however righteous. A generous temper implies courage, in Aphra's case even daring, physical as well as of the finer sort. Incidentally in the course of her narrative she refers to herself as a strong, athletic girl, fond of hunting and of sport, yet so highly strung that excess of feeling often made her ill; inclined to melancholy at times, like most vivacious and witty people, desirous of learning and of pleasing, susceptible, responsive, and, as always, through her adventurous and laborious life, "more ready to forgive an injury than do one."

We are told that she was a most beautiful woman. Her portrait, by Lely, painted in her prime, shows her dark but comely with some of the glow and fire of the tropics in her animated irregular face, dusky, wavy hair, and eyes that were neither sleepy nor languishing like those of the beauties of Hampton Court. She was slim and straight as a spear, slight enough to wear easily the long, laced straitjacket of current fashion, and round enough to curve gently above its bondage, like the bust of a nymph emerging from a stovepipe. Her nose was of the curious, witty variety, just escaping impertinence, what her neighbors across the Channel called *"un nez à la Roxelane";* her mouth, delicately sinuous, was more reflective than expansive; hers were not those overripe, scarlet lips that Lely bestowed impartially on his models. Her face was long from the eyes down, and ended in a slightly doubled chin. The painter gave her the columnar throat and falling shoulders that were evidently studio properties in the seventeenth and eighteenth centuries, at the disposition of every sitter.

There is a pen-portrait of Aphra written in terms too glowing to be quoted, though this flaming eulogy is printed among the Memoirs collected by the Unknown. Evidently Aphra was "a man's woman," one of those sirens whose supreme attraction defies definition. For all her sweetness there was plenty of spice in her sugar. Her anonymous friend says of her at the close of the Memoir: "She was of a generous and open temper, something passionate, very serviceable to her Friends in all that was in her Power; and could sooner forgive an injury than do one. She had Wit, Honor, Good-humour, and Judgment. She was Mistress of all the pleasing Arts of Conversation, but us'd 'em not to any but those who love Plaindealing. She was a Woman of Sense and by consequence a Lover of Pleasure, as indeed all, both Men and Women, are. . . . For my Part I knew her intimately, and never saw aught unbecoming the just modesty of our Sex."

IV

When the news of the death of her father's successor, who was lost at sea on his voyage to Surinam, reached her, Aphra "was awaiting the Arrival of the next Ships to carry her back to her desired England; where she soon after, to her Satisfaction, arrived." She had ample reason to be satisfied; for the year following, Aphra tells us in "Oroonoko" the English were driven out of their homes and most of them killed by the Dutch, who were soon afterwards massacred by the savages they had failed to propitiate as the prudent English had done. In "Oroonoko" again she assures us that his life would have been celebrated by a worthier than a "Female Pen," if the Dutch, "who immediately after his Time took that Country, had not killed, banished, and dispersed all those who were capable of giving the World this Great Man's Life much better than I have done it." Unfortunately a massacre of settlers by aborigines is too common an occurrence in the history of colonization to be a marking one, and does not help to fix the date of Aphra's landing in England. Her biographer laconically states that on her arrival Aphra "gave King Charles II so pleasant and rational an Account of his Affairs there, and particularly of the Misfortunes of Oroonoko, that he desired her to deliver them publickly to the World."

It is just at crucial moments in Aphra's career that her biographer becomes most mysteriously and irritatingly reticent. Aphra's arrival in England, her reception at court, her marriage are dismissed with a few words. Mr. Gosse places Aphra's return in 1658, Mr. Summers in 1663; apparently from the Fair Unknown's account King Charles had not only come to his own again, but was comfortably settled, at leisure to hear stories; so Aphra could not have been at court at least until the end of 1660, and probably later. The Unknown, who devotes whole pages to elaborate accounts of practical jokes and lively episodes, can only spare a line to "Oroonoko," her friend's "best seller." Indeed the more important the event the more succinctly is it mentioned. Perhaps the Unknown took it for granted that her readers were already familiar with the career of her friend, and therefore avoided its well-known features to dwell on side issues. As for dates, they are taboo, and not one is to be found in the seventy-three pages of the Memoir.

The grouping of events in many biographies, notably this one, recalls the serenely irresponsible way in which the old engraver, or landscape-painter, treated a historic site. Was Piranesi ever deterred by reverence for realities from transporting a temple to a more picturesque position, from rebuilding a palace to his own taste, from lengthening a staircase, or suppressing a façade? To fit harmoniously into the lines of his composition did not the mountain come to Claude Lorrain more meekly than to Mohammed? Were not rivers diverted from their sources, and forests uprooted by this chartered libertine of landscape? The biographer was no more shackled by realism than the painter, and unabashed took the same liberties in the arrangement of his material. For her own reasons the Unknown chose to telescope the events of this brilliant period of her friend's career, but much can be read between the few lines vouchsafed it.

The year 1660 saw a prodigious scene-shifting: Aphra's old world was upside down; her "desired" England was once more under the rule of the Stuarts. The cavaliers were drunk with joy—and other intoxicants—and Aphra, stanch little Royalist, rejoiced with them; the England of her childhood, the stern-browed and helmeted England, devout and pure, had vanished utterly. What was the new England to stand for? What ideals was restored royalty upholding, what virtues was it honoring? What influences were to shape, and what examples determine the character and the nascent powers of an impulsive, ardent, and impressionable girl? Gone was the grim Puritan concept of life, with its enthronement of duty, its distrust of happiness, its scorn of delight, its strait intolerance. Aphra consciously and temperamentally had rejected it always. Warm-hearted, detesting cruelty and injustice, she would have eagerly welcomed a more humane ideal of conduct. What did the new order of things offer her?

England was merry, for the orgy of the Restoration had begun. All that was accursed had become blessed, the forbidden was the enjoined, and what was sin in the past was salvation in the present. The people had turned a moral somersault, and were dizzy and dazed by the whirl of it. Away with long faces and short locks! Down with psalm-singing and sad-colored doublets! A forest of Maypoles sprang up in a night. Herrick's Julia, unrebuked, spiced her bride's cake; bear- and cock-pit, prize- and bull-ring flung open their doors. The younger seamen "heard the Common-prayer, and God-damn-ye for the first time on the "Naseby" that brought home his Majesty." Swearing was a mark of loyalty, and society was clothed with cursing as with a garment. Gaming and drinking were rehabilitated. Dancing was counted a duty, "a thing useful to any gentleman," and he who figured well in a coranto at court found Fortune compliant. The bells were unmuzzled, the pictures and statues unveiled. Serenade and madrigal sang out the short spring nights; tavern and ale-house echoed once more to jolly catch and ringing rouse. The playhouses, dark for fifteen years, lighted their candles, and to their old-time magic added sexual sorcery, young and beautiful women playing Desdemona and Fidelia.

Dress, so long legislated into simplicity and modesty, broke out again into vivid color and extravagant form. The kerchief slipped from the shoulders, the tuckers shrank away; there was more lace and more ribbon on a cavalier's rhingrave than on a lady's petticoat, and twice as many curls on his head, and feathers on his hat. The plumed and crested male creature far outshone his mate, and as Dame Pullet to Chanticleer was Mrs. Pepys to her lord.

England was merry again. The watch was beaten blithely, poor folk returning from work late at night to their dens were set upon by lively cavaliers, slashed, larded, stabbed—sometimes mortally—in sheer high spirits and pure fun. To trick a difficult, puritanical jade with a mock marriage, to throw billets of wood at a tethered fowl until it was bruised to death, to hire bravos to thrash an impudent actor, or slit the nose of a rival, were popular manifestations of the prevailing lightness of heart. But the best sport of all was that liberally furnished by a merry monarch to his joyous people: the drawing, hanging, and quartering of Republicans. The gibbeting of dead Puritans, though diverting, was comparatively lacking in comic and dramatic incident, but an execution, especially the droll antics and contortions of the condemned at the end of their ropes, afforded more merriment than any puppet-show. Decent, self-respecting folk hired windows to see Sir Harry Vane, or Algernon Sidney, die. Pepys having been on April 11 to the Cockpit where, during the play a very pretty lady who sat by him "called out to see Desdemona smothered," noted on April 13: "I went out to Charing Cross to see Major General Harrison hanged, drawn, and quartered, which was done there; he looked as cheerful as any man would look in that condition." After this morning entertainment Pepys spent the afternoon "setting up shelves" in his study. Indeed the observant

Samuel who seldom missed a play or a gibbeting mentions several times the "cheerfulness" of the condemned. It was of a feeble variety compared to that of the spectators.

He who contributed so much to the general amusement had many reasons to be merry; from the hour he landed at Dover his life had been a royal progress. The sorrows of his boyhood, the humiliations and dangers of his young manhood, were only a prelude to a triumphal march. England had thrown herself at his feet in a passion of penitent loyalty. The return of the Stuart seemed to have taken the heart out of the nation, so contrite was it for the Commonwealth's conquests, so desirous of atoning for two decades of republican glory. England craved forgiveness for her sovereignty of the three seas, for the defeat of Van Tromp, for sweeping the Mediterranean clean of pirates from Gibraltar to Candia; she begged pardon for having dominated Germany, cowed Spain, despoiled Holland, overawed France, and menaced Italy; for having raided Tunis and Algiers, humiliated Lisbon and seized Jamaica. Above all, she cried *peccavi* for having become the defender of the Protestant faith. Never was so swift a change of heart, so agile a change of front. The most redoubtable power in Europe was suddenly transformed into the flunky of France, the suitor of Portugal, the quintain of Holland, the proselyte of Rome! Who now could doubt the royal power to work miracles?

Under the King's touch the national pride and valor shrivelled and disappeared, England was cured of her king's evil.

Charles II's spaniels never cringed and fawned as did his courtiers, with Clarendon at their head. Were there ever such supple spines, such pliant knees? The only plaindealers at court were my Lady Castelmaine, and devil-may-care wits like De Grammont, who when the King drew his attention to the gentlemen serving at table on their knees, answered: "O, I thought they were begging your Majesty's pardon for giving you such a bad dinner." In general the English were as enamoured of their self-abasement as women are of their petty vanities, and to fetish-worship of the King was added the fervor of reaction in the carouse that followed the long fast of Puritanism.

Merry the monarch was not, saturnine rather and haunted by the fear of ennui, but it was always carnival time with his friends. A feverish pursuit of sensations urged them to every form of enjoyment —the finer as well as the baser sort. A new world for voluptuaries and epicureans was discovered, men of leisure and fashion gave the tone to life and literature. With the rake and the fop, the wit and the dilettante came to the fore. Though the Restoration did not restore taste, it "brought back the arts" (Walpole). The painters Lely, Cooper, Verrio, the medallists Rottier, the architect Wren, the musicians Purcell and Blow found not only patronage but appreciation at court. Never before had actors been so highly honored or actresses so nobly dishonored; Westminster Abbey opened its doors to the dead mime. Light literature was in favor. Men of fashion, who were also men of letters, wrote comedies as twenty years before they had written songs. Every scribbler had a play up his sleeve, as every poet had a tragedy on his desk. Belles-lettres were greatly esteemed; exquisite verse was written by roysterers, perfect songs by worldlings. As in mediæval times, nobility was doing its own singing, though people of fashion kept a poet as they did a coach. Music was added to verse. At court a band of violins, tenors, and basses supplanted the old viols, lutes, and cornets. The fine seventeenth-century engravings show the lute and the guitar on every toilet-table, with a copy of the newest air and the latest play. The *novella* was revived; not so often written as told. The recent translation of the "Arabian Nights" stimulated many imitators; the "*Quatre Façardins,*" and "*Le Bélier*" of Count Hamilton, unequalled for caustic wit and variety of incident, are still almost as diverting as the more famous Memoirs of his brother-in-law, De Grammont.

There was more than a pinch of Attic salt in the highly spiced entertainments at Whitehall or Hampton Court. The ladies, even of the dishevelled duchesses' circles, did not always sit on the floor in a ring to play "I love my love with an

A," as Pepys saw them; the *belle* Stuart was considered a simpleton because she liked building cardhouses and romping in Blind Man's Buff, and La Mazarine owed her place and her pension in England more to her wit than to her overblown beauty. Courtiers who read Hobbes, and carried "Hudibras" in their pockets, and played in masques, were not lacking in love of letters. Waller and Saint Evremond were of the court as well as Rochester and Buckingham, and Rochester and Buckingham could talk well and write admirably. That "literature had become a matter of study rather than inspiration, an employment of taste rather than enthusiasm, a source of amusement instead of an *emotion*" (Taine), is incontestable. But if the muse of epic poetry, turned Puritan, had retired to "a low chamber hung with rusty green tapestry" in a humble house in Bread Street, her looser-zoned sisters remained in the world.

Where there are leisure and highly developed social conditions, conversation is included among the pleasures of life. Conversation, in the French sense, there was not except at Will's coffee-house, or at Mr. Evelyn's, or occasionally at Mr. Pepys's men's dinners, or at Knowle, or in Milton's cottage, whither lettered folk made constant pilgrimage to honor the last of the Elizabethans. But there was constant talk in most court circles—banter, raillery often brilliant, sometimes bitter, that occasionally hardened into satire or lampoon. A bout of verbal fence between two such old hands as Etherege and De Grammont must have been diverting to ears not overnice. Talk among men of their kidney was not an exchange of ideas, a clear and carefully considered expression of opinion, with an amiable, or at least a decent, deference for the views of others, but an encounter of personality, a contest where wit sought to wound as often as to surprise or illumine.

Gossip was virulent in tone, and any story about anybody was accepted and repeated if it were sufficiently amusing. Amusing it generally was when Hamilton or Buckhurst retailed it, and surely when propriety and amenity are alike disregarded, it is not so difficult to be witty. Every conversational barrier was down. Neither age, nor sex, nor rank, nor achievement were respected. Imagine a society in which an accomplished cavalier on the day that the Protector's body was taken from Westminster Abbey and hung on the gibbet at Tyburn, could tell Cromwell's daughter that he had just seen her father, and that he smelt very evilly!

This brutality occasionally took a more courageous form, and Talbot astounded French courtiers by his reply to Louis XIV. The King, after remarking Talbot's extraordinary resemblance to himself, asked him: "Was your mother ever at my father's court?" Talbot answered instantly: "No, sire, but my father was!" Reckless Killigrew appeared booted and spurred one morning at Whitehall, and told the King that he was "starting for Hell to beg the Devil to send back Oliver Cromwell to take charge of the affairs of England, for his successor is always employed in other business." Charles II's fellow-feeling for jesters made him as lenient to them as he was ruthless to Republicans. His pleasantries were less cruel than those of his courtiers, and the royal wit pardoned their quips on the King. "His was a plain, well-bred, gaining, recommending kind of wit," we are told. He was an admirable story-teller, and anecdotes and tales were popular at court. His own career was rich in adventures which he told well, said Buckingham, and too often, Rochester averred, wondering, "how a person who possessed so good a memory as to repeat a story without missing a word, should have so bad a one as to forget that he had told it to the same company but the day before."

Lounging lends itself to long talks and story-telling. Though the King was a fast walker, and an expert tennis-player, his mornings were delightfully wasted strolling in Green Park with his pack of little dogs, feeding the water-fowl on Duck Island, of which Saint Evremond was facetiously made governor, as Zamor was of Louveciennes by Louis XV. Here Charles walked with Hobbes, or Evelyn, or (his taste for society was eclectic) hummed a song leaning on honest Tom D'Urfey's shoulder, or that rogue Rochester's. In these rambles formality was doffed like a stiff court costume.

Perhaps it was during one of those strolls that Aphra told her King the story of the royal slave. It was a sad tale, suited for sober morning hours rather than for postcenal ones. Local color enhanced its human interest, first-hand news from a remote colony was rare, and the animation and charm of the story-teller counted for something. Southerne said of "Oroonoko" that "she always told his Story more feelingly than she writ it." Aphra had brought illustrations to her tale; the skin of a huge serpent "to be seen at his Majesty's Antiquary's," marvellous butterflies, and a set of feather ornaments, "the dress of the Indian Queen," presented by the natives to Aphra, and given by her to the King's Theatre. "It was infinitely admired by Persons of Quality, and was inimitable," Aphra averred. Conjecture is useless as to whether or not these exhibits enhanced the vogue of the story. Probably royal and court patronage sufficed; in any case, "Oroonoko" was finally published, and at once became one of the books that have moulded public opinion.

V

Did Aphra's marriage precede or follow her appearance at court? The Unknown refers casually to these nuptials *en passant*, and not even a silhouette remains of Mr. Behn, "a Merchant of this City tho' of *Dutch* extraction." Indeed he seems an unsubstantial being, a kind of male Mrs. Harris, or Diotima, and is thus summarily dismissed by a sceptical modern biographer: "On her return to London she [Aphra] is said to have married Mr. Behn, a merchant of 'Dutch extraction' residing in that city, of whom nothing has ever been known, if anything more ever existed." A strong aversion to the Dutch, and especially to Dutchmen in love, is the only side-light cast by Aphra herself on this subject. It has been suggested that a rich marriage secured her an *entrée* at court, and a position in society, but this is a mere supposition as the Dutch were out of favor in Charles II's time; Aphra in caricaturing them in her plays was perhaps only following the Royalist fashion of aspersing the courage and good sense of a brave and astute enemy. Perhaps Mr. Behn as a mere commoner, a city man, adding no lustre to his wife's fame, was ignored by Aphra's biographer.

So much for Mrs. Behn's husband! His wife learned to know London well in the roistering sixties. Apparently for some years she was a lady of leisure, if not of quality. Familiarity with the court was already a liberal education in folly; Aphra completed it by a postgraduate course in the dissipation of the Town. London was a bustling Vanity Fair for a pleasure-loving young woman. There were diversions of all kinds, for all tastes, from the prize-ring to the conversation of wits and wise men. The day of any lady with money and time to waste was a full one; generally it began at eight o'clock with prayers and chocolate in bed. At eleven, when "the long labours of the toilet" were but half finished, came Bohea and bread and butter, shared with early visitors, and flavored with gossip. Between the tiring- and the tea-table the morning was dawdled away. Visits were also received in bed when the lady though willing to appear undressed had "put on her best Looks" and slipped into a French nightgown. Interludes diversified the toils of dressing. Addison's Sempronia talked politics with her hair down her back, divided her discourses between her woman and her visitors, made sprightly transitions from an opera or a sermon to an ivory comb or a pincushion, and "held her tongue in the midst of a moral reflection by applying the tip of it to a patch."

In the pretty clutter of silver, crystal, and ivory on the toilet-table, a lute or a guitar found room; there were playbills under the rouge-pot, and the curling-tongs were wiped on copies of verses. Letter-writing and beautifying went on together. There was always a little shelf for scribbling a note, a compartment for pen, ink, and paper in the toilet-tables, and old letters may owe something of their ease and spontaneity to these comfortable conditions. When the visitors were gone and the letters written, there were suits of ribands to be sorted, new "heads" to be tried, orders given to have Cupid or Veney "washed and combed"; indeed, there was scant time before the three-o'clock dinner to hurry over a new song, glance at a lampoon or the latest play. Sometimes, indeed, ladies huddled on their clothes, or went masked "in their mobs," to consult a fortune-teller in the morning hours, and in the spring even sluggards were up and out before dawn to gather May dew for their complexions.

Occasionally, too, the lady was dressed betimes to sit for her portrait. She had a fair choice of painters. She could be immortalized by Cooper, "the great limner in little," for thirty pounds, or "done in chiaroscuro" by Halys for fourteen pounds. (That is what Mr. Pepys paid for his own portrait.) Mary Beale, Lely's pupil, John Riley (both of them painted Aphra), or Wissing, might be depended upon for good, though not brilliant work. If her purse were long, and her taste docilely followed the fashion, Lely (who made an engaging portrait of Aphra) would be a fine lady's first choice. Were she chaste as Diana, diligent as Penelope, learned as Circe, he would see her, and make others see her, as a languishing, ogling coquette, half nude in her elusive draperies, her hair in a fine disorder, apparently just out of bed, ready for her chocolate and the playbills, or the early visit of an admirer. For background the sitter could have a cellar, a noble park, or a rich curtain. Military or nautical gentlemen were allowed a battle or a sea-fight as an adjunct, on which they frequently turned their backs. To scholarly male persons, globes, books, and maps were supplied; Mrs. Knott was exceptionally favored by Wissing with one book. The maternal portrait was quite out of date; offspring, unless they were illegitimate, or costumed as attendant Cupids, were considered old-fashioned, and worse—Puritanical. Small hounds, little shock-dogs, and negro pages replaced children and showed the white, lazy hands of the sitter to better advantage.

There was a great liking for the attributes of virgin saints, and the vesture of the most respectable of the Pagan goddesses. Both the Duchess of Cleveland and the Duchess of Richmond wore "indifferent well" the panoply of austere Athene, and the "belle Stuart" appropriated Diana's bow and quiver. Less imposing beauties, like the fair Middleton, and the baby-faced Duchess of Portsmouth, were content with the fruit and flowers of Pomona and Flora. The lamb of St. Agnes, St. Catherine's wheel and palm, her sword and scroll were pre-empted first by the King's mistresses, in compliment to the queen, Catherine of Braganza! Later many women of fashion and quality followed suit, and the costume and attributes of the Alexandrian saint finally were assumed by the city ladies. The loveliest of the many St. Catherines was the Duke of York's Mrs. Bellasys; Nell Gwyn preferred the lamb, when she was not costumed as Cupid or Venus.

But whether her portrait was painted or not, these mornings were so well filled that the meat was often as cold as the punctual husband's temper was heated, before the busy lady was ready to dine, at three o'clock. Dinner despatched, a chair or the coach was ordered for a round of visits, a little shopping, and a turn in the Park. St. James's Street offered the most tempting shops and the finest houses. It was the gay heart of the city, and ran from Piccadilly or Portugal Street down to St. James's Park, which then included Green Park as well, and was an open meadow. Charles II had cut a canal through it, planted it with lime-trees, and made of the footpath that crossed it a wide, smooth road called Pall Mall. People of fashion had settled in this pleasant quarter, and it lodged wits as well as beaux, Mr. Waller among them. For air and good company Pall Mall had no rival, but the New Exchange, an arcade leading out of the Strand filled with tempting shops, beguiling chapmen, and pretty girls selling fans and ribbons, scents and gloves, was a favorite lounge. A whole afternoon could be agreeably squandered there, cheapening china, haggling over a yard of lace, flirting and gossiping *al fresco*. Mrs. Trinkett's shop for modish toys and perfumes, gay as a net full of butterflies, was always crowded. There love-letters were exchanged and messages sent, for Mrs. Trinkett was an elderly Iris to the fop touching his eyebrows with essence of jessamine, and the coquette choosing a favor for her lap-dog.

Such folk were too nice to dance at "The Bear" in Drury Lane, where the fiddles were hard at it day and night, though for a snack or a frolic they went to "The Folly," a curious floating restaurant anchored in the Thames with something of the scow, and something of the excursion-steamer about it, if old prints are to be trusted. There were other pleasure resorts—Mulberry and Spring Gardens, but the favorite of the moment was Fulke's Hall, or Foxhall, a strip of land on the Lambeth side of the Thames, once part of the domain of Foulques de Bréauté, King John's minister, now a garden for collations and music. There was the puppet-show at Covent Garden if one liked horse-play and broad jests, and the bear-gardens if a lady's nerves were strong, and she did not mind having a mangled dog tossed onto her lap, or seeing a fine horse baited by curs. There was stronger whet for jaded pleasure-seekers in the matches between couples of bargees, butchers, and sometimes women, stripped to the waist and hacking at each other with cutlasses. Ladies of delicate sensibilities, however, always went to matches masked, or in men's clothes. Even such means could not win them an entrance to the symposia at Will's coffee-house, at the corner of Russell and Bow Streets where all the town wits from Dryden the poet and Mr. Harris the player to "Mr. Hook of our college" met for sober revelry. These staid suppers were not for Aphra; her feasts were less delicate; treats at fashionable taverns, country frolics where city folk danced on the green and ate curds and whey, and trips to Bartholomew's

Fair to have fortunes told, buy fairings, and see the Pig-faced Lady.

Finer pleasures were Aphra's also: English music was in its lovely noble youth. Simple and gentle alike loved and practised it. From the shepherds piping on "oaten straws" to rigorous Colonel Hutchinson playing his viol da gamba all English folk were making music; in it Puritan Milton and Pagan courtier found fellowship. The mastery of a musical instrument was included in a liberal education, and part-singing was an every-day accomplishment. There was music everywhere: at chapel, at the play, "on the leads," and on the Thames, that borrowed something of Venetian gayety and splendor when furrowed by beflagged and beflowered barges freighted with lutes, guitars, and violins.

Late afternoon saw Aphra at the opera or the play. The theatre was a drawing-room for informal receptions. People visited from box to box; fops combed their periwigs; ladies chattered, orange girls peddled their fruit, deadhead critics audibly damned the play, and the audience to a man, in spite of its purfled laces and pale satins, sucked oranges.

From the play to the Park was not far in a smaller if not cleaner London. The glass coach, with its gilding and color, its arms and devices, its caparisoned horses and belaced coachman and footman, was a more brilliant setting than the rather dingy theatre-box. It was not only fine in itself, but it stood for

APHRA BEHN 169

so much: position, achievement, wealth, and success. Remember Mr. Pepys's flutter of pride, fear, and anxiety when on the memorable first day of May (1669) he and his wife first rode in their own coach after weeks of consultation and ceaseless superintendence of its varnishing and furnishing. Pity Nature was unsympathetically inclement; it was "dusty, windy, and cold, and what made it worse, there were so many hackney coaches, as spoiled the sight of the gentlemen's," especially such as were airing their own equipages for the first time. Hamilton celebrated the battle royal between the Duchesses of Cleveland and Richmond, the King's past and present, for the *éclat* of a first appearance in Charles II's new glass calash fresh from France, the gift of De Grammont.

Evening brought revels. There were the court balls, elaborate ballets, superbly costumed, danced by the King and the princes; masques played by royal and court ladies in beautiful fantastic dresses, sewn with jewels. Even pious Miss Blague, Evelyn's platonic flame, wore £20,000 worth of gems when she appeared in the title rôle of Crowne's "Calisto." Of the brilliant hunting-parties and the gorgeous masquerades Aphra may have been a spectator if not a participant; to her nimble wit and high spirits, the masked ball afforded endless opportunities for mystifications and practical jokes. Jests were rather cruel, and no respecters of persons when Rochester disguised himself as a fortune-teller to shame court ladies, and even irreproachable Miss Hamilton made a laughing-stock of the Marquis de Brisacier and the saintly Miss Blague. The mask was a constant factor in Aphra's plays, and an easy means of creating dramatic imbroglios.

Did Aphra know the feverish delights of gaming? If she did not she was an exceptionally prudent person, for everybody gambled from the courtiers whom Evelyn saw on Sunday evening "at basset around a large gallery table, a bank of at least £2,000 in gold before them," to the quiet county families over their fireside picquet. Bets and wagers were as popular as basset, and as expensive, and to play cards without a stake would have seemed as impossible as getting drunk on cinnamon water.

It is not a pleasant process to follow, that of the coarsening and hardening of a fine, generous spirit. We have no data by which to measure Aphra's descent into Avernus, but after a few years of court and town life vice had no veil, evil no mystery for her, and the seamy side of things was always before her eyes. She was essentially a woman of her time, and, in spite of her chivalrous temper, could no more escape the influence of her environment than a planet can change its pressure and its atmosphere. The heat of the compost forced the flower, withering while stimulating it, Hobbes's philosophy was no aid to noble living, and the maxims of La Rochefoucauld were as blighting to ideals as the example of the Duchess of Portsmouth or the patronage of Nell Gwyn.

Apparently the death of Mr. Behn (possibly of the plague, in 1665) closed this stage of Aphra's progress and threw her on her own resources. Clever, handsome, experienced, a nimble wit and an engaging talker, she found court favor and general popularity a slight defense against the wolf and turned her talents to stocking her larder and replenishing her wardrobe. She had a facile pen, an engaging address, a knowledge of men and tongues for sale, no prejudices and few illusions, so she soon found a market for her wares. She was not contented to be a mere scribbling creature, but aspired, like many brother writers, to a larger career, and longed to poke her small finger into the political pie. There were plums to spare in it in the early days of Charles II's reign. Most things and most people were for sale, and Aphra's experience and training had not steeled her against considering herself a negotiable commodity; in a word she became a political spy, and was despatched to Antwerp. Her business was to send news of the movements of the Dutch fleet to England. Her Dutch name, some knowledge of the Dutch language, and familiarity with Dutch customs were her assets. Sardou's captivating Countess Ziska, the bewitching betrayer of political men, has familiarized us with a type of secret agent not uncommon in Europe even to-day.

VI

In 1662 the old rivalry between Dutch and English had broken out afresh. By the cession of Bombay, which opened India to England, and the formation of a London company to trade with the African Gold Coast, Holland's jealousy was reawakened. Nor did England lack cause for quarrel. The sturdy Republic, no respecter of persons, had formerly flouted the pretensions of Charles II, a prince without dignity or credit, a seedy, poverty-stricken Pretender who skulked about dodging his creditors and boozing in pothouses. The King of England still smarted from Dutch gibes and Dutch caricatures. Naturally, then, the ruin of an odious republican government, with no reverence for the Lord's Anointed, and a flourishing trade with the Far East, would be doubly grateful to him. Fortune hitherto had been even-handed and divided honors between the combatants. In 1665 the obstinate battle of Lowestoft ended with the defeat of the Dutch. The next year De Ruyter after a three days' fight off the North Foreland drove Monk and the English ships into the Thames. In a third battle the English had their revenge, chased the Dutch into the Texel, and sailed along the coast, burning the unfortified town of Brandaris (1666).

Holland soon reformed and refitted her fleet and meanwhile extravagance and mismanagement had weakened the English navy; plague and fire had harried and impoverished London; her treasury was empty, her forts undefended, and her ships unmanned. The King and his brother, who had thousands of crowns to throw into an actress's lap, or to stake on a cast of the dice, had no money to pay their sailors. The situation was grave. How would Cornelius de Witt profit by it? What would be his next move? What was Holland planning? Aphra, and undoubtedly many other spies, were sent to find out.

There are two widely differing accounts of Aphra's mission to Holland. The first is her own, slightly touched up, it may be, by her biographer, or her editor, Charles Gildon. It is a highly colored, romantic story, full of interest and dramatic situations. Some of them suggest that the Italian novelists were as useful to the English writers of the seventeenth, as they had been to the dramatists of the sixteenth century. Plots and ruses, billets-doux, disguises, rival lovers, a charming confidante, an irresistible leading lady, and an intriguing duenna, a series of Decameronian episodes in a setting by Rubens, gay, debonair, and voluptuous, furnish material for a sparkling, bustling comedy. Aphra, then, according to her biographer, enlivened her political mission with plenty of fun and feasting. Antwerp, the scene of her labors, was a *pays de Cocagne*, and life in the Low Countries was softly wadded with material comforts. Was there ever more domestic luxury, more intimate charm than in those cosey, deliciously painted interiors of the "little" Dutch Masters? Was Aphra as snugly housed as those flaxen-haired, chinless ladies who, in their canary-colored satin sacques edged with swan's-down, or in long-waisted, trimly laced brocade gowns, make music, lightly touching the lute, or daintily fingering the harpsichord? Did she play at cards with rubicund, high-booted cavaliers? Were her despatches written in a quiet-toned study with burnished panes and clear gray walls, enriched with paintings and maps like that of Netscher's "Letterwriter"? Where else in Europe were there such clean, warm houses, dignified by the beauty of Eastern stuffs, the cool sheen of rare porcelain, the bluish lights and deep shadows of well-polished wood? They were ready-made backgrounds for a colorist, those richly toned chambers, where the subdued light, struggling through banks of vapor and leaded glass, fell upon gleaming floors of black and white marble, on tulips flaring at the casement's ledge, on parrots vivid as the flowers, preening their flaming plumage in dusky cages, on the pearly hands of a lace-maker, or the pale gold of a long-stemmed glass of white wine. It is always there, the white wine, flanked with other good things, plump oysters, or deep-colored fruit. Pleasant was the lot of the home-keeping dame in such chambers as those in which Vrouw Mieris plays with her silky spaniels, or Terborch's young ladies read their love-letters, or Vermeer's white girls clasp their pearls; Holland could show scores of such interiors radiating peace and domesticated beauty. Did Aphra spread her nets and weave her webs in some such enchanting corner of Antwerp? She does not say, but while she was cozening her dupes she thriftily made notes for a new novel, finding her material in the life and adventures of a Flemish heiress and beauty.

Some practical jokes, Shakespearian in their breadth and heartiness, more to the taste of the jolly Queen of Navarre than of Julie d'Argennes, enlivened Aphra's sojourn in Antwerp. They would have alarmed a less intrepid lady, but Aphra dominated a dubious situation with such frank gayety, such a rush of high spirits, that her critic is surprised into tolerance of such verve, and such irresistible joy in life. To play upon the vanity and the senile passion of a doting old man, to make him a butt for guests and friends, very much as the Merry Wives fooled the fat knight, was venial if unkind; only the bloom was rubbed off the ladies in the process: playing with fire sometimes smirches when it does not burn. There was, however, more mischief than malice in these adventures.

One of them had a serious sequel. In a short time after Aphra arrived in Antwerp she had besieged, taken by storm, and occupied the weakly defended hearts of two Dutch gentlemen: Van Bruin, vain, obese, stingy yet showy, well past his prime, and Van der Aalbert of Utrecht, ardent, handsome, young and rich. He was in the confidence of De Witt, hence a useful tool for Aphra. By what surprises, what false sorties, what feigned retreats, what sudden sallies, what mines, and traps, Aphra won the confidence of her admirer, had best be left to those versed in such tactics to imagine. Doubtless by the same subtle arts that Dalilah, Circe, and Diana of the Crossways practised with equal success, or probably they were not subtle arts at all, but the old primitive method of betraying the vain and amorous male. But then man was always a primitive creature.

This is a sorry episode in Aphra's life which one would gladly obscure in a picture, but cannot omit in a portrait. Thackeray, apologizing for avoiding some dubious passages in Becky Sharpe's career, advises us only to look at the golden locks of the sirens, to listen to their sweet voices, and to keep our thoughts away from their scaly, hideous tails, crawling and twining about dead men's bones, and wrecked ships under the waves. The student of sirens, however, is obliged to note submarine phenomena.

Probably secret service always will have its apologists as well as its heroes and martyrs. Aphra herself and her biographer regarded her mission as an honorable and patriotic one and, being so considered, it was not degrading. If we could look upon Aphra as a character in fiction, as one of the disguised duchesses of the cycle of the "*Trois Mous-*

quetaires," who plot and intrigue, and lie with unfailing dash through two or three enthralling volumes, we should judge her very leniently or not at all, but from the friend and advocate of "Oroonoko" more is expected.

Van Bruin was played with, poor fat mouse, but Van der Aalbert was taken more seriously; though enamored he was not submissive, though devoted he proved masterful; Aphra had her wolf by the ears, and her hands were full. In a tender moment he betrayed his country and his friend, the Stadtholder by confiding to Aphra Cornelius de Witt's project "to sail up the River Thames and destroy the English Ships in their Harbours," which had been carefully timed and planned. It was more in the nature of a manifestation than a descent, a counter-stroke for the recent ravaging of Brandaris, but it would at once shame and cripple England already weakened and needy, and inflict an irreparable loss of prestige on the island that safe behind her "silver streak," had remained proudly inviolate since Norman William clutched and conquered her.

Aphra's despatch was sent post-haste to London. The Dutch fleet was to sail in June, there was no time for hesitation, only instant action might save England. But England as always was averse to instant action. More stolid than their stolid Dutch foes, the English councillors refused to move, dismissed Aphra's warning with an "Impossible!

They would never dare!" So the news was pooh-poohed with a laugh and a jest on the broad-beamed enemy, a sceptical raising of eyebrows, and perhaps a fleer at the credulity of women. If Aphra had had stomach for revenge she could have glutted it. On June 11, the punctual Dutch fleet appeared in the Nore. Nothing had been prepared to meet the enemy. "The Duke of Albemarle rushed down in his shirt with a great many idle lords and gentlemen," says Marvell, and raised a few score of dock-hands, and sunk ships in the Medway to obstruct the channel. Meanwhile the Dutch, unopposed, rather like a sea-pageant than an invader, sailed up the stricken Thames to Gravesend, forced the booms and broke the chains in the Medway, burned the English ships of war which lay at anchor in the river, carrying off the *Royal Charles*, which had brought the King to England in 1660, and withdrew only to patrol the coast and proclaim the Dutch masters of the Channel. Old Van Tromp's broom had never swept the sea so clean of Englishmen. Aphra was too good a patriot to enjoy the bitter-sweet of revenge; her kind heart would have ached could she have seen the terror and mortification of England in those long June days of 1667. "The alarm was so great that it put both city and country into fear, a panic and consternation . . . everybody was flying, none knew why or whither." On the 28th of the month the Dutch were still in the Nore blockading London, "a dreadful spectacle as ever Englishmen saw, and a dishonor never to be wiped off," wrote Evelyn, while Gossip Pepys added: "Everybody nowadays reflect upon Oliver and commend him; what brave things he did, and made all the neighbour princes fear him." The King, however, was calm, even merry, and joined with spirit in a chase after a moth at Lady Castelmaine's after supper, while the Dutch guns were booming in the Medway.

Meanwhile Van der Aalbert, having delivered the goods, presented his bill. He naturally expected to be well paid for his treason to his friend and his country, and when in return for his perfidy he himself was perfidiously treated (or, as Aphra's biographer plausibly puts it, "she contrived to preserve her Honor without injuring her Gratitude") his indignation at Aphra's breach of faith cried for revenge; angry, jealous, and tricked, he was not scrupulous in his choice of means, anything was fair against his betrayer. Aphra's sheep-dog was "an old, decayed Gentlewoman whom out of Charity she kept as her Companion"; but she, "guilty of the common Vice of the Age, was corrupted by Aalbert's Gold" to sell him an interview with Aphra; the beldame lent him the door-keys, and a suit of her clothes, so that disguised in them he could enter the house at will.

Aphra, since she had wheedled him out of his secret, had been inaccessible, almost invisible, and he had been unable to have a word with her, even to reproach her for her treachery. The false one, unstung by remorse, was always in company, and especially affected the society of two young ladies of Amsterdam, and that of their brother. One evening, the little party returned to Aphra's lodgings after a gay supper. Young people full of fun and white wine could not separate without a frolic. Some one proposed that as a fitting conclusion to a jovial evening the brother, "a brisk, lively, frolicksome young fellow," should rush into the old companion's room, which was also Aphra's, and surprise her with a declaration, "whilst they should all come in with Candles and compleat the merry Scene." As was agreed so they did, but the young spark was in his turn surprised when "the decayed old Gentlewoman," instead of squawking and shaking, instantly seized him in two muscular arms, and held him close prisoner until the lights and the ladies arrived and discovered Van der Aalbert in cap, kerchief, and gown clasping the adventurous young gentleman to his broad breast. The surprise was universal and complete, surpassing the fondest expectations of its authors. Such adventures were not uncommon even in the best circles; a similar one got Bonnivet a well-scratched face, and furnished Queen Marguerite with a most diverting tale which she told to a group (including her husband) of friends of the discomfited hero. Evidently a century later ladies still possessed the same robust sense of humor. Van der Aalbert's misadventure, while making him ridiculous, did not render him repulsive; indeed when were not women lenient to the offenses provoked by their charms? Evidently the delicate sentiments of the Hôtel Rambouillet had not been acclimated in Holland;

"Her Cupid was a blackguard boy."

The scene had the usual comedy denouement. Van der Aalbert, evidently still considering himself defrauded and ill-used by Aphra, "was appeased by her Promise to marry him at her Arrival in England. But Aalbert, taking his Leave of her with a heavy Heart, and returning into Holland to make all Things ready for his Voyage to England, and Matrimony, died at Amsterdam of a Fever while Aphra proceeded on her journey to Ostend, and Dunkirk where . . . she took shipping for England."

A very different aspect of a secret agent's experiences is gathered from the documents collated by Mr. Summers from Aphra's letters to Lord Arlington, Secretary of State, to James Halsall, Cupbearer to the King, and to Thomas Killigrew, Groom of the Bedchamber, and her three petitions. From them it appears that Aphra's first business in Holland was to find and communicate with William Scott, son of the regicide, Thomas Scott, who was executed after the Restoration. Scott was desirous of earning his pardon by spying on the English, many of them stanch Republicans, who were plotting against the King. As he was as hard up as Charles II had been before 1660, presumably Scott was to be bought at a moderate price.

Aphra started on her mission at the end of July with only forty pounds. In a letter of August 15, she writes that she has found Scott, whom she poetically styles Céladon, and who is eager to help her. Unfortunately he is himself a suspicious character and is closely watched by the English exiles, therefore great caution is necessary, and his meetings with Aphra must be sceret. Her succeeding letters are pleas for money, with which she was scantily provided. Discreet messengers are expensive, Scott is penniless and must be supported, Aphra's own living costs her ten guilders a day and, as she receives no remittances from England, by the end of August she is eighty pounds in debt. By September 4 she was in desperate need, and though she was faithfully forwarding Scott's letters under cover of her own, sending news of the Dutch navy, and of the illness of De Ruyter, she gets no answers and no pay.

The culpable neglect with which her information and her services were treated is easily accounted for by the general *laisser aller*, and disregard of public interests characteristic of the Merry Monarch's reign. Aphra continued to write, however, and the government continued to ignore her letters. Her finances went from bad to worse. On November 3 she sent a moving appeal for help to Lord Arlington;

she is without money or credit, has pawned everything, and is to be sent to prison for debt; the destitute Scott is already jailed. On December 26, in dire want she made a final effort. She begs for a hundred pounds as she is utterly discouraged, is disgusted with the whole business, and is only desirous of returning to England; she complains bitterly of her harsh treatment, and would be stark mad if she were not sustained by the justice of her cause and the consciousness of duty performed.

As this letter, like the others, was unnoticed, Mrs. Behn contrived to raise a loan of a hundred and fifty pounds from an Englishman, one Edward Butler, with which she paid her debts and her journey back to England. There more suffering and mortification waited for her. It was impossible to get a penny of her salary. The royal purse remained closed; prayers and arguments failed to open it, Butler pressed her for his money, and the horrors of the debtor's prison loomed before her. Three petitions tell the piteous story of Aphra's sordid woe. In the first describing her two years of constant effort and severe privation she begs for an order on the Keeper of the Privy Purse, Mr. May, for the one hundred and fifty pounds due her. To her second petition, enumerating her services, she appended a letter to Killigrew, a pathetic little document on gray paper in a fine Italian hand. Even to this appeal there was no answer, as in a third petition Aphra urges that the one hundred and fifty pounds be paid to

Edward Butler who, when neither money nor order was forthcoming, sent Aphra to prison. There is no record of her stay there, or of her release. Perhaps her mother succeeded in "throwing herself at the King's feet," and presenting Aphra's very moderate bill for service rendered. As Mr. Summers suggests, perhaps, finally, Killigrew came to her rescue. His own espionage on Charles II had been far better paid by Cromwell. As Aphra was always on good terms with Killigrew in after-life, this seems probable. Possibly some newer friend, touched by her undeserved misfortunes, helped her. In any case she was finally paid and vowed never to serve the state again, but thenceforth to devote her life "to pleasure, and poetry."

The two accounts of Aphra's failure as a political agent are not irreconcilable. Light-hearted Bohemians in dire straits are often able to amuse themselves with reckless abandonment. A dun at the door is but a *memento mori* to some temperaments. *Atra cura* is not so black as it is painted in letters to debtors or creditors, and a conviction of the dreariness and aridity of life as a whole, is not incompatible with appreciation of the delectable oases that stud its weary waste. Aphra may have pleaded, despaired, raged, wept herself sick, and then washed her face, put on a touch of Spanish vermilion, a pretty gown, and been the life of a gay supper. If there is no documentary evidence to support her assertion that she warned the English Government of De Ruyter's descent there is no evidence against it. In favor of Aphra's story is the English habit of procrastination, of undervaluing the enemy; the Englishman's belief in his invincibility, and his notorious unpreparedness, and if the excuse given by Aphra for her fiasco as secret agent was not true it was at least well found. Another lady, more happily circumstanced, had great difficulty in convincing Englishmen that their coast could be ravaged and that the Armada was coming. There is, if Aphra's story is entirely an invention, a gallant spirit in the effort to conceal the sordid misery of her misadventure under the bright frippery of her *novella*. But the Aphra of the documents is an honest and sympathetic person, working conscientiously at her unpleasant task, the coquettish Célimène of the "Memoir" is the false, vain, artificial fine lady of Restoration comedy.

VII

Aphra, then mortified at her fiasco in secret service, resolved to dedicate her life "to pleasure and poetry," or more prosaically to earn her bread by writing. Such a decision seems natural enough to-day; then it was revolutionary to an incalculable degree. No Englishwoman had ever written for a livelihood. There were few professions open to her sex. Aphra had tried the most lucrative and failed; "witchcraft and needle-work" remained, for Aphra had neither the accomplishments nor the disposition for a housekeeper or a gentlewoman's woman. A born scribe, she chose the quill, though it was hardly more respectable than the broomstick. She was without resources, she had no pension from the crown, which is a kind of certificate of virtue, proving that she had not rendered the kind of service that the King always rewarded, but though misfortune had been busy with her, and she was shipwrecked on her home voyage, she believed still that the world was her oyster, and eventually could be pried open by her pen. Very naturally she turned to the most lucrative branch of her chosen profession, playwriting, for with the reopening of the theatres in 1662 men of letters again became playwrights. There was a demand for new plays and they were fairly well paid. A dramatic author received all the third night's profits from his play, and what he could obtain from a bookseller for his copyright, for any play that ran nine nights appeared soon afterwards in book form. New plays were as eagerly read as new novels are now, and were an important source of revenue to a popular dramatist.

Under these favorable conditions a fresh crop of plays sprang up, a rank, weedy growth, "which was not literature or art or nature." Men of fashion like Killigrew and Howard wrote for the stage in a stilted, artificial style, then as the drama grew in popularity and influence and again began to take its place among the arts, Dryden, Etherege, Wilson, and Shadwell vitalized the play by bringing it into truer relations with life. When Aphra returned to London these were the four best-known names on the playbills, and very naturally their work was that most studied and imitated. Dryden was, of course, Aphra's model in tragedy. For her master in comedy she chose Etherege, when she was not imitating Molière, or borrowing from the Spaniards. Indeed Etherege has been credited with founding English comedy in his "Comical Revenge." Undoubtedly with him "the Ben Jonson comedy of humors, always with a kind of moral, and always with a *parti pris*, became an objective observation of morals and characters" (Gosse). In his maiden play (very reminiscential of "*L'Etourdi*," and "*Le Dépit Amoureux*") the valet Dufoy filled the rôle of hero, and the villains and traitors were Puritans; innovations hailed with delight by the gentry's flunkeys in the gallery, the King's lackeys in the boxes, and promptly adopted by Aphra and others. Four years later (1668) "She Would if She Could," won even greater popularity, and was followed nearly a decade afterwards (1676) by "The Man of Mode, or Sir Fopling Flutter," which tyrannized English comedy of manners for many years; it was a *pièce à clef*, Dorimant was Rochester, Medley stood for Sir Charles Sedley, and the minor characters were well-known people under a transparent disguise.

The success of "The Man of Mode," was immediate and immense. This comedy artificial as it remained, was partially vivified by the introduction of contemporary characters, studies from life, of actual scenes in London, of every-day conversations flavored with wit, and allusions to current events. Humor, vivacity, and bustle, if not action, accompanied characterization, and what was relatively realism.

As Aphra's successes were in comedy, no apology is required for dwelling on her exemplar; she needed a master as well as a model; playwriting was a new trade for her, with a new technic. Like all tyros, she wanted the advice and criticism of an old hand at her new business, for she had neither familiarity with the stage, nor the acquaintance of actors, so enlightening to a student as to the practical side of their art, nor a workaday familiarity with the requirements of dramatic presentation. She had not the successful playwright's knack of taking goods (other people's goods) wherever they were to be found. Plagiarism was universal, dramatic material, plots, situations, characters, were as truly common property as compositions, movements, and color arrangements were to the artists of the Renaissance. The greatest borrowed freely from every available source, and were held to honor what they appropriated; Dryden culled in every garden from Shakespeare's to Mademoiselle de Scudéry's; Molière's was an open common for a generation of dramatists to browse in at will.

APHRA BEHN 189

Aphra so far had lived on her own harvest, she needed an instructor in picking and stealing. Gossip would have it that she discovered her Fagin—a talented, witty Fagin—in Edward Ravenscroft. Like many of his fellows, he had deserted the law to follow a vagabond Muse, for Themis versus Thalia always loses her case and her votary. A member of the Inner Temple, "he had beguiled a fortnight's illness" with the composition of his first play, and afterwards "he spent some idle time after a similar fashion" to some purpose, for in 1672 his "Mamamouchi or the Citizen Turned Gentleman," an adaptation of Molière's "Bourgeois Gentilhomme," was produced at Dorset Gardens, ran nine nights, and was played thirty times before it was published with a dedication to Prince Rupert. This was a fair sample of a successful play.

Ravenscroft was a born adapter, the Dion Boucicault of his time. Not one of his *soi-disant* offspring but was a changeling. "Great wits oftener write to please themselves than the public," he remarked in one of his prologues and he acted as a literary middle-man, selecting and arranging their wares to catch the public eye. Aphra in her prentice days could have had no better master than this expert handler of dramatic goods. When and where Aphra and Ravenscroft met, how soon their acquaintance mellowed into friendship, cannot be guessed. Probably their lines converged in the Bohemia which lies on the lowest slopes of Parnassus. However, it was only in pilfering and stage-craft that Aphra could say: "Ravenscroft *magister erat*"; her style was unaffected by him. John Hoyle, an intimate friend of Mrs. Behn's, was also called her collaborator by the Grub Street *chronique scandaleuse*, but as he never wrote anything that resembles her authentic work, we may assume that Aphra was an exception to Heine's rule that the woman who writes always has one eye on the paper and the other on a man.

A dozen well-known playwrights were matriculated at the same time; between 1670 and 1675 Wycherly, Buckingham, Lacy, Settle, Otway, Lee, Crowne, Aphra Behn, and a host of minor writers, Ravenscroft among them, published their first plays. For twenty years this group dominated the English stage with only one addition: Southerne, "who belongs in age to the earlier and by genius to the later school." It was among these playwrights that Aphra found friends and comrades. Her first essay, "The Young King," was a failure; for it she could find neither manager nor publisher; undiscouraged, however, Aphra pursued the reluctant Muse. Her first battle was lost, but she soon won two others: "The Forced Marriage" (1670) and "The Amorous Prince" (1671) were presented at the Duke of York's Theatre with a fair measure of success, and amply justified her choice of a profession.

Two years later (1673) a lively comedy, "The Dutch Lover," showed Aphra still sore over England's humiliation in 1667, and "The Town Fop" her familiarity with the earlier dramatists' work and methods (1676). She held fast to a corner of Marlowe's mantle in "The Tragedy of Abdelazar" (1677). For this, Aphra says in a letter to a friend, the world treated her "as a Plagiery," and "not with Injustice." "But," she continues, "I have sent you the Garden from whence I gathered, and I hope you will not think me vain, if I say I have weeded and improved it." "Abdelazar" contains some lovely verse, and was produced as a kind of opera with musical interludes, and songs; for these Henry Purcell wrote the music, a sufficient proof that Aphra was gathering bays if not guineas. Like some of the happy rhymesters of the silver age, she possessed the special gift of song-writing: the linking of tuneful syllables that sing of themselves; a nice choice of vocables that coax open the lips and gently unclose the throat, and the felicitous selection of final vowels that prolong the sweetness of note and word. With "The Rover," a rollicking daredevil comedy (Duke's Theatre, 1677), guineas followed the bays. The play, produced anonymously, pleased royalty, and took the town by storm. The author was supposed to be a man, a man after the heart of Charles II and his crew; in it Aphra beat Wycherly at his own game of audacity, "The Rover" could give points to "The Plain Dealer," and Aphra was now to be reckoned with in her profession. "Sir Patient Fancy," her adaptation with new characters of "*Le Malade Imaginaire*" (1678), roused some adverse criticism, against which she defended herself in a sportive preface to the first edition of the play. One of her next year's comedies, "The Feigned Courtesans," was dedicated to Nell Gwyn (1679). The same year "The Young King," written in Surinam, revamped and dedicated to one of Aphra's admirers, Philaster, finally appeared. In the dedication the play is called "an American whose country rarely produces Beauties of this kind, the Muses seldom inhabit there . . . but for variety a Dowdy Lass may please." This "Dowdy Lass" is founded on an episode from La Calprenède's "*Cléopâtre,*" and one which never fails of dramatic effect, be the hero of it Abou Hassan or Christopher Sly.

In 1681 the second part of "The Rover" appeared under Aphra's own name. Like Farquhar's "Sir Harry Wildair," "The Rover" lost nothing of his dash and spirit after his resurrection. In 1682 "The Roundheads" and "The City Heiress," in which the Puritans were drearily vilified, were played to the joy of packed Tory audiences; Aphra was following in the track of "Hudibras," an inexpensive and short cut to success. "The False Count," an adaptation of Molière's "*Précieuses Ridicules,*" was well received the same year. At times Aphra was as prolific as a modern French poetess of whom it is said, "*Elle n'écrit pas ses poèmes, elle les pond.*" In 1687 a farce pantomime, "The Emperor of the

Moon," and a comedy, "The Lucky Chance" (1686), were added to her list of plays. Her works continued to appear after her death, as though her unlaid ghost still lingered where she had labored, and could not at once acquire the habit of repose. "The Widow Ranter or Bacon in Virginia" (1690) was published by one "G. J. her Friend," and "The Younger Brother" (played in 1696) by Gildon with a short Memoir. The prologue of the latter ended with these lines:

"Oh! then be kind to a poor Orphan Play,
Whose Parent while she lived obliged you all;
You praised her living and you mourned her Fall.
Who could like her our softer Passions move,
The Life of Humour, and the Soul of Love?
Wit's eldest sister; thro' out every Line
You might perceive some female Graces shine,
For poor Astrea's Infant we implore,
Let it then live tho' she is now no more."

In 1694 Southerne's tragedy, "Isabella, or The Fatal Marriage," founded on Mrs. Behn's novel, "The Nun, or the Fair Vowbreaker," and a favorite of Mrs. Siddons, appeared, followed two years later by the tragedy of "Oroonoko," Aphra's old friend Purcell writing the incidental music for them. Aphra's plays, published by the faithful Gildon in 1702, reached an eighth edition in 1735, a ninth in 1751. "The Rover," modified, remodelled, and rechristened as "Love in Many Masks," held the stage until 1790, and carried its author's name through another century.

Aphra's success had justified her audacity: another was added to women's vocations, which Mrs. Centlivre and Mary Pix soon adopted. Amiable and kind-hearted as Aphra was, each of her hardwon triumphs made her new enemies. She answered their gibes and abuse tartly enough in some of her dedications and prologues. When her rivals could not deny her wit they aspersed her character or asserted that her plays were the work of her lovers. She was accused of plagiarism at a time when every dramatist, from Dryden to a drollwriter, ignored all distinctions between mine and thine. She was rebuked for her indelicacy by admirers of Wycherly and Rochester. She was ordered back to her spindle because she handled the stylus too successfully. She paid the usual price of achievement to detraction and envy.

VIII

A catalogue of dramas, even a *catalogue raisonné* with analyses of plots, specimens of dialogue, lists of characters, and a carefully ticketed exhibit of the stolen goods the plays contain, is dreary reading. It is a handful of seeds in lieu of a nosegay. Even a play published with various readings and notes historical and technical, is but a pressed flower, the wraith of the live thing. Still some idea of its lost color and life may be guessed at, even faintly pictured, perhaps, by an evocation of the actual conditions under which a dramatic work was originally produced.

A drama is such a complex work of art that its mere shell and setting count for much in its effect. The theatre which supplies environment, the stage which furnishes background, the actors that vitalize the characters, and also the nature and temper of the audience are all factors in the success and life of a play, and consequently in the popular estimate of its value; not of masterpieces, nor of such works as are "not for a day, but for all time," but of a mere workaday play to be acted, not read in the study. A glance at audience, greenroom, actors, and stage may aid understanding of the phenomenal success of Mrs. Behn's "Rover," which a century could not stale, and which pleased a generation of playgoers and actors, from Nell Gwyn to Mrs. Jordan, from Betterton to Kemble.

In the last quarter of the seventeenth century attendance at the theatre had become a habit among the higher and middle classes in London. Not to have seen the newest play was to be as much in the rear of the mode as to cling to an old peruke or an antiquated farthingale. The drama was not only a mental diversion, it was a means of social reunion. The theatres, particularly that first gallery where beauty and fashion glowed in a radiant half-circle, were enlarged drawing-rooms of rather mixed companies. It was at the play that novelties in the fashion of attire, as well as of thought and speech, made their bow to a critical public, and were approved or condemned, that Mr. Pepys sought a model for a new coat, and that the playwright avenged English defeats by ridiculing the Dutch. Aside, however, from these exterior attractions the play *was* the thing that a handsome proportion of the audience found of paramount interest.

The last comedy, the newest tragedy, was a topic of conversation in circles polite as well as learned; mischievous fops quoted its dubious witticisms, and pensive young ladies learned its tender speeches by heart. If roisterers infested the theatre to sit in the orange girls' laps, or to hustle the footmen on their way to the second gallery, if the worn gamesters of the basset-table lent but an unheeding ear to Dorimant's jests or Imoinda's plaints, on the other hand the Mæcenases, the noble patrons of literature, and the patronized who have made their patrons and their age illustrious were present in force.

Leavening the lump, binding the ruder and grosser to the finer and subtler elements of the audience, ran an electric current of intelligence. Scattered over the playhouse were connoisseurs of literature, fellow-workmen, appreciative of verbal felicities, virtuosi in language, sensitive to each nicely turned phrase, or well-balanced antithesis, as instantly responsive to a witty sally as they were indulgent to breadth of jest or audacity in situation. For if in the pit lolled Mrs. Flirt and Betty Flauntit, there also sat in judgment critics of taste and discrimination: Saint Evremond, Hamilton, staid John Evelyn, when he could be lured from his books and gardens at Sayes Court, De Grammont, not too eager in the pursuit of a new beauty to miss a fine line or a telling hit. There too were the poets: worldly Waller in some duchess's box, and "the mob of gentlemen who wrote in verse," that aristocracy of literary cultivation, who loved letters generously, cherished literary men with a fraternal affection, and sacrificed to the Muse themselves always with ardor, often with success. Authorship was the fashion. "Without his song no fop is to be found," laughed Lord Mulgrave, but all courtly singers were not fops, and some fops were sweet singers. Among the poet-lovers of the play were Roscommon, admirer of Milton and friend of Dryden, who in Charles II's reign was the only poet-peer to boast "unspotted bays"; Dorset, "the grace of courts, the muse's pride," the earliest writer of society verse, the friend and host of poets at Knowle, where he renewed the symposia of Lorenzo de' Medici; Sedley, whose sprightly graceful verse possessed

> "that prevailing gentle art
> That can with a resistless charm impart
> The loosest wishes to the chastest heart,"

and who was a discriminating dramatic critic. Pepys always enjoyed sitting near him at the theatre, where his comments on a new play were more interesting than the piece. Rochester, who was a lover of plays as well as of actresses, rarely missed a first representation, sometimes lending a hand himself by contributing a prologue or a song, sometimes, as in the case of Mrs. Barry, intelligently and tirelessly training a player for the boards. Prince Rupert on the contrary was only lured from his crucibles and alembics when pretty Mrs. Hughes played. A constant theatre-goer was magnificent, insolent Buckingham, author of a successful and witty burlesque, "The Rehearsal," that killed the heroic comedy, as "Don Quixote" had murdered the heroic novel.

Did Herrick in his old age desert his pets and Prudence Baldwin for London and the play? Was Cowley, whose Latin poems Aphra versified in an English translation, ever lured from his tranquil retreat in Chertsey for the pleasures of theatre and coffee-house in London? Did that noble old Puritan, Andrew Marvel, who could pity Charles I and praise Cromwell, and remain constant always to Milton and his republican ideals, find relief from cares of state at the play? Who knows? He would hardly choose Aphra's comedies as his diversion.

There were always fellow-dramatists in an audience to whom a playwright could appeal, sure of their understanding, if not of their good feeling: Wycherly, in the full flush of the success of "The Plain Dealer," leering impartially at the beauties in the side-boxes and the beauties on the stage; Etherege, the most popular playwright in England, and himself "The Man of Mode"; Settle, not yet reduced to playing the dragon in a leather case of his own invention in low drolls at Bartholomew's Fair; Shadwell, whose comedy of "Epsom Wells" was second only in popularity to "The Man of Mode," and who dared the thunders of Dryden's ire, and deserved them, for he wrote of his own arrangement of Shakespeare's "Timon of Athens": "I have made it into a play." Nat Lee, author of "The Rival Queens," having failed as an actor, was just beginning his long career as playwright when "The Rover" appeared.

Otway, we may be sure, would be in the house, full of good wishes on the first nights of Mrs. Behn's plays. They had been friends since 1670, when the poet, just turned twenty and badly stage-struck, managed to slip into the greenroom of the Duke's Theatre; Mrs. Behn's play of "The Forced Marriage or the Jealous Bridegroom," was being rehearsed; to her Otway confided his craze to act, and the amiable creature, touched by his young enthusiasm, and perhaps by his boyish beauty, gave him the small rôle of the aged King in her play, where Betterton, then middle-aged, acted the young lover. It was an excellent part for a novice, that of the King, with only a few lines until the fifth act, where he unites the lovers and closes the comedy with a kindly speech bound to please the audience, and insure applause. Poor Otway was seized with stage fright, was inarticulate and benumbed; "The full house put him to such a sweat, and tremendous agony, that being dash't spoilt him for an actor." Twelve years later he wrote the prologue for his constant friend's "City Heiress," and to a great lady who censured the indelicacy of the plot of his own "Soldier's Fortune," he replied: "I have heard a lady (Mrs. Behn) that has more modesty than any of these she-critics, and I am sure more wit, say that she wondered at the impudence of any of her sex who would pretend to an opinion on such a matter." That he could consider Mrs. Behn a censor of decency shows what good and loyal friends Otway and Aphra continued to be through successes and failures. In an age of constant quarrels between authors, when writers assaulted each other as foully and fiercely as did the Humanists of the Renaissance, Mrs. Behn was not immune from abuse, but she was on friendly terms with most of her fellow workers, and generally stood aloof from the squabbles and the scandals of her comrades. Was she too busy or too kind to join in the frays? Perhaps both. Dryden, the greatest poet of a little age, was her friend and wrote with his usual generosity (to those he liked) of her work. From his own forest of laurels he could easily spare a leaf or two for an amiable, hard-working woman who minded her pen instead of her neighbor's sins, who was occasionally sharp-tongued in her own defense, but never bitter, and had kind words for her co-laborers when they treated her with decent fairness. So Aphra may have counted the playwright of "All for Love," who wrote the prologue of her play, "The Widow Ranter," in her first-night audience.

In that audience also were literary ladies, fair runners in the race for dramatic honors. The Duchess of Newcastle in an outlandish garb, with seventeen patches on her face, whose plays Pepys declared the silliest ever seen, we suspect because he personally disliked her Grace. The poetess and future Countess of Winchilsea, maid of honor to Mary of Modena, may have been in attendance, and in a vizard mask, at the Duke's Theatre on some "Rover" night, but young Mistress Anne Killigrew, the poetess whom all poets praised, would hardly have been a spectator, even masked, of so lively a comedy. It was in the side-boxes that the disturbers of the peace of players sat enthroned. There royalty blazed with brilliants, old favorites "looked like fire" upon new ones, the heroes of the Dutch war could be admired at close range by plain citizens, and their daughters could note the length of La Mancini's side-locks, and decide if the belle Stuart was really like her effigy on the penny.

From Mr. Pepys we learn how important a part theatre-going played in the life of the plain people. It was their court-calendar, their fashion-paper, their portrait-gallery of celebrities, their *chronique scandaleuse*, and often their forum where, with something of the license accorded the Roman populace in the amphitheatre, they expressed their opinions. The sight of the King's new French doll, La Kérouaille (so dearly bought with English gold), at the play inflamed Protestant zeal; the house was soon filled with curses, drawn swords, and lighted torches, and a riot followed. It was at the theatre that the Duke and Duchess of York made their bows to the public after their romantic marriage; that her curious subjects got their first good look at the new queen, Catherine of Braganza, and that the actress Mrs. Davenport, after Lord Oxford had gulled her with a false marriage, finally reappeared in the gay world in the "chief box in a velvet gown, as the fashion is." The auditorium must often have been richer in dramatic episodes than the stage.

But the patronage of King and court and city could not support more than two theatres in Charles II's reign: that of the King's Company in Lincoln's Inn Fields (1672), later in Wren's new playhouse (1674), and the Duke's Company in their fine house in Dorset Gardens also built by Wren, and decorated by Grinling Gibbons (1671). It was not until 1682 that the two companies united at the new Drury Lane Theatre, again the work of Wren.

The hour of the performance varied as the century grew older, and as the dinner-hour was advanced. In Charles II's earlier years the playhouse opened at three o'clock. Colley Cibber tells us later, "plays used to begin at four o'clock, the hour that people of the same rank are now going to dinner" (1740). In any case with people of fashion, the play followed dinner, as the Park followed the Play, and after her dessert the lady of quality freshened the roses on her cheeks with some Spanish wool, set a fresh patch, slipped on a Phillamot hood, and sent for a chair. Then once properly packed in, her little shock-dog with the belled collar tucked under her arm, her snuff-box and comfit-case and Turkey fan dropped into her deep pockets, she set off for the theatre. Nor was the vizard mask forgotten, lest some allusion in the play should cause the British cheek, once so prone to blush, to hang out its red signal of distress. Behind her trotted the faithful Pinner or the handy Toilet, the henchwoman of the past, now extinct as the dodo.

The scene at the doors of the theatre was as animated as any behind the footlights. Such hustling of linkboys, for even two hundred years ago in a London smaller, whiter, and cleaner, the smoke had already laid a sooty hand on Wren's cornices and columns, and night early folded the city in her sombre mantle. Such jostling and crowding of chairs, and hackney coaches, and gilded carriages! Such spattering and fouling of footpassengers! Such pushing and scrouging in the doorways! Such quarrels for precedence between tall footmen clearing the way for their masters, and sturdy citizens with a wife or daughter on their arms! And the language! The vigorous, nervous

English of our forefathers, used by a nation who easily held the belt for the most consummate swearing and cursing in Europe, though in blaspheming it was distinctly inferior to the Italians. Nor were hostilities confined to mere verbal assaults. Here a dispute about a cab-fare had led to fisticuffs between cabby and passenger, the bystanders forming an orderly but enthusiastic ring about the combatants; there Oyster Doll and Black Betty were pulling caps, the watch standing disinterestedly by, waiting until they were both sufficiently exhausted to be easily bundled off to Bridewell. A more genteel fracas between two fops promised to end more seriously, the curl of a periwig accidentally caught on the button of a rocklow, a string of lusty oaths, a refusal to apologize, a series of taunts, ending in a challenge to a meeting in St. James's Park:

"Were you, Sir, stap my vitals, rooking my periwig, Sir?"

"Nay, Sir, split me, were I for stealing I could easily find a better, Sir."

"You lie like a villain, Sir. If you liked it not, why did you not let it alone?"

"Gad, Sir. The periwig's well enough; 'tis the ugly phiz under it that mars it."

"S'blood, I'll make yours an uglier one, Sir."

"Impossible, Sir."

"Damn you for a coward if you do not meet me at St. James's Park within the hour."

"Dammee, Sir, I'll meet you at your own time and place. God b'w'ye."

Episodes of this sort were frequent enough to make the attendance of a brace of stout footmen a necessity rather than a matter of display. Added to the frequency of street rows were the covert assaults of thieves, who plied their trade intrepidly even in the shadow of Tyburn, and the cynical rowdyism of young noblemen of the type of my Lords Jeffreys or Mohun. It was not necessary to enter a theatre to witness drama of poignant, even tragic interest.

The entrance, a veritable passage perilous, once effected, courage and persistence were still required to push on through the crowd to the box on the stage, or in the first gallery. These boxes cost from 18d. to 4s., though Pepys complained that on first nights the prices were sometimes doubled. As for the half-crown places in the pit, they could be occupied and kept for their owners by footmen who were sent on some hours before, until Jeems's manners offended the usual habitués, and a new law, "No Persons to be admitted to keep places in the Pit," was promulgated, closely following that other edict—"No Person to stand on the stage."

"The Pit [which was long left unroofed] is an Amphitheatre filled with Benches without Backboards, and covered with green cloth. Men of Quality, particularly the younger Sort, some Ladies of Reputation and Vertue, and abundance of Damsels that hunt for Prey, Sit all together in this Place, Higgledy Piggledy, chatter, toy, play, hear, hear not. Farther up, against the Wall, under the first Gallery, and just opposite to the Stage, rises another Amphitheatre, which is taken up by persons of the best Quality, among them are generally very few Men. The Galleries, whereof there are only two rows, are filled with none but ordinary People, particularly the Upper One." This upper gallery was the footmen's Paradise, where they paid nothing as they were supposed to be in attendance on their masters. They formed a power to be reckoned with, and their employers were often obliged to hiss them into silence.

The candle-snuffer was a necessary and hard-worked person when stage and house alike were lighted by dips "that shed their soft lustre, and tallow on head-dress" and mantle, and ranging over the house those picturesque precedents of our prosaic ice-water boys, the orange girls, pert hussies, went peddling their fruit and their graces, if one may believe Colley Cibber. They were in any case ready enough to further other people's love-affairs, and part of their perquisites was the fetching and carrying of billets and nosegays, from pit to gallery, from gallery to greenroom. Commissions to that greenroom deserved a generous reward. It was not the orderly and busy anteroom to the stage that the complicated "sets" and elaborate lighting of the modern play have made it. From the time of Mr. Pepys, who spent no inconsiderable number of his evenings there, to that of Dr. Samuel Johnson, who frankly told his friend, Mr. Garrick, that he felt obliged to shun its allurements, it seems to have been more like a slave-market than a portico to the temple of Thespis. The "stars" perhaps had their own tiring-rooms, but for the rank and file of the actors there was little or no privacy, and Hogarth's picture of "Strolling Players Dressing in a Barn," is probably only a picturesque exaggeration of the conditions that existed in the theatres. A stream of visitors poured in and out of the greenroom and robing-room during a performance, not court gallants only but citizens and their wives. Mr. Pepys, who enjoyed a glimpse of "the inside of the stage, the tiring-rooms, and the machines" thus records his impressions: "What a mixture of things there was; here a wooden leg, there a ruff, here a hobby horse, there a crown, would make a man split himself to see with laughing; and particularly Lacy's wardrobe, and Shotrell's. But then again to think how fine they show on the stage by candle-light, and how poor things they are to look at too near hand, is not pleasant at all." He admits, however, that the machines are fine and the paintings very pretty.

It was John Kemble who first lighted the stage properly, but scenery and flats were perfected earlier. The Opera, and the example of the elaborate and beautiful "sets" produced in Italy by a series of as yet almost unknown but gifted artists, soon affected stage decoration generally. Betterton was sent by Charles II to Paris to study scene-setting and many improvements were made by him in stage-craft. Comfort had increased; there was no greater luxury than under Elizabeth, but there was more *diffusion* of luxury, and greater things were expected of the scene-setter. The scenes of the comedies varied but little: a drawing-room, a bed-chamber, a closet (or boudoir), a street, a garden, a public park, an inn, or a country road, but the tragedies admitted of, often required, spectacular effects, and were elaborately costumed and staged.

The "stars" of the Augustan age had already risen when Aphra wrote, years before they shone in the plays of Congreve, Vanbrugh, and Farquhar. These artists seemed, however, to enjoy the perpetual youth of the Sociétaires of the Comédie-Française, and can any one who remembers Delaunay at the age of sixty, playing the rôle of a young lover, or who has seen Ellen Terry at forty-odd, floating across the stage as Olivia, doubt their possession of perennial charm? Perennial charm while they lived and moved in the enchanted realm behind the footlights—yes, but fleetest, least enduring spell when once the dark curtain has fallen, and the lights are snuffed out. A few lines in some little-read history of the stage, an occasional high-flown description, or quaintly worded panegyric in a worm-eaten book that evoke smiles rather than admiration, at best a portrait by some cunning hand, or a tomb in Westminster Abbey. *Pulvis et umbra!* That is all that remains of the golden voices, the eloquent faces, the fire and tenderness of these incarnations of a poet's vision or a wit's invention. It is so difficult to realize what they were like, these exponents of the most evanescent of the arts. The appreciations of contemporaries leave so much to be desired. Of the company of the Duke's Theatre where Mrs. Behn's plays were generally given there are many descriptions, but few portraits. Aston does little to paint the personality of Betterton when he writes: "He has a broad face, a little Pock fretten, a Corpulent Body and thick Legs, with large Feet. His voice was low and grumbling, yet he could tune it by an artful *Climax* which forced universal attention, even from the Fops, and the Orange Girls." What a caricature of the man whom Pepys called "the best actor in the world," of whom Colley Cibber, a fellow-actor and accomplished critic, wrote: "I never heard a line in tragedy come from Betterton, wherein my judgment, my ear, and my imagination were not fully satisfied," and to whom Steele paid a moving tribute: "Mr. Betterton . . . from whose action I have received more strong impressions of what is great and noble in human nature, than from the arguments of the most solemn philosophers, or the descriptions of the most charming poets I have ever read." A consummate actor in his versatility, he was equally at home in the parts of Sir John Brute, Valentine, and Hamlet. The latter was his finest, and the public thought *the* finest impersonation on the English stage throughout Betterton's theatrical career of over fifty years. He possessed the Shakespearian "points," the stage tradition piously handed down a precious heritage, by Burbage to Taylor, and by Sir William Davenant who had seen Taylor act, to Betterton himself.

Mr. Smith, the first to play "The Rover," was the original Sir Fopling Flutter of Etherege's comedy, and was the *jeune premier* in many of the plays of the period. Mr. Jevorne was a wit as well as a comedian. At the coffee-house, when a waiter expostulated, "You are wiping your dirty boots with my clean napkin," Jevorne retorted: "Never mind, boy, I'm not proud—'t will do for me," a witticism which has been as often revamped as one of his own farces. Underhill, or Cave Underhill, to whom the part of Blunt in "The Rover" was given, was generally cast for an old man, as he excelled in the delineation of every variety of obnoxious ancient from an amorous old dotard to a malicious withered wit. Downes is not very enlightening in his portrait of Verbruggen, the actor who created the rôle of Oroonoko: "Verbruggen is Nature without Extravagance, Freedom without Licentiousness, and vociferous without bellowing." Sandford who played Daring in Mrs. Behn's "Widow Ranter," was usually cast for a villain and his audiences were so accustomed to him in this part that once when he played an honest man they hissed him and the piece in which they considered him so wasted. His specialty was, of course, melodrama, and his declamation was especially praised. Scudamore was the second "juvenile lead" after Smith, and played the lover and the fine gentleman; in his gallant old age he married an heiress who had fallen in love with him or his youthful rôles. Anthony Leigh, who often acted in Mrs. Behn's comedies, was one of Dorset's commensals, and his portrait still hangs at Knowle. The portrait of another actor, Mr. Pepys's friend Harris, in his best part, that of Cardinal Wolsey, painted by Hailes, still remains in the Pepysian Library at Cambridge. Harris was a popular actor, a fine singer, dancer, and talker, and one of the accomplished coterie that Dryden assembled at Will's.

James Nokes, the delight of the court and the city in comedy, began his career in women's parts. His first success was as Juliet's nurse, and as Nurse Nokes he was known even in later life. Like Dogget, he was "very Aspectabund, wearing Farce in his Face, his Thoughts deliberately framing his Utterance congruous to his looks." He scarce ever made his first entrance in a play, but he "was received . . . by a general laughter which the very sight of him provoked . . . yet the louder the laughter the graver was his look upon it." Though the most "comic Original," he observed character closely, studied every detail of his parts with scrupulous care, and in his most mirth-provoking characters remained true to nature.

Mr. Kynaston, the famous boy actor of women's characters, was billed as Bellamour in Mrs. Behn's "The Lucky Chance" (1687). He made his début as Olympia in Beaumont and Fletcher's "Loyall Subject," and was "the loveliest Lady" Pepys ever saw in his life. Again in Ben Jonson's "Epicæna" he appeared three times in different parts, and was in turn the prettiest woman and the handsomest man in the house. He was spoiled, of course; ladies of quality took him in his stage-clothes to drive in Hyde Park after the play and when he was late at the theatre King Charles waited patiently for him to appear after the manager had explained that "the Queen was not yet shaved." He, Kynaston, mimicked and ridiculed Sir Charles Sedley on the stage and was waylaid and soundly beaten by Sedley's flunkeys. Later in life he appeared in many famous masculine characters and won fresh fame, not only in Wycherly's comedies, but in the rôles of Shakespeare's kings. He had already shed his petticoats and made a gallant and winning Bellamour at the age of twenty-eight, still boyishly handsome and singularly graceful.

Though many spectators besides Mr. Pepys preferred Kynaston's interpretation of women's characters to those of any actress, the public had shown

APHRA BEHN

a whole-hearted approval of giving female parts to women, a novel custom imported from France at the Restoration. A new career was thus opened to them, one of the very few in which they have equally shared honors and rewards with men of the same profession. By 1671 actresses had long ceased to be a new dramatic feature, and the most talented of them appeared in Mrs. Behn's plays. A glance at the bills shows the names of Mrs. Betterton, Mrs. Barry, Mrs. Mountfort, Mrs. Bracegirdle, Mrs. Hughes, Mrs. Davies, Mrs. Davenport, Mrs. Cook, Mrs. Currer, Lady Slingsby, and Mrs. Gwyn.

Mrs. Betterton married the famous actor early in her career. Their courtship began in "Hamlet" and lasted through their lives. For thirty years Mrs. Betterton played continuously in many different rôles. There is much testimony to her ability and charm. Her Lady Macbeth was unequalled, and if she does not figure as prominently in dramatic annals as some actresses of less achievement, it was because her life was as irreproachable as her art was rounded. She is one of the best examples of the stock actress.

Mrs. Hughes was the first woman who played Desdemona. She was better known to playgoers as the conqueror of the grave, studious Prince Rupert, who until he saw her at Tunbridge Wells had loved only his forge and minded only his chemicals. "The impertinent gypsy chose to be attacked in form," sneered Hamilton, and the court rejoiced at seeing "The Alchemist" play Romeo. Mrs. Hughes owed her success more to her beauty than to her art. She played the young lady's rôles in Mrs. Behn's comedies, where looks were of more value than talent. Pepys vouches that she was well qualified for them; he records kissing her in the Drury Lane greenroom, and calls her "a mighty pretty woman." Mary Davies was another actress whose face was her fortune, aided by a sweet voice. The King, touched by her singing of "My lodging is on the cold ground," in "The Mad Shepherdess," promptly presented her with a more comfortable one in Suffolk Street and soon the stage knew her no more.

Mrs. Barry, Mrs. Mountfort, and Mrs. Bracegirdle were the leading ladies of Mrs. Behn's comedies. Mrs. Barry was the daughter of a barrister who had lost his fortune in the Royalist cause, and was obliged to allow his daughters to earn their living; she chose the stage as a profession, failed to learn her business under the tuition of Sir William Davenant, but after six months' study with that universal genius, the Earl of Rochester, who took infinite pains with her, she made her début. She failed to please at first, but in ten years was at the head of her profession. The Duchess of York not only took lessons of her, but presented her later with her own coronation robes. "And yet," adds Aston, "this fine creature was not handsome, her Mouth opening most on the Right Side, which she strove to draw t'other way, and at times composing her face, as if sitting to have her picture drawn. Her Face somewhat preceded her Action, as the latter did her words, her Face ever expressing the Passions, not like the Actresses of later Times, who are afraid of putting their Faces out of the form of Non-Meaning lest they should crack the Cerum, Whitewash, or other Cosmetic troweled on." She created many rôles in Mrs. Behn's plays.

Mrs. Mountfort's life was a tragedy, though her name figures constantly on the lists of comedy rôles, and she was mistress of more variety of humor than was ever known in one actress. A vivid sketch of her by Colley Cibber has preserved something of her verve and *vis comicæ*. Her first husband, Will Mountfort, played "The Rover" Willmore, so admirably that it was remarked by many, and particularly by Queen Mary, that "it was dangerous to see him act, he made vice so alluring." Mountfort was killed for protecting Mrs. Bracegirdle from the dissolute Lord Mohun, and Mrs. Mountfort's father was drawn into an "Assassination Plot," against King William. He was pardoned at his daughter's intercession by Queen Mary, who could afford to be kind to other people's fathers, but he died from the harshness of his imprisonment. Mrs. Mountfort afterwards married Jack Verbruggen, the actor, and one wonders if the happiness of her married life with him, as described by Aston, requited her for earlier sorrows: "She was the best Conversation possible, never captious nor displeased at anything but what was Gross, or indecent, for she was Cautious lest fiery Jack should so resent it as to breed a Quarrel, for he would often say: 'Damme! Tho' *I* don't much value my Wife, yet nobody shall affront her, by Gad!'"

The successor of beautiful, impudent Sarah Cook, Mrs. Bracegirdle, Aston depicts with evident gusto: "She was of a lovely height, with dark-brown hair and eyebrows, and a fresh, blushy complexion . . . having continually a cheerful aspect, and a fine set of even, white teeth, never making an Exit but she left the Audience in an imitation of her pleasant Countenance. Genteel Comedy was her chief Essay, and that too when in Men's cloathes, in which she far surmounted all actresses of that Age." It was as a débutante that she appeared in Mrs. Behn's "Widow Ranter" in the rôle of the "Indian Queen Semernia beloved by Bacon."

Like Reade's Peg Woffington, she was truly charitable, and would daily go about Clare Market, feeding the hungry and clothing the naked; unlike Peggy and most of her fellows, her life was stainless. It was the fashion to adore her; men toasted her, fought for her, courted her, tried to carry her off; Tom Durfey, an unsuccessful lover, celebrated her virtue, and Congreve, the all-conquering Congreve here only failed to conquer.

Betty Currer, a pretty, spirited Irish girl who possessed something of the witchery of Dora Jordan, created several of Mrs. Behn's rôles, notably "The Widow Ranter"; and Mary Lee, afterwards Lady Slingsby, the first English actress to wear a title, a noble, statuesque creature, with the bearing of a stage queen, began her triumphant career at the Duke's Theatre in Mrs. Behn's "Young King." Again, when she had become the first tragic actress of her day, she appeared as the amorous and maleficent Isabella of "Abdelazar." Aphra and Lady Slingsby were imprisoned a few days in August, 1682, for a prologue written by one, and recited by the other, containing an allusion to Monmouth. Was the Mrs. Gwyn who appeared in two of Mrs. Behn's comedies in 1677 and 1678 the famous Nell Gwyn? Genest says that Mrs. Ellen Gwyn returned to the stage in 1677 (she had retired in 1670), to act Angelica Bianca in Mrs. Behn's "Rover," while Peter Cunningham maintains that Almahide in Dryden's "Conquest of Granada" (1670) was the last rôle Nell Gwyn ever played. Mr. Gordon Goodwin, in his notes to Peter Cunningham's "Nell Gwyn," suggests that the Mrs. Gwyn of Aphra's plays was a misprint for Mrs. Anne Quin, an actress also of the King's Theatre. It seems improbable that Nell Gwyn after seven years of an easy and dissipated life should have returned to the stage. She had money, position, and admiration, nothing to gain by going back to an adoring but possibly capricious public. She could hardly have been tempted by the character of Angelica Bianca, the beautiful Venetian from Padua in "The Rover." It was a professional beauty's part, rather tame for as vivacious and temperamental a person as Mistress Ellen. On the other hand, the character of Lady Knowall (in "Sir Patient Fancy"), for which she was billed in 1678, "an affected, learned woman," would have afforded ample opportunity for the comedian to play her prettiest tricks. Imagine those pouting lips rattling off a list of "favorite Philosophers." One can almost see the bewitching grimace with which she would have mouthed a line of Greek, and the comic turn given the pedantry by one of the most mischievous, audacious little rogues that ever delighted an audience. Her reappearance in "The Rover" would have added to the success of the play, which became at once, and long continued to be, a popular favorite. Comedians are proverbially whimsical; a quarrel with her royal lover, the rise of a new favorite, may have inspired a fancy to go back for a time to her constant admirer, the public.

"A turned-up nose . . . a full nether lip, an out-mouth . . . the bottom of your cheeks a little blub, and two dimples when you smile: For your stature, 'tis well, and for your wit, 't was given you by one that knew it had been thrown away upon an ill face." This is Dryden's portrait of Florimel in "Secret Love," and perhaps, as Mr. Saintsbury suggests, of Nell Gwyn who created the part. Lely's portraits sustain the suggestion.

APHRA BEHN

Nature formed Nell for comedy, and naturally enough in a tragedy (Dryden's "Tyrannic Love," 1669) as Valeria, daughter to Maximin, "she did very vilely," until the epilogue, when the dead princess jumped up and angrily rated the bearers who attempted to carry her off:

"Hold, are ye mad, you d——d, confounded dog,
I am to rise and speak the epilogue."

The verses that followed promptly revived the spirits of an audience depressed by a bloody play. Prologues and epilogues the coarser the better, were Nelly's forte. After the dullest play she could always be depended upon to awaken sleepers, and to raise a laugh. The saucy verses given to Lady Knowall in the epilogue to "Sir Patient Fancy," one of the earliest declarations of the rights of women, were cunningly adapted to the pretty bravado of her manner.

Aphra dedicated a comedy, "The Feigned Courtesans; or a Night's Intrigue," to Mrs. Ellen Gwyn. This extraordinary composition equals some of Dryden's epistles dedicatory in fulsomeness of flattery; surely stomachs were as solid as back-bones were elastic when such nauseating adulation could be gravely received and humbly offered. Here is a sample of Mrs. Behn's style: "I with shame look back on my past ignorance which suffered me not to pay an adoration long since where there was so very much due; yet, even now, though secure in my opinion, I make this sacrifice with infinite fear and trembling; well knowing that so excellent and perfect a creature as yourself differs only from the Divine Powers in this: the offerings made to *you* ought to be worthy of you, while they will accept the *will* alone!" "Flattery is the chief art in a monarchical age," but there is a point where it ceases to be art. Aphra was, however, only one of a mob of offenders. Dedications were sold higher than books sometimes, and each piece of adulation meant a purse of guineas; patrons paid more than publishers, and Aphra's offense was a venial as well as a venal one. These considerations, however, leave us still in the dark about Nell Gwyn's possible return to the stage. Even without her there was a galaxy of "stars" to illuminate a brilliant play and add lustre to a dull one.

Such were the actors, such the theatre, such the playwrights of the drama of the Restoration. What were the requirements of their audience? What did it demand of those who sought to please? Wherein did it differ from the spectators who filled the Globe, or the Cockpit a century before?

The radical difference between the public of Shakespeare and that of Congreve may be expressed in few words: decline of imagination. The men who listened to Hamlet and Mercutio were sons of morning, they came into being in the fortunate years of the rebirth of England, out of civil and religious strife, out of sanguinary anarchy and fettering formula. What Salamis was to the Greeks, the defeat of the Armada was to the English. The magnificent outburst of patriotic feeling that united all creeds and classes against the invader was only one manifestation of the activities of the nation. What had they not seen, and done, and felt, those ruffling and gorgeous gallants, those bronzed and scarred sailors, those grave, yet eager scholars who sat on the stage, or looked down from the galleries of the Elizabethan theatre? Could the enchantments of Prospero's isle seem strange to men who had cut their way through the flower-forests of South America, who had heard eye-witness's tales of the glittering roofs and jewelled walls of the Incas, who had waded ankle-deep in the gold and pearls of captured Spanish galleons, and seen the many-colored marvels of Southern seas?

A poor mimicry of battle could easily awaken the memory of men whose feats of arms had equalled those of the half-mythical heroes of rude chronicles. If Earl Waltheof Sigurdson held the gate of York against an Army, had not again and again one small English ship engaged a whole Spanish fleet? Did not Surrey travel over Europe with a standing challenge to any knight of any land who would not agree instanter that the "Fair Geraldine" was the purest and loveliest of all the ladies in Christendom? Gentlemen, who for years had been "singeing the King of Spain's beard," who had sailed under Cary and

Grenville, and had looted and ravaged under Drake and Hawkins, had a lively imagination where war and images of battle were in question. They were not merely fighters, and freebooters either; they were exquisites as well. They talked Euphues with Lilly, studied verse-making, read Spenser and Sidney, wore big pearls in their ears, and a whole manor on their backs. They had as youths made the Italian tour. When the sign-boards on the Cockpit's stage were lettered, Sicilia, Verona, Mantua, Venice, Rome, in ardent imaginations avid of beauty, stately cities, snowy or rosy towers, the delicate curve of an undulating coast, groves of lemon-trees, marble colonnades, seemly backgrounds for Juliet or Portia, rose like mirage before their mental vision. What mattered the dingy actual surroundings of the *dramatis personæ* when the playwright could appeal to memories stored with such glowing pictures, to imaginations at once poetic and pictorial. A line, an allusion was sufficient to evoke mental images more vivid or more lovely than any stage-decorator could supply.

To the folk who crowded the King's and the Duke's Theatres, life had grown tamer. The creative impulse of the Renaissance had been succeeded by a calmer, more self-conscious attitude of the mind. Men had begun to take stock of their intellectual possessions. They were ceasing to be poets, and were becoming prose writers. The intoxicating inrush of new impressions, the ardor of conquest in all fields of thought and action had diminished, and fallen into narrower and well-defined channels, and the rampant individualism of the Renaissance was deeply modified by the restraint resulting from more highly developed social conditions. A stable government, insuring personal security, favored social expansion, while the imitation of French models lent an appearance of a much higher degree of polish and culture than was really attained.

To resume: decline of the figurative imagination created a demand for realism; the passing of the heroic age narrowed the scope of the emotional appeal; the rise of a new social ideal, with a new order of interests, naturally influenced a sensitive form of art; the adoption of French customs, and French forms of social observance, the importation of classical models, still further transformed the romantic, idyllic, poetic comedy of the Elizabethans into the realistic, prose comedy of the age of Charles II. There was also in these comedies a grossness, a deliberate indecency due, not only to the natural reaction after the enforced austerity of Puritanism, but to the patronage of the Merry Monarch and the Court. Wycherly's loathsome parody of Molière's Alceste, his disgusting travesty of the innocent Agnes of the "*École des Femmes*," were the product of the desire to please the Duchess of Cleveland and her ilk, not entirely the rebound from the enforced decency of Puritan ordinance nor the desire to satirize vice and expose hypocrisy. Loose talk and indecorous situations gratified the roisterers, and the plain people, having acquired the taste for strong waters, craved more and more of them—hence the aqua fortis in the plays.

In every comedy of this period two characteristics can be observed: first, the imperative demand for an exact reproduction of every-day life, of commonplace occurrences, and of ordinary types of humanity capable only of prosaic sentiments; in the second place, decidedly in the second place, a desire for wit and fine language. This new-born craving for style and elegance was the age's substitute for elevation of thought and poetic imagery. These were not missed by the gentleman who, when he dropped into the play, after he had combed his wig and saluted his friends, wished above all else "to see a literal picture of the life he had just left outside the theatre, and a faithful reflection of himself on the stage." (Taine.) Therefore, away with heroes. The man of quality is a rake, or would be one, therefore the leading male characters, young and old, are libertines; the man of the world is a spender and a waster, he hates Puritans and piety, he scorns the Quakers; he borrows the clothes and his manners from France, just as he took French bribes, but he despises Frenchmen and other foreigners; he is litigious and occasionally has to pay his lawyers, therefore he considers them as pettifogging rascals. He owes money to tradespeople, therefore tradespeople, merchants, bankers, and their ilk are cheating knaves, or miserly usurers. He quarrels with his father about money or property, therefore all fathers are selfish and cruel tyrants, or foolish dotards. His business is gambling, raking, drinking, and dressing, his object to marry an heiress, or obtain a sinecure at court. He is idle, profligate, dishonest, and untruthful, but he is sometimes brave and generous, often brutal, and occasionally malignant, always witty, generally light-hearted, and never prosy. At his best he is a fine human animal, with the language of the drawing-room, the bow of a dancing-master, and the principles of a bashi bazouk.

And the lady of quality, who forms a pendant to the man of the world, she would be safer, we feel, behind a veil with a guardian like the bashi bazouk's female kind. She is witty, she is diverting, she is absolutely unreliable. She is not only an animal but a perverted animal, pampered and greedy. We watch her with the same delight that children experience in looking at the quick movements, the sudden darts, the iridescent plumage of a hummingbird. She is at the mercy of all her sensations, the slave of every fugitive whim, and is as futile as she is irresponsible. We cannot confine this radiant butterfly in a net of duties, let us rather enjoy the flower-like tints, the soft flutter of its wings as it floats from blossom to blossom in quest of sweets. But the fair honey-seeker grows old, and such a youth as hers is a poor preparation for a sweet and dignified old age. The brilliant and capricious coquette withers into a covetous, bibulous hag, a shrivelled sheaf of appetites. If we turn in distaste from the grander folk to plainer people we find no better principles and much worse manners; the citizens' wives are every whit as vain and light as the women of quality, and their husbands are either knaves or scamps.

This scorn of the middle class, so constantly expressed, was playwrights' and actors' revenge for eighteen years of exile from the stage. The mass of Cromwell's followers were of the third estate. The Commonwealth had persecuted players, the city, largely Puritan, had been hostile to the stage. Now again the mummers were in favor, and the ridicule and contumely heaped on the Puritan, the Republican, "the Oliverian," was the throwback for the Long Parliament's closing of playhouses and imprisonment of "those proud parroting players, and superbious ruffians," as they were styled in the ordinance of suppression.

The officers are the most respect-worthy of the *dramatis personæ*, and even among them are bullies and cowards. The lawyers are sharpers, and the doctors of divinity are fawning rascals—nothing could render more vividly the disrepute into which the priesthood of the established church had fallen. As to the servantry—I should have to borrow the unabashed language of the plays properly, or rather improperly, to describe them.

If tiring of this urban corruption we journey to the country for purer air we breathe the odors of the pot-house, the scent of the kennel and the stable. The indulgent view that the French writers of the eighteenth century took of the rustic and the savage is here replaced by a pitiless contempt. Man stripped of his fine clothes and polished manners is shown to be but a sorry brute, or a bundle of uncurbed instincts.

In borrowing plots, and characters, and manners from the French, the English playwrights omitted to add to their shoplifting restraint, urbanity, and the appeal to the mind. The French writer of comedy, *real* comedy (not farce), has always been a moralist; ethical and social questions are his theme. In England the comedy writer has been a jester, with the whimsicality and irresponsibility of a jester. In France it has always been the custom to *exhort* on the stage and *amuse* in the novel. In England this process has been exactly reversed. It is curious to see the same author, for instance Mrs. Behn, writing simultaneously licentious plays and moral (though coarse) tales. Later Fielding had two entirely different tones in his comedies and in his novels, and Goldsmith, following instinct and tradition, made a novel of "The Vicar," and a play of "She Stoops to Conquer." In comedy the English had never sought an incentive to righteous living.

Perhaps the reason is not far to seek. The Frenchman is mentally stimulated and perfected by society and conversation; the Englishman is intellectually developed by solitude and reflection. The English-man is not so great when he is witty and sportive as when he is moved or impassioned. His hand is heavy in pleasantry, his jests are often tart, his sallies acrid. When his heart ceases to speak he becomes brutal, sometimes virulent. His comedy has but seldom the genial good nature, never the noble humanitarian spirit of Molière; indeed social intercourse often seems to rouse the Englishman's dominating, instead of his social, instinct.

To the pertinent question—Of what value then are these comedies to us; why should they not be cast into the dust-bin with the other broken toys of the past?—three answers have been made. In the first place, because of their language; never was the English tongue better spoken or written. The clearness, the justness, the delicate precision of this style render it a tempered and exquisite instrument; it was perfected at an unique moment in the evolution of the language. Milton was still a living memory, Dryden was still its artificer when to amplitude and energy, limpidity and celerity were added.

Furthermore, it is a precious human document. In its crystalline forms is preserved a distinct phase of social development. Many of its characters possess the vigor of a Franz Hals, or a Jordaens portrait. Beside the vehemence and directness with which these primitive types of man are rendered, the characters of later comedy look like the figures of Watteau beside the figures of Rubens. Finally, these comedies are amusing. True, theirs is a world of drones and butterflies where the bees are always robbed, and the ants outwitted. But there is in the depths of our unregenerate nature, a faun, a strange, frolicking, mischievous creature, the foe of the didactic and the literal alike, who when we are very young, loves to see Mr. Punch hang the policeman, and likes to tweak Lord Fauntleroy's angelic curls. To the piping of these audacious revellers the faun breaks from his decorous prison and dances, pricking his pointed ears, and kicking up his cloven heels. Let him dance a little, not for long, lest he grow into a bloated Silenus, or an ugly satyr. His will be merely an intellectual orgy. You will be none the worse for a capriole or so, you will return to a strenuous world presently, and the adventures of these scamps and flirts, of these bullies and beaux will leave you in merrier mood than will the theses of modern French drama, or the problems of Ibsen.

Not one of these excuses is valid for Mrs. Behn's plays. Though her language is rich and sonorous, vigorous and racy, she cannot be counted among the group of comedy writers who clarified and disciplined our tongue. She has none of the filed and polished elegance of Congreve, none of the finish of the Augustans. She wrote hastily and carelessly, her style is often uncinctured, unmanicured, *en negligé,* its slipshod easiness is that of *billets du matin* dashed off on a toilet-table; indeed, Gildon noted that Aphra wrote while talking with her friends or receiving visits.

The second contention, that Restoration comedy portrays the manners of the society of its time, is only half true. We could as well unquestioningly accept De Maupassant's French peasants as studies from nature, or D'Annunzio's novels as accurate pictures of modern Italian life. Aphra's flirts and bullies and rascals are "society" people; when not the conventional stock characters of Spanish comedy they are hangers-on at court, needy cavaliers with Worcester and Marston Moor behind them, and a sponging house before them, swaggering fortune-hunters—Bassanios vulgarized, and thirsty Petruchios. The ladies are—when they are ladies—pert minxes, and highly born romps, all touched by the taint of Whitehall. Their manners and conversation are those of the court. The intrigues, disguises, practical jokes, heartless gallantry, indecent jests are those of the courtiers. The heroes are modelled after Rochester, Buckingham, Sedley, Killigrew, and the gentlefolk of their circle. Hardly an incident in Aphra's plays but can be paralleled by an episode from Hamilton's "Memoirs" and Pepys's "Diary," or even from grave Evelyn and Burnet. Queen Catherine and the Duchesses of Richmond and Buckingham in peasant's dress jog off to the fair at Audley End, on cart-jades, maids of honor garbed as orange girls sell fruit in the theatre, Killigrew inveigles the soft little fool Miss Temple, disguised in Miss Hobart's clothes. Lady Chesterfield contrives a series of dramatic scenes to flout De Grammont, Rochester "sets up a stage as an Italian mountebank" and sells drugs (Burnet). Lord Oxford arranges a false marriage with the help of his trumpeter and kettle-drummer to deceive Mrs. Davenport. Not merely dramatic episodes, but complete little comedies which might be called, *The Treacherous Green Stockings, The Mocking of Lady Muskerry, The Faithful Lover of Miss Warmistre*, are acted in Hamilton's pages; a playwright who knew the court had not far to seek for plots and situations.

Such a view of life was intensely artificial, it was parochial as well. Aphra may call her scenes Naples or Madrid, they are always Hampton Court, St. James's Park, Foxhall, or Bartholomew Fair, though in "The Widow Ranter," where the scene is laid in America, and Bacon is hero, there is a dash of the local color so distinctive a feature in "Oroonoko." Aphra's outlook in her drama is no narrower than that of her contemporaries and followers, but it is a small loophole from which to observe life. Certainly humanity *is* a sordid affair if we eliminate its finer elements, and nature *is* a sickening spectacle if we confine our observations to dung-hills. The choice is ours, the fertilizer and the flower lie close together, we can contemplate the flower or we can "concentrate" on the fertilizer if so inclined, but we must not insist that only the latter is real. Who would imagine that this world of Aphra and Etherege and Wycherly was that of Lady Rachel Russell, of Algernon Sidney, of saintly Baxter, of heroic Lucy Hutchinson, of pious Herbert, and kindly William Penn, of heroes, martyrs, poets, sages. We cannot too often remind ourselves that the comedy of the Restoration was a court-jester. The theatres were the King's, the actors were protégés of the courtiers, the actresses generally their property, the playwright their client when not one of themselves, and the drama was the mouthpiece of the court. The English nation had other spokesmen. In 1678 while Aphra was jotting down the witty ribaldry and cruel jests of "Sir Patient Fancy," a poor tinker's immortal vision of the pilgrimage of the soul from earth to heaven appeared to the perennial delight and inspiration of the people. Ah! here was drama indeed, the Divine Comedy of England, a world of characters, gentle and simple; dialogue, action, scene-painting (who does not know the wicket gate, the slough, and the green valley of Humiliation dotted with snowy sheep?); above all, here was the creative faculty, a puissant imagination, tireless and fruitful, and an ideal that still commands reverence.

Aphra and her kind dwelt contented in "Vanity Fair." No shining visions floated before her as she drove her busy pen and took her plays to market.

APHRA BEHN

To write what would sell was her business, to please her public was her ambition, and after a false start and a couple of failures she fell into her stride and kept up the pace until the end of her busy life. No author of her time save Dryden was so prolific. Her material was ready to hand, her manner varied with her subject. Body of doctrine had she none, nor convictions, nor purpose, nor standard. She labored to amuse and surprise. She succeeded. Like those of all the playwrights of her time her characters were generally immoral, her situations often equivocal, her language frequently gross. Therefore, in spite of their undeniable qualities, their humor, sprightliness, and movement, her work has deserved oblivion, and no one, even to-day, would wish to revive her plays. Nor is their coarseness their only offense. In them humanity is on a low plane; their tone is debased, the heroes for all their high-flown talk are brutal, the roguish, lively ladies are stony-hearted. Mediæval barbarity, its ruthlessness to the weak and lowly, lives on in them. In Michelet's words describing the inhuman humor of the middle ages, "*les grimaces du pendu, les pleurs du battu, le désespoir du cocu,*" were excellent fooling for his Grace of Buckingham and Lady Shrewsbury. Such mirth is not merely "the crackling of thorns under the pot," as Thackeray said, but the cracking of whips over bowed backs. Rancor and hatred edge this wit, the playwright's pen is dipped in vitriol. He is stabbing at the Puritan, cutting at the sober citizen, thrusting at the clean-liver. The Republican is pilloried, the Nonconformist pelted with mud, and after five brisk acts vice is rewarded, and the hypocrites who pretend to be decent folk are properly despoiled or ridiculed. The harshness and acridity of this drama can only be accounted for when we remember that it had wrongs to avenge and the power to avenge them; the playwright was the long-oppressed actors' spokesman.

Enough has been written of the inhumanity and licentiousness of Restoration drama in general, of Mrs. Behn's in particular. On her little brown head many posthumous phials of wrath have been poured; when men and women sin it is still the woman who is stoned. What interests us is why a woman who, tradition has it, in her life was amiable and generous should have contributed to this coarseness and cruelty.

Because Aphra was beneficent she was not necessarily delicate-minded. A desire to help one's fellow-creatures is not inevitably accompanied by good taste. The merciful, even in the Beatitudes, are not always the pure in heart. Aphra could easily pen atrocities and oblige a needy author synchronously. It is to be feared that her grossness was part of her stock in trade; many successful modern plays have proved its marketable value. It is a cheap substitute for wit, and the easiest way to amuse; even a trite anecdote, or a mild jest spiced with profanity or indecency, is sure to please a certain portion of the public. No better apology has ever been offered than that of Dick Steele's to the young lady who rebuked him for a ribald sentence in a new play. (*Vide Spectator*, Vol. I, 306.) A certain length of tether had been allowed to comedy from time immemorial. How great was the license of Aristophanes! How chaste and restrained were the Greek tragedians! It was not a question of *kind*, but of *degree;* Aphra went to the limit, and she was in numerous, if not in good company.

If her plots were filched, her characters conventional, Aphra's dialogue if not always witty was always lively, and there are no languid moments in her plays. She has "the gift of pace," as essential to comedy as Miss Terry finds it to the comédienne. She was deeply in debt to Molière, and, like her contemporaries, she often soiled what she borrowed, but something of his dramatic action was hers by nature. The imbroglios of her plays are so complicated that they must have taxed the attention of an audience that we have always imagined was none too attentive. From the Spanish school of comedy came these three-ply intrigues, intricate plots, and continual disguises that weary and bejuggle a modern reader.

IX

Aphra's plays were only part of her product. Besides her dramas, in the eighteen years of her literary life, she wrote thirteen novels; most of them are negligible. "The History of the Nun, or the Fair Vowbreaker" (1688), recently discovered and republished by Mr. Summers, is a seventeenth-century version of the tragedy of "Enoch Arden," the story of a fickle-minded lady, and two faithful lovers, of bigamy and murder, a brutal *fait divers*, served with a sauce of sentimental reflections; on it Southerne founded his "Fatal Marriage."

"The Fair Jilt, or the Amours of Prince Tarquin and Miranda" (1688), is the true tale of a siren, a northern Countess of Cellant, beautiful, malignant, and venomous, who charms men to their destruction, lures a page to poison his mistress, persuades her husband to kill her sister, is condemned to stand by the scaffold while one of her victims is hanged, and though execrated by the whole city of Antwerp, is beloved by those she has ruined, and ends her days peacefully with a devoted husband. Not one of Aphra's other tales show a trace of the charm and originality of "Oroonoko." They are generally spiced with crime, flavored with conventional moralizing, and hastily thrown together. They were written while Aphra, unable to work for the stage, was suffering from the torturing complications of ills that soon after caused her death. As thrillers these stories have merits, and with a very free application of blue pencil they might qualify Aphra for a lucrative position on the staff of a "yellow" journal.

People were reading French novels when Aphra delivered "Oroonoko" "to the world" in 1688. Light literature was an *article de Paris*, like perfumed gloves, apricot paste, and other elegant trifles. The "best sellers" were the "Astrée" of d'Urfé (though a little old-fashioned), the "Cassandre" of La Calprenède, and "Le Grand Cyrus" of Scudéri. France had imported her novels until after the defeat of the League when the heroic Spanish romance lost popularity. Giants, dwarfs, enchanters, and paladins ceased to please and were shut up in the mighty tomes where they still remain. As Spain retired, Italy advanced. Favored by a *roi galant*, and an Italian Queen, the *"Pastor Fido"* of Guarini, and the *"Aminta"* of Tasso peopled French fiction with amorous shepherds and tuneful shepherdesses. England had already entered "Arcadia" with Sir Philip Sidney, and Spain in her turn had deserted her knights for the sophisticated rustics of Montemayer's *"Diana,"* when the French novel became bucolic.

In 1609 Henry IV, who had little time between making romances to read them, was condemned to loveless desuetude by a fit of the gout. Between twinges the first volume of a new book, the *"Astrée"* of Honoré d'Urfé was read to him. The King listened, approved, and accepted the dedication of the second volume. With "*Astrée*" the pastoral style triumphed, and with it platonic love and agricultural implements became the fashion. The crook was mightier than the sword, and the charger was driven from the hero's side by a sheep. A novel celebrating "*l'honneste Amitié*" was sure of success with *précieuses*, and "*Astrée*" was admired and imitated by the inner circle of the Hôtel Rambouillet. The long, romantic courtship of Julie d'Argennes, Madame de Rambouillet's daughter, by the devoted and indomitable Monsieur de Montausier (the model of Molière's Alceste), reads like a chapter of d'Urfé's novel, which it also resembled in length.

Only a leisure class could have enjoyed "*Astrée*" and the interminable novels that followed it. Beside them "Clarissa" is alert, and the pace of Thackeray's "Virginians" furious. The first volume of "*Astrée*" appeared in 1608, the second in 1610, the third nine years later, a fourth in 1624, one year before the author died, leaving the novel unfinished. Had he been spared he might have continued to issue a volume every lustre for many years more, for the texture of the tale was such that it could have been cut off or spun out at will.

But d'Urfé's novels were short and scant of breath compared with the long-windedness and prodigious length of those of his successor, La Calprenède. He also owed something of his success to royal favor. Like Aphra, he *told* his novels first, not to the King, but to the Queen's gentlewomen. Ladies in waiting truly they were and grateful to the ingenious storyteller who charmed weary waiting at late levees, or tedious vigils at the convent in the rue St. Jacques, while Anne of Austria prayed and plotted.

Before long the Queen was persuaded to join La Calprenède's audience. She gave him not only a hearing, but her patronage and a pension. Did the stories please this daughter of monarchs because in them bucolic characters gave precedence to royal and princely folk? Their names, it is true, were borrowed from kings and conquerors of antiquity, but though their language was that of languid and tender shepherds of romance, their characters (!) were those of contemporary nobles. These exalted persons entertained only elevated sentiments which they expressed in elegant periods. The gentlemen were always brave and faithful, the ladies chaste and tender. Love and valor were the alternating motives of their conversations and ample reflections. Feelings, though never precipitated into actions, were minutely described; every degree of a grand passion was accurately delineated and the technic of love-making tenuously elaborated. This stately gallantry captivated the amazons of the Fronde, who though they had plotted, and fenced, and galloped over half France with pistols at their belts, appreciated the highflown sentiments and verbal delicacies of the Hôtel Rambouillet. The ten volumes of *"Cassandre"* left them unsatisfied, and eager for its successor. "*Cléopâtre*" (1647–8), which Madame de Sévigné read in odd moments, trailed its formidable length, a veritable serpent of old Nile, through two dozen volumes. The author's vogue was undiminished when his life and the seventh volume of "*Faramond*" ended in 1663. Meantime the Hôtel Rambouillet, which had founded the *salon*, remodelled domestic architecture, added conversation to the pleasures of life, ennobled love, and refashioned language, had formed a novelist in its own image: Madeleine de Scudéri. She refined on La Calprenède's refinements, and added to them her own delicacy of feeling and the taste and tone of the society she frequented. Her first novel, "*Ibrahim, ou l'illustre Bassa*" (1641), was published under her brother George's name. Like many other successful novels it was dramatized, and later Dryden borrowed much of it for his "Mock Astrologer." In 1649 "*Artamène ou le Grand Cyrus*" appeared in ten volumes. It was a portrait-gallery of the *habitués* of the Hôtel Rambouillet. Among these portraits that of Artamène, the great Condé, occupied the centre of the collection, while adventures (here Scott found the scene of Rebecca and the Templar in the tower), chivalrous feats, chastened gallantry, and elevated sentiments, but best of all charming letters and interesting conversations enchanted all the circles of reading Paris. "*Clélie*," a story of Ancient Rome, really that of the

Fronde followed, also in ten volumes (1656). The togas and stolas thinly disguised the intriguing cavaliers and fighting duchesses, who are as much of their own time as the map of the *pays du Tendre* is unlike the Rome of the Republic. Mademoiselle de Scudéri's characters are fine lay-figures, draped in the ermine and purple of an elevated or précieux style. They are high-minded but tedious, virtuous but prolix, and to a modern reader inexpressibly wearisome. They seem refined out of all human interest, yet so relative is realism that their readers recognized in them piquant likenesses of the notabilities of the period, and even of the smaller social fry. "The authors of these novels under the name of their heroes sometimes paint the characters of their own friends, people of no importance," commented Boileau. Characters! Portraits from life! These heroes and princesses seem as far above peccant humanity as are the duchesses and sirens who stare haughtily, or smile impersonally from hairdressers' windows. The cavaliers and ladies of the seventeenth century saw them with other eyes, to them these insipidities were at once models of elegance and incentives to noble living. "Nothing burnishes the wit, forms and prepares it for society like the reading of good novels . . . they teach morality better and more forcibly than the most able philosophers," was the opinion of a man of the world and the other world, Bishop Huet.

No *ruelle* was without a copy of "*Clélie*"; the well-bred lived by its rules, and it might have been called the book of etiquette of the emotions. But how unfixed is fame! Already in 1660, when Aphra was telling her story to the King, Paris was yawning over "*Almahide,*" Mademoiselle de Scudéri's "latest." Readers had begun to tire of double-distilled sentiment, superfine language, and superhuman propriety. High dilution of feeling was becoming insipid, even flavorless.

In England, however, the three-decker French novel held on its triumphant course for many years more. Ladies wasted tears and candles over it. Men of fashion quoted it, and read it aloud in polite circles. It was well translated; "*Cassandre,*" for instance, was beautifully done into English by Sir Charles Cottrell. No library was complete without "twelve vast French romances, neatly gilt." Mr. Pepys bought "*L'illustre Bassa,*" "*Cassandre,*" "and other French books" for his wife's closet, though on one occasion he records checking her "in her long stories out of '*Grand Cyrus*' which she would tell tho' nothing to the purpose, nor in any good manner." Addison, years afterwards, noted in a lady's library, "Cassandra," "Cleopatra," "Astræa," "The Grand Cyrus," "with a Pin stuck in one of the middle Leaves," and "Clelia," "which opened of itself in the Place that describes two Lovers in a Bower." All through the eighteenth century the ponderous tomes found English readers, even such readers as Dr. Johnson and Mrs. Chapone, and were still considered to furnish exemplars of gallantry and heroism, of noble deportment and fine language.

Into this realm of subdued half-tints, of discreet, reflected lights, of faintly defined forms, "Oroonoko" dashed like a tropical bird into a dove-cote. It is easy to imagine the stir it caused, the surprise and interest it aroused after people had recovered from the first shock of its novelty. New indeed was a story told straightly, undeflected by digressions, its force undiluted by discussions; the abstract banished, and the concrete not only presented but visualized by all the means at the writer's disposal. The personal experiences, the autobiographical form, heightened interest, and the pictures painted from actual scenes and people added color to the narration. The action was not clogged by a multiplicity of minor episodes, attention was not disseminated by the abrupt intervention of new characters and their recital of adventures that had no immediate connection with the plot. Languors of all kinds, those of the "*Roman Comique,*" as well as those of "*Clélie*" were avoided. There were no delays in the development of the simple story, and none of the contemporary clogs on swift movement. The group of characters was a small one, and no elaboration of detail wearied the reader or diverted interest from the principal personages of the tale. The sentimental straw-splitting, the finikin refinements, the wire-drawn casuistry of the French novelists were forgotten; indeed in "Oroonoko" affairs of the heart are treated with a straightforwardness characteristic of the jovial gossips of the Queen of Navarre. The form and pace of "Oroonoko" recalls the directness of attack of the Florentine *novella*, it has hurried away from the stately advance of the slow-paced seventeenth-century novel. In short, "Oroonoko" is composed; it focusses interest in one central figure. Its alertness is somewhat akin to that of Voltaire's tales. It could not, like its contemporaries, and many of Ibsen's plays, be continued indefinitely. Compared with the swift allure of this simple story the epistolary and picaresque romances of Aphra's distinguished successors are prolix and desultory. For the form of "Oroonoko," for equal succinctness and concentration, we must hark back to the story-tellers of the Renaissance.

It is naturally an aid to clear relation of facts to possess facts at first hand to relate, and for the expression and communication of emotion, the capacity for, and experience of, emotion is valuable. Aphra was deeply moved by the sufferings and tragic fate of her savage hero; admiration, pity, a horror of cruelty and injustice, are potent incentives to expression. The revolt of a high young heart against wrong finds eloquence ready to hand. Here *le style c'est la femme;* Aphra recounted an actual emotional experience. Local color, studies from life, a narrative of personal adventure were as new in fiction as a plea for the oppressed, or an arraignment of ruling powers. Here was a frank departure from the Arcadia of aristocratic shepherds, and shepherdesses, exquisite and artificial as Dresden china rustics; into this fantastic throng, strode a bleeding slave, with manacled wrists and furrowed back to take his place among the paladins of romance and the princesses of fairy-land. Oroonoko was a prince also, it is true, but his court life was only an introduction to his adventures as a captive and a slave. The description of Coromantien reads like a concession to convention. In the seventeenth-century novel high rank was as necessary an attribute of a hero as personal beauty; Oroonoko was endowed with both as a matter of course, but it was as a man and not as a deposed prince that he was interesting.

The story of the captive prince was that of many African chieftains who had died unsung, sold or betrayed into slavery. It was through Mr. Trefry who had bought him and treated him like a brother that Aphra met Oroonoko and heard his story from his own lips. Although he was the grandson and heir of the King of Coromantien, curiously enough his education was that of a French gentleman owing to the teachings of a "Frenchman who had been banished out of his own country for some Heretical Notions he held." He "found it profitable to be a sort of Royal Tutor to this young Black" and, finding him "very ready, apt and quick of apprehension, taught him Morals, Languages, and Science." The tutor "tho' he was a Man of little Religion, yet had admirable Morals, and a brave Soul." Judging from the sentiments and conduct of his pupil, the exile may have been a Huguenot of the Montausier type, for Oroonoko's code was that of the heroes of the Hôtel Rambouillet. He was of course a soldier, like all African chieftains, and early in life became the betrothed of Imoinda, the daughter of a savage general, his master-in-arms. Oroonoko's grandfather, though a hundred and odd years old, was no longer an amateur, but still a connoisseur and collector of beauties, and during the absence of Oroonoko on an expedition he added Imoinda to his harem. With the aid of a fellow slave Imoinda contrived to meet Oroonoko on his return from war, but they were surprised by the King's attendants. Imoinda persuaded her lover to escape, assuring him that she could make the King believe that Oroonoko had tried to carry her off, but that she had resisted him. Oroonoko reached camp safely, but Imoinda was immediately sold to an English slaver, while her lover was told that she had been killed. His despair and desire for death urged him to fight so desperately that he won a signal victory, and returned to court, loaded with loot and safe from the old King's vengeance.

Shortly after Oroonoko's return an English captain to whom he had often sold his prisoners of war invited the prince, his French tutor, and his friends to a dinner on board the slave-ship. This captain was a man of parts and of learning, superior to his profession, and an old friend of Oroonoko's. They had spent many hours together, the captain "entertaining the Prince every Day, with Globes, and Maps, and Mathematical Discourses, and Instruments." His invitation was accepted. When the guests were warm with wine they were overpowered and manacled at a signal from their captain by the English sailors, while the ship hoisted sail, and stood for the open sea. Oroonoko endeavored to starve himself to death; he had fasted for four days when the thrifty captain, fearing to lose a valuable piece of property, with abundance of "Crocodile Tears besought forgiveness," pleading that he had yielded to a sudden temptation, which he repented, and promising to free his captives as soon as they reached land. Oroonoko, who was as trusting as he was honorable, pardoned the captain, and persuaded his companions to agree to his conditions.

On arriving at Surinam they were all sold to separate masters with the exception of the Frenchman, who was set free. Mr. Trefry became the master of Oroonoko whom he brought to Parham House, the seat of the governor, where Aphra met him. His appearance quickened an admiration which a further acquaintance heightened. He was as handsome as Hiawatha, as dignified as Uncas, as intelligent as *l'Ingénu*, as gentle and courteous as Ramona's hero; indeed with Oroonoko the noble savage entered the domain of fiction. To his naturally keen mind and his acquirements he added a French urbanity of manner and address, "an extreme good and graceful Mien, and all the Civility of a well-bred Great Man."

For several days Oroonoko remained at Parham House, treated like a distinguished guest before he went to the plantations with Mr. Trefry. There the slaves, many of them from Coromantien, having heard of his capture, and his arrival in Surinam, honored him as though he was still their chief. Among them he discovered his Imoinda. She also had been sold to Mr. Trefry. Even Aphra's tropical exuberance of style failed to describe the transports of this reunited and sorely tried pair. They fainted at the sight of each other like the lovers in the "Arabian Nights," but soon recovered to an ecstasy of joy. For a little while they were in Eden, and then these wild creatures began to chafe against their light bondage. Oroonoko longed for his army and his liberty, Imoinda grieved because her child would be born a slave. Mr. Trefry had promised them that as soon as the new governor arrived from England they should be sent back to Coromantien, and Oroonoko had pledged himself to pay a large ransom for Imoinda and himself, either in gold or slaves, provided that some security were given him of the good faith of the governor. His recent experience had shaken his faith in the word of a white man. The lord-governor was long in coming, and both the prince and the colonists grew uneasy and suspicious of one another. The latter, surrounded by Indians, and possessing slaves vastly exceeding themselves in numbers, feared that the impatience and discontent of Oroonoko might lead to a revolt. Aphra, to whom he was devoted and whom he called "his Great Lady," was begged to soothe and divert him. "They knew that he and his wife," she says, "were scarce an hour a day from my Lodgings, that they eat with me, and I obliged them in all things I was capable. . . . I entertained them with the Lives of the Romans, and Great Men, which charmed him to my Company; and her with teaching her all the pretty Works that I was Mistress of." Aphra even made some timid and fruitless efforts to convert them to her own faith; she was more successful in inducing Oroonoko to join hunting and exploring parties, wherein his great strength and courage won the admiration of the planters, for as he could not drink, he generally shunned their company.

Although Oroonoko had assured Aphra that she and her friends should never in any event be harmed, he would not promise to forego any opportunity to regain his freedom. "One Sunday, when the Whites were overtaken in Drink," he persuaded the negroes in Parham Plantation to make a dash through the forest for the coast, where they might be able to seize a ship and with it return to Africa. The slaves, fired by his words, followed him, and on

Monday morning the overseers found the fields deserted. The militia, that grotesque militia which Aphra scornfully described, was summoned, and started in pursuit. The trail was easily found, for the fugitives had been obliged to fire or fell the trees; so the English followed them easily, and soon overtook and overcame them.

Oroonoko, his friends, and his wife, resisted to the last, intending to kill themselves rather than be captured, but Mr. Trefry, who had joined the expedition with the hope of saving them, persuaded them to lay down their arms. Byam, the treacherous deputy-governor, swore that they should receive the honors of war, and be sent back to Coromantien by the first ship that sailed for the African coast. No sooner had Oroonoko surrendered than he was seized, bound, and whipped, "until the Flesh was rent from his Bones." He was then chained, fastened to the ground, and Indian pepper rubbed into his wounds.

Aphra, who, when the revolt of the slaves became known, had, with the women of the colony, left the plantations, returned in time to save what remained of Oroonoko from further torments. Her presence would have prevented those he had already endured. He was tenderly cared for, and his bodily hurts were healed, but his self-respect had been mortally wounded. He had resolved not to survive his degradation, but to live until he had revenged himself on Byam, who had betrayed, and then whipped him; unwilling to leave his wife in slavery he decided to kill her first, then his enemy, and finally himself.

As soon as he could leave his bed he begged his devoted nurse, Mr. Trefry, to let him take the air alone with Imoinda. No sooner had they entered the forest than he told her of his resolve, of the impossibility of escaping, and the necessity of dying. He found her far more eager for death than he was to slay her; "filled with joy that she should die by so noble a Hand, and be sent into her own Country (for that's their Notion of the next World) by him she so tenderly loved, and so truly adored in this." There in the enchanted woods of the tropics, vibrating with the stir and hum of myriad creatures, resonant with the sweet calls of wooing birds, where all Nature teemed with life-giving forces, these poor children, for they were children still, in years, in soul, in everything but sorrow, took leave of each other. All that love could say being ended, Imoinda received her death-stroke like a last caress. No sooner was she dead, and buried under a mound of flowers, than physical weakness, and the fatal infirmity of purpose, characteristic of his race, overcame Oroonoko. He was powerless to leave the grave, to pursue his vengeance, or even to put an end to himself. A week later he was found, still alive, lying by his wife's body.

Again he was carried back to Parham House, and tenderly nursed by Aphra and Mr. Trefry. He lingered on, the spectre of himself, though the surgeon who cared for him assured his friends that he could not live. All that they hoped for him was a painless death. They were too sanguine, for while Aphra, who was ill from watching and sorrow, had gone to Colonel Martin's for a short visit, the Deputy-governor Byam sent Mr. Trefry up the river on some feigned business, and carried off Oroonoko. The dying man was tied to the whipping-post, and slowly dismembered while still alive. He told his torturers that he would encourage them to die by his example, and he kept his word. He asked for tobacco, which was given him, and smoked in silence, while he was hacked to pieces, "without a Groan or a Reproach" until Death freed him.

Oroonoko was the first character in English fiction possessing a definite personality, a personality marked by racial characteristics as well as individual traits modified by a foreign education. In spite of his French breeding Oroonoko was depicted as a negro, and a savage, noble and kind by instinct, as the dog is faithful, and the blood-horse mettlesome. He was not a white man painted black with a white man's nature and innate ideas, he was not a negro St. Francis like Uncle Tom. There still was much that was fierce and untamed in Aphra's hero. He lacked, like most savages, sequence in action, constancy of purpose; his fortitude was physical only. He was not the gentle savage who illustrated

APHRA BEHN

the superiority of Nature over civilization, dear to the eighteenth-century philosophers. Though his instincts were those of the primitive man, no doubt his French training furnished him with a code of honor, and its language. A hero of Corneille would have shamed his betrayer in the same spirit and terms with which Oroonoko answered the scoundrelly slaver. His declaration of love would have delighted the most fastidious précieuse who ever talked *Phébus* and professed Platonism. To Imoinda he vowed: "that no Age or Wrinkles should incline him to change; for her Soul would be always fine, and always young; and he should have an eternal *Idea* in his Mind of the Charms she now bore, and should look into his Heart for that *Idea* when he could find it no longer in her Face." We might believe that Aphra supplied these sentiments, and idealized the character of her black hero, if she had ever lent the Corneillian tone, or platonic refinements to any of her other lovers, or the numerous *jeunes premiers* of her comedies, but *they* are all kinsfolk of the Plain Dealer, a world removed from Alceste. The words and acts of Oroonoko are consistent, they are never out of character, and consequently are convincing. With the exception of the adventures in Coromantien, which Aphra had at second hand, and which read like a twice-told story, the rest of the novel has an accent of truth, as well as an atmosphere of realism. Besides the vivid figure of Oroonoko, how shadowy seem the shepherds of "*Astrée*" and the Romans of "*Clélie*." It was the heroic naïveté of Oroonoko, an innate magnanimity that led him to trust still in human nature after its baseness had been rudely exposed to him, that won Aphra's admiration. This same quality charms us in Voltaire's engaging Huron, a younger brother of Oroonoko, who, however, would never have forgiven, far less have accepted benefits from the man who had dishonored his betrothed; Oroonoko was in spirit far more akin to Horace and Rodrigue than to *l'Ingénu*.

He was as handsome, however. Aphra grew eloquent while describing him: "The most famous Statuary could not form the Figure of a man more admirably turned from Head to Foot. His Color was a perfect Ebony," his eyes piercing, "the White of 'em being like Snow as were his Teeth." "His Nose was rising and Roman, his Mouth the finest Shaped that could be seen. . . . There was no Grace wanting that bears the Standard of true Beauty"; in fine, an Antinous in black basalt.

Perhaps this pen-portrait added to the interest aroused by the virtues and misfortunes of the ill-starred prince. In any case through pity and admiration for this royal slave, a sentiment against slavery was awakened. Aphra's simple appeal to the emotions was more potent than a direct pleading or a protest. No ethical generalities, no preaching could have so touched the heart and quickened the imagination, and the readers of "Oroonoko" became the first Abolitionists. He was the Uncle Tom of the seventeenth century. "Oroonoko" then was not only new in treatment and subject, but it was also the first novel with a purpose. Mrs. Behn was a pathfinder in fiction. It was not until 1740 that "Pamela," another novel with a well-defined central character, appeared, nearly three-quarters of a century after "Oroonoko" was published (1688). Its success was instantaneous and permanent; it was translated into French and German, and like many successful modern novels was dramatized. For three decades its vogue was undiminished. By 1735 it had passed through eight editions. "The original editions are now extremely rare," we are assured, and probably the older copies of a popular novel, read, reread, borrowed, stolen, and cried over, have literally disappeared. A unique example of the *editio princeps* of "Oroonoko" is in the library of Mr. F. F. Norcross of Chicago. In dramatic form it was even more enduring; Southerne's tragedy of "Oroonoko," which closely follows the novel, appeared in 1696, and was remodelled in 1759. When the comic scenes which Southerne had introduced were left out the play thus reconstructed followed the original story more faithfully than before, and held the stage for nearly a century and a half after Mrs. Behn was buried in Westminster Abbey. Famous actors filled the rôles; Jack Verbruggen was the original Oroonoko, and won such a signal success that the name stuck to him for life; in time Garrick played Oroonoko and Aboan, and—final and indisputable proof of popularity—a brand of tobacco was named after the unhappy hero! Curiously enough, the essential originality of the novel persisted in the play. Southerne in adapting the story to the stage, exploited, perhaps unconsciously, a new realm of dramatic emotion. The appeal to pity, the pathos of defeat, the helplessness of innocence, employed as major motives, were rare in tragedy. "Glory to the conquered" struck a new chord in men's hearts; "Oroonoko" and the dramatization of another novel of Mrs. Behn's, "Isabella, or the Fatal Marriage," initiated the sentimental drama of the eighteenth century which Steele was supposed to have founded, and the adjective generally applied to these plays—"feminine," "almost feminine," in their appeal to the sensibilities—was as unconsciously literal as it was descriptive.

"Oroonoko" has not escaped unassailed by modern German criticism, destructive as many other Teutonic activities. Dr. Ernest Bernbaum considers the story a pure romance with no foundation in reality. He is less drastically sceptical than Aschbach, however, who labored to prove there was no such person as Hrotsvitha, and, admitting the existence of Aphra, regards Oroonoko and Mr. Behn only as fictitious characters. Dr. Bernbaum disbelieves also Aphra's account of her journey to and sojourn in Surinam, and doubts whether she was ever in America. As her father was a professional barber, argues Dr. Bernbaum, he would not have been appointed governor of a colony; consequently Aphra's reason for her presence in Surinam falls to the ground. There exists no proof that Aphra's father was a barber, and Dr. Bernbaum leans very heavily on the unsupported statement of the Countess of Winchelsea, who never knew Aphra personally, and who, when she wrote that misleading note in her manuscript, was probably chronicling a bit of Grub Street gossip. The Countess misstated Aphra's father's name; is there any reason to believe that she was not equally mistaken in regard to his calling? It is hardly prudent to put one's trust in the noble poetess solely, and to ignore the negative testimony of the parish register at Wye. Aphra was too well-known and too envied to assume an alias, and to invent a mythical husband and a distinguished parent with impunity. Her fellow-scribes would have made short work of such pretensions.

Dr. Bernbaum suspects that Aphra's knowledge of Surinam was gleaned from a book published in London (1667) by George Warren, twenty-one years before "Oroonoko" was written. It is curious, then, that, with this "Impartial Description" before her, Aphra's "perfectly fantastic account of the scenery and flora of Surinam should indicate, as far as it is evidence at all, that the author had never been in that part of the world." Mr. Bernbaum does not take into account her interest in the life, and her familiarity with the conditions in the English colonies, and he attaches no value to the evidence of Aphra's friends and contemporaries: of Gildon, who saw her write "Oroonoko"; of Southerne, who said "that she always told his story [Oroonoko's] more feelingly than she writ it." Could a vamped-up tale, padded with descriptions from Warren's book, have moved Aphra and her auditors? Would it possess the indescribable accent of truth, of personal emotion at first hand? The biographical form counts for little; the older romances teemed with narratives told in the first person; Aphra's friends were themselves writers, old hands at the business, familiar with literary tricks. To argue that, because "an amorous and sensational romance" has been woven about Aphra's adventure in Antwerp, "Oroonoko," and the voyage to Surinam were, therefore, pure fiction, is to overlook the spy's necessity for secrecy and the fact that the romance may have been invented to conceal the object of her political mission. Secret-service agents do not often publish accurate accounts of their movements.

In fine, to have deceived so many people all the time (including historians and critics of English literature) Aphra must have been either a consummate artist, or an enthusiastic but sincere biographer. The balance of evidence inclines one to believe still that "Oroonoko" was a study—an embellished and idealized study—from life.

X

Aphra's poems, collected by Mr. Summers (1915) from many sources, amply justify the praise of Swinburne and prove that she had more than "a touch of lyric genius." Her first book of verse was published in 1684. It contained, besides some of Aphra's best pieces, several poems by Rochester and others, and a collection of poetic eulogies of the poetess herself, by friends and admirers, comparing her to Sappho, Virgil, and the greatest of her contemporaries. As for Ovid, the "Incomparable Astræa" is assured that had the Roman poet known her and her works, he would have gone out of business himself, neglected Julia, escaped exile, and lived happy as Aphra's lover, resigning his lyre to her abler hands. Evidently the great had no monopoly of flattery. To these "Poems on Several Occasions," "The Voyage to the Isle of Love" was added. It is a free translation in verse of Paul Tallemant's "*Voyage de l'Isle d'Amour,*" inspired by Mademoiselle de Scudéri's "*Carte du Tendre.*" Aphra's is a graceful and easy rendering of the pleasing but somewhat tame original. It was followed by other translations, "The Lover's Watch" (1686) and "The Lady's Looking-Glass," also from the French, an admirable doing into English of Baltazar Bonnecorse's "*La Montre*" and "*Le Miroir,*" a series of delicate meditations on love, interspersed with daintily alembicated verses.

These manuals of devotion would not be out of place in the famous blue room of the Hôtel Rambouillet; indeed their author was a protégé of de Scudéri, then arbiter of elegant sentiments. If "The Watch" was a lover's breviary, "The Lady's Looking-Glass" was his litany, and handling such airy trifles is a delicate task; they are woven from threads of gossamer in hours of love in idleness; but Aphra was catholic-minded, and could write for maids and youths as well as for rakes and worldlings. The thick air of the greenroom had not lessened her relish for the scent of spring meadows.

A "Miscellany" of 1685 is rich in "Pindarics," among them one on the death of Rochester. Some spirited verses are marooned in the rather dreary and trite allegory of "Lycidus, or The Lover in Fashion" (1688). Gildon's collections (1692-4), published after Aphra's death, preserve her imitation of Sappho, her poem to Dr. Burnet, several songs, and the elegiac verses on the death of the poet Waller, which had been contributed originally to a volume of poems to his memory, by various authors (1688). Of course, Aphra did the usual stint of official verse-making, that to-day solely devolves on the Laureate. More spontaneous were her tributes to her friends: to Dorset on his marriage, to Creech on his "Lucretius," to Stafford on his translation of an episode in Virgil, to Greenhill the painter, and to certain noble ladies of her circle. A quantum of this verse was a kind of poetic exercise, a form of diversion common to Aphra's contemporaries, who not only lisped in numbers but also conversed in couplets, drawing on a conventional stock of images, comparisons, and sentiments, arranged in a set form. The happenings of domestic life, a quarrel, the demise of a pet, a birthday, a little journey, a picnic, were subjects constantly treated with skill, in fluent verse, well named of society.

The popularity of songs was a stimulus to this form of poetic invention; most of Aphra's were written for her plays. This exquisite little lyric is from "Abdelazar." The form is of the school of Waller and "the mob of gentlemen who wrote in rhyme," but a richer vintage has been poured into the worn wine-skin, and the artificiality of the conceit melts away in the glow of genuine feeling.

LOVE ARMED

"Love in fantastique Triumph sate,
   While Bleeding Hearts around him flow'd,
For whom Fresh paines he did Create,
   And strange Tyranick power he show'd;
From thy Bright Eyes he took his fire,
   Which round about in sport he hurled;
But 'twas from mine he took desire
   Enough to undo the Amorous World.

From me he took his sighs and tears,
   From thee his Pride and Crueltie;
From me his Languishments and Feares,
   And every Killing Dart from thee;

> Thus thou and I, the God have arm'd,
> And sett him up a Deity;
> But my poor Heart alone is harm'd
> Whilst thine the Victor is, and free."

The following is simple and tender enough for "The Faithful Shepherdess":

> "'Tis not your saying that you love,
> Can ease me of my smart;
> Your Actions must your words approve,
> Or else you break my Heart.
>
> In vain you bid my Passion cease,
> And ease my troubled Breast;
> Your Love alone must give me Peace
> Restore my wonted Rest.
>
> But if I fail your heart to move,
> And 'tis not yours to give;
> I cannot, wonnot cease to love,
> But I will cease to live."

Hippolyta, in "The Dutch Lover," is less resigned.

> "Ah! false Amyntas, can that Hour,
> So soon forgotten be?
> When first I yielded up my Power
> To be betrayed by thee?
>
> . . . .
>
> I had not one Reserve in store,
> But at thy Feet I laid,
> Those Arms which conquered heretofore,
> Tho' now thy Trophy made.

> Thy Eyes in silence told their Tale
> Of Love in such a way,
> That 'twas as easy to prevail,
> As after to betray."

Some of the pastoral songs are more joyous. The shepherdess of "The Invitation," is an optimist, not averse to accepting the second best.

> "Damon, I cannot blame your will,
> 'Twas Chance and not Design did kill,
> For whilst you did prepare your Charmes,
> On purpose Silvia to subdue:
> I met the Arrows as they flew,
> And saved her from their harms.
> . . . .
> Content thee with this Victory,
> Think me as faire and young as She,
> I'll make thee Garlands all the day,
> And in the Groves we'll sit and sing,
> I'll Crown thee with the pride o' th' Spring
> When thou art Lord of May."

These verses should be presented with a gilded cage of doves, or tucked into a nosegay of spring flowers:

> "Oh! how the Hand the Lover ought to prize
> 'Bove any one peculiar Grace,
> While he is dying for the Eyes,
> And doating on the lovely Face!
> The Unconsid'ring little knows,
> How much he to this Beauty owes.
>
> That when the Lover absent is,
> Informs him of his Mistress' Heart,

> 'Tis that which gives him all his Bliss,
> When dear Love-Secrets 'twill impart.
>   .   .   .   .   .   .
> 'Tis that which Treasure gives so vast;
> Even Iris 'twill to Damon give at last."

Ocasionally some touch of color in the neat lines reflects the rosy afterglow of the Renaissance. Lysander, hearing music, suggests this Tiepolesque picture:

> "So look young Angels, Listening to the sound,
> When the Tun'd Spheres Glad all the Heaven's around:
> So Raptur'd lie among the wondering Crowd,
> So Charmingly Extended on a Cloud."

The counsels to the little Loves Aphra summoned to mourn the death of Rochester, evoke memories of antique altars, a glimpse of pearly plumes on snowy marble.

> "Cold as his Tomb, Pale as your Mother's Doves;
> Bewail him then, oh! all ye little Loves.
> Upon your hands your weeping Heads decline,
> And let your wings encompass round his Shrine."

Though Aphra's love-poetry is sometimes indecorous, venal love inspires her with an aversion expressed in many different ways. Willmore in the "Rover," will not hire his Love's heart,

> "Nor Tenant to your Favors be;
> I will not farm your White and Red,
> You shall not let your Love to me,
> I court a Mistress not a Landlady."

Most of these songs are like Byron's young lovers,

"Half-naked, loving, natural and Greek,"

but the poetess sometimes forgets that, "*Si l'amour est nu, il n'est pas crotté.*" For if Aphra's chosen land was Arcadia, it was Arcadia peopled by a colony from Bohemia, which the original settlers of Sir Philip Sidney would have cut dead. To please these sophisticated pastoral folk was Aphra's aim.

> ". . . my careless Muse no higher strove
> T' inlarge her Glory, and extend her Wings;
> Than underneath Parnassus Grove,
> To sing of Shepherds, and their humble Love;
> But never durst, like Cowly, tune her Strings,
> To sing of Heroes, and of Kings."

The moral standing of the shepherd in the later English pastoral was low; often he would have been better or more congenially employed as a swineherd. The high-minded, punctilious *bergers* of French pastoral romance were vulgarized when they crossed the Channel. Amaryllis sporting in the shade is a legitimate subject for poetic effusion, but Aphra omitted the shade. She ignored, wilfully perhaps, the force and charm of suggestiveness; lovelier far are the nymphs, a glimmering whiteness among the distant willows, than when they are rudely unzoned before us. Aphra evinced no appreciation of the artistic value of reticence. Her own experience had coarsened her. In entering a literary career she had necessarily abandoned certain reserves and defied the conventions; in succeeding in her profession she became a target for calumny. Forced to admit that her work was good "tho' writ by a woman," her detractors found it easy to account for its excellence by accusing her of passing off some man's productions as her own; Aphra refers again and again to this aspersion of her ability and good faith. "Obliged to earn her bread, and not ashamed to own it," she found its taste bitter even when flavored with bay leaves. When pushed into a defiant attitude foreign to her nature did she break with essentials, as she had with appearances? Did she live as she wrote, like a literary man? It is unjust to judge her own conduct by that of her *dramatis personæ*, as she sold the public what it would buy, but it is difficult to believe that one who habitually dealt in forbidden fruit never nibbled at her own wares. The personal note is of course more marked in her poems than in her plays, there are a dozen or more lyrics addressed to Amyntas, Lysander, Lysidas, Damon, Alexis, *e tutti quanti*, in which the poetess betrays as intense an appreciation of virile comeliness and strength, as of manly wit, and understanding.

Were all these shepherds flames of the poetess? As the grenadier said of the English at Waterloo, "*Ils sont trop*," especially for an extremely occupied person. Were they not rather masculine substi-

APHRA BEHN

tutes for the visionary nymphs which were part of every rhymester's stock in trade, a literary tradition which obliged the most modest bard to keep a poetical harem? The poems to J. H., however, are too distinctly personal, too informed with feeling (feeling often resentful and exasperated) not to betray the expression of real sentiments, and real suffering. J. H. was not a tender shepherd. He had much of Richardson's Lovelace in him, a passion for mastery, a desire to hurt, and a talent for wounding. If he was John Hoyle, and there is good reason to suppose that he was, he gave ample cause for Aphra's complaints.

Hoyle was a lawyer, a wit, and a rake. He was handsome and accomplished, and his arrogance and apparent indifference to them appealed irresistibly to women. His friendship, however, would have compromised a Godiva, and with Aphra he seemed to be on most intimate terms. He was not a lover to foster fine ideals, and for him apparently Aphra felt a wretched, degrading passion; a passion that scorned and despised even while it desired, against which reason, self-interest, pride, even disgust, revolted in vain. Living with lawless people, breathing an atmosphere surcharged with excitement, a denizen of an artificial world where amorous caprice recognized no restraints, she was unarmed against impulse. Hoyle's perverseness, his infidelities and exactions embittered but did not cure her. No pain is spared to a warm-hearted and generous woman who loves unworthily, who is a poet naturally doomed to illusions and deceptions, and not the least of Aphra's sufferings was the consciousness of her folly. Fortunately she was a worker also who had little time for the indulgence of an unhappy passion. There was a gaunt shadow athwart her threshold that only an active pen could keep at bay. And there is no doubt that to mourn in numbers relieves a full heart, and the artistic expression of its burden lightens a heavy mind; the woes of the literary should not too deeply grieve the gentle reader. The same penful of ink served for Byron's "Fare thee well and if forever, Still forever fare thee well," and "Hurrah! Moore, we're off." Without imputing to Aphra the extent and variety of George Sand's emotional experiences one may say that "she loved not like a lady but like a gentleman"; and it may be surmised that Aphra had her distractions: admirers and friends, who prized her society, and appreciated, perhaps overappreciated, her talent. She wrote to an accompanying chorus of praise, and often actually in the midst of her little court, for to her, like many writers of her time, verse-making came easily, almost too easily. Her practice knew neither the file, nor the lamp, and her poems, unrevised and uncorrected, were often either a fine careless improvisation, or a slipshod jingle. All her verse sings, however, and though often trivial is never unmusical. More even than her prose it bears the marks of haste, but from time to time her poor, jaded Pegasus, jogging along at a shilling the hour, unfolds shining pinions and soars into the empyrean. In the midst of a formal panegyric to Sir Francis Fane we happen on a fine image:

"Your nobler flights will wing my Callow Muse;
So the young Eagle is informed to fly
By seeing the Monarch Bird ascend the sky.
And tho' with less success her strength she'll try,
Spreads her soft plumes and his vast tracks pursues."

These tripping verses lead up to a lovely line:

"What would a Lover not endure,
His Mistress' Fame and Honour to secure.
Iris, the Care we take to be discreet,
Is the dear Toil that makes the Pleasure sweet;
The Thorn that does the Wealth enclose
That with less saucy Freedom we may touch the Rose."

Aphra's portrait of J. H., the heart-taker, in "The Cabal," is not engaging to modern eyes:

"Next Lysidas the haughty Swain,
With many Beauties in a Train,
All sighing for the Swain whilst he
Barely returns Civility.
 .   .   .   .

His eyes are black and do transcend
All Fancy e'er can comprehend;
And yet no Softness in 'em move
They kill with Fierceness, not with Love;

> Yet he can dress them when he list
> With Sweetness none can e'er resist
> His Tongue no Amorous Parley makes
> But with his Looks alone he speaks.
> And though he languish yet he'll hide
> That grateful knowledge with his Pride."

He will only impart love enough

> "To gain and to secure a Heart."

When he is sure of it he prepares for new triumphs, and leaves it to despair. This simple technic appears to have been very successful, and through it Lysidas "has gained more hearts than all the rest of the 'Pastoral Cabal.'" Whatever his magic was Aphra has not succeeded in communicating it.

In spite of her voyages to Cythera Aphra could write gravely and tenderly; witness these verses on a baby's tomb:

> "This Little, Silent, Gloomy Monument
> Contains all that was sweet and innocent;
> The softest prattler that e'er found a Tongue
> His Voice was Musick, and his Words a Song;
> Which now each List'ing Angel smiling hears,
> Such pretty Harmonies compose the Spheres."

In the elegy on the death of Waller a deeper, sadder note is struck:

ON THE DEATH OF WALLER

> "'How to thy sacred Memory shall I bring,
> (Worthy thy fame) a grateful Offering?
> I, who by Toils of Sickness am become
> Almost as near as thou art to a Tomb?

While every soft and every tender Strain
Is ruffled and ill-natured grown with Pain.
But at thy Name my languid Muse revives,
And a new Spark in the dull Ashes strives;
I hear thy tuneful Verse, thy Song Divine,
And am Inspired by every charming Line.
But Oh!
What inspiration at the second Hand,
Can an Immortal Elegy command?
Unless, like Pious Offerings, mine should be
Made Sacred, being consecrate to thee.
Eternal as thy own Almighty Verse,
Should be those Trophies that adorn thy Hearse,
The Thought illustrious and the Fancy young,
The Wit sublime, the Judgment fine and strong,
Soft as thy Notes to Sacharissa sung;
Whilst mine, like Transitory Flowers decay,
That come to deck thy Tomb a short lived Day,
Such Tributes are, like Tenures, only fit,
To show from whom we hold our Right to Wit.

Long did the untun'd World in Ignorance stray,
Progressed in nothing that was Great and Gay,
Till taught by thee, the true Poetick way;
Rough were the Tracts before, Dull and Obscure;
Nor Pleasure nor Instruction could procure;
Their thoughtless Labour could no Passion move,
Sure, in that Age, the poets knew not Love,
That Charming God, like Apparitions, then,
Was only talked on, but ne'er seen by Men.
Darkness was o'er the Muses land displayed,
And even the Chosen Tribe, unguided, straid,
'Till by thee rescued from the Egyptian Night,
They now look up and view the God of Light,
That taught them how to Love, and how to Write."

Pain, lassitude, and incessant labor leave her little leisure for meditation, yet her later verses show their chastening.

"Do thou, oh Lord, instruct me how to know,
Not *whither*, but *which way* I am to go,"

Aphra asks in her "Paraphrase on the Lord's Prayer." In the same poem she uses Omar's impressive figure, but with Christian humility not Oriental fatalism:

"For thou, oh Lord, art Holy, Wise, and Just,
And raising Man from forth the common dust,
Hast set thy Sacred Image on his Soul,
And shall the Pot the Potter's hand controul?
Poor, boasting, feeble Clay that Error shun,
Submit, and let th' Almighty's Will be done."

XI

Eight "Love Letters to a Gentleman," written during the last year of Aphra's life, were published after her death by the Unknown. A sharper contrast to the Dresden-china idyl of Damon and Iris could not be imagined. Here are no *concetti*, no artificial flowers, nor rosy ribbons, no devices of happy young hearts to say "I love you" again and again yet with a difference. Lycidas, to whom the letters were addressed, was no Damon but an indolent, critical, saturnine man of the world, reluctantly, in spite of himself, charmed by Astræa, dreading the possible ascendancy of her positive character over his negative one, and of her fixed will over his vacillation. To her sincerity he opposed mockery, and to her frankness silence, or evasion. He was cold yet jealous, exacting while neglectful, censorious though indifferent. He made laws and rules for Aphra, meanwhile carefully guarding his own liberty. He blamed her freedom of life, her lack of "the little Arts of her Sex," even while profiting by her unconventionality. Lycidas ruled her *salon*, proscribed her old friends, and shut her doors on her admirers. There are constant allusions in her letters to promises "to see no Man" until Lycidas returns, or to cloister herself with her servants. Though exiling her companions, he never presented her to his, or tried to fill the void he made in her social life. How a large-minded nature could have wasted itself on such a petty, peevish creature is one of love's mysteries. The poor fond lady taxed her wit in trying to *understand* him, to plumb his shallows, and to warm her chilled heart at his feeble, fluttering flame. It is pitiful to see this brilliant woman, a celebrity and a wit, held to an accounting of her time, her words, her smiles, and to witness her supine acquiescence in this mean despotism. Love rode Aphra with a long spur, and Van Aalbert was avenged.

These letters are sad reading. What jading anxiety, what sick fears at having unwittingly offended, what heart-quakes at the thought of losing her dear tormentor darkened the close of Aphra's life. Occasionally she realized her folly, beat at the closed gates of her dungeon, struggled against the torturer; but the revolt was only momentary, she soon stretched herself on the rack again, and the pincers tore her kind heart. There were even sadder lucid moments in her madness when she saw for what a poor thing she had bartered her peace, to what a miser she had played the prodigal, and her pride winced and bled under the lash of her self-scorn. But this lucidity was transient, and she soon slipped on her manacles again.

How piteously grateful she was for a little tenderness: "My Lycidas says He can be soft and dear when He pleases to put off his haughty Pride, which is only assumed to see how far I dare love him ununited. . . . Since then my Soul's Delight you are . . . shew me all the Love thou dissembled. . . . And if thou hast Love, shew that Love, I beseech thee."

She evidently besought him in vain, for in her next letter, she complained again of his having misinterpreted her actions and protests against his disheartening censure of her words. "Do not shame me with your perpetual ill Opinion, my Nature is proud and insolent, and can not bear it. I will be used something better. For God's sake do not misinterpret my excess of Fondness. . . . Pray make haste to see me Tomorrow, and if I am not at home when you come, send for me over the Way, where I have engaged to dine, there being an Entertainment on purpose tomorrow for me." Like a spaniel at its master's whistle, she will leave the friends who prize her, in the midst of a dinner in her honor, at a sign from Lycidas.

She was well rewarded, apparently, for she soon writes: "I conjure thee if possible to come Tomorrow about seven or eight at Night that I may tell you in what a deplorable condition you left me Tonight. I can not describe it but I feel it. . . . Love and Rage, Fevers and Calentures, even Madness itself! Indeed, indeed my Soul I know not to what Degree I love you: let it suffice I do most passionately, and can have no Thoughts of any other Man while I have Life. . . . Farewel—I love you more and more every Moment."

Astræa is more resigned in her next and last letter. . . . "Oh to what Purpose is all this fooling. I was born to ill Luck, and this Loss of my Heart is, possibly, not the least Part on't. . . . For as I am satisfied I love in vain . . . I am satisfied that nothing but the Thing that hates me could treat me as Lycidas does, *and it is only the Vanity of being beloved by me* can make you countenance a Softness so displeasing to you. How could any Thing but the Man that hates me entertain me so unkindly? Witness your excellent Opinion of me, of loving others, witness your passing by the End of the Street where I live, and sqund'ring away your time at any Coffee-house, rather than allow me what you know in your Soul is the greatest Blessing of my Life, your dear, *dull* melancholy Company; I call it dull because you can never be gay or merry where Astrea is." Why did he not tell her plainly: "My Friend Astrea, I neither do love thee, nor can, nor ever will"? Why does he not love unreservedly, why these whims, and ill-humors, and sudden coldnesses, why this capricious chilling of genial currents? And when Astræa in her turn shuts her door, does not write, feigns (with what difficulty!) an equal indifference, he reproaches her. Where are her professions, her vaunted affection? "Why truly, my dear Lycidas, where it was and ever will be . . . you have in your Astrea all she possesses. I should be glad to see you as soon as possible. . . . I beg you will not fail to let me hear from you today being *Wednesday*, and see you at Night if you can."

One wonders if he came on Wednesday night, who he really was (what is known of the talented and disreputable John Hoyle from Aphra's poems resembles Lycidas), and how long this devastating passion endured. There was, of course, a final break, and the letters, returned to Aphra, probably were flotsam from the wreck. Perhaps the Unknown by printing them unedited, without comment, in her Memoir hoped to strike at a flinty heart. They immediately precede the account of Aphra's last illness and death. Truly a grand passion should be a forbidden luxury to a literary woman. Balzac with his curious tendency to estimate most things, feelings included, in coin of the realm, calculated how many volumes an affair of the heart costs an author. What a wasteful discharge of nerve-cells, what a prodigal expenditure of force to no real purpose was squandered by Aphra in this swan-song of her heart. How the spendthrift had lavished tears, and fever, and insomnia, how she had thrown away on an obscure and unappreciative individual, imagination and emotion sufficient for half a dozen plays, with a poem or so thrown in! What an expense for a woman whose daily work made great demands on her strength! How extravagant, how unwise, was such indulgence at forty odd years, when Daudet's *quatrième étage* had been reached and one could look down quietly on the ascent successfully climbed. Elderly philandering has a comic element in its tragedy which could not have escaped a humorist like Aphra; and probably she never pitied herself without a wry face. If "*au cœur on n'a jamais de rides*," the mind grows wrinkled after such experiences as hers, and it is then that the intelligent are doubly tortured. The woman, I might say surely the *man*, of the world in her jeered at the mature Juliet's infatuation, with bitter jests that sear but do not cauterize the wounds of the heart. She had too often ridiculed the decayed beauty's belated flame in her comedies to play that mirth-provoking rôle without shame.

Her own last act was not lacking in dignity. She had her consolations—friends, praise, success, best of all, work. The constant excitement of a playwright's life, the palpitating drama of the production of each play from the initial reading to the joys and terrors of the first representation, superseded, for a time at least, all other preoccupations. With the author's anxiety, the gamester's excitement was mingled; each play was a stake, and she could no more count on its success beforehand than she could on winning at the basset-tables.

Had she no higher source of consolation than that afforded by occupation? Between her plays and novels Aphra had slipped in some translations: "The Maxims" of La Rochefoucauld (1685) and Ovid's "Epistle of Œnone to Paris" from a paraphrase, as Aphra was no Latinist. Dryden wrote of it in genial praise: "The Author, who is of the Fair Sex, understood not *Latine*. But if she does not I am afraid she has given us occasion to be ashamed, who do." Aphra, Nahum Tate, and other writers whose names have been forgotten, Englished Cowley's Latin verse, "Sex Libri Plantarum," published after his death (1689). Two years before she had versified Æsop's Fables for a fine illustrated edition of them. In 1688, Fontenelle's "*Pluralité des mondes*" was done into English by Mrs. Behn, preceded by an essay on translation.

The study of astronomy hardly seems a healing balm for lacerated affections, yet it may have proved a cooling one. The august spectacle of the march of worlds through infinite space awes a personal sorrow into silence. Before such a mighty manifestation of eternal law, the wildest heart, the most rebellious will tenders—at least for a time—its submission, a submission that is acceptance, not despair. In the presence of this radiant permanence how infinitesimal and how fugitive seem human passion and pain! From the unplumbed abyss of the sky, a dim conception of the Great Design, the pattern so vast that only shreds of it can be apprehended, is revealed to the star-gazer. Something of the harmony of the celestial choir descends on fevered brain and bruised heart, desire and will unconsciously attune themselves to that unheard music, and on awe and humility reverence waits.

To translate a book is to read, and reread it, and no mind as impressionable as Aphra's could have remained unaffected by such study of "The Plurality of Worlds," in which for the first time, the wonders of the firmament were shown to other than special students of the stars. An active and receptive mind is often a Good Samaritan to a broken heart and nature is a cold but sure friend. In looking up through nature to nature's God, in the knowledge and acceptance of law, it may be hoped Aphra found peace.

The old order had crumbled away about the ardent Royalist in those last days of 1688. James II, Aphra's patron, had been driven out of the England he harried and tortured, "Kirke's Lambs" had ravaged the western counties, Alice Lisle had been beheaded, and Elizabeth Gaunt had been burned alive at Tyburn for sheltering Monmouth's followers. Jeffreys, the blood-maniac, had gone to his Judge. Mary of Modena, with her horrible pin-money from the sale of hundreds of English prisoners into slavery on Jamaica plantations, was a refugee in France. For three years the sons, not of Belial only, but of Moloch, flown with insolence and blood, had terrorized England. Aphra lived long enough to see another Convention Parliament and to read the "Declaration of Rights"; William and Mary were crowned three days before Aphra passed away with the passing of the world she knew. For some time her health had been precarious, weakened by years of exciting and unremitting labor. The output of even the last months of her life was extraordinary. She lived in every sense; her writings, numerous as they are, were only part of her endeavors. She loved society, and her door was seldom shut even in working hours; she entertained while composing, laying down her pen to look over a new French book or, perhaps, to mix a bowl of the milk-punch she is said to have introduced to English palates. Gildon saw her write "'Oroonoko' and keep her own in Discoursing with several then present." She was a genial hostess and counted among her friends distinguished men of letters: Waller, Dryden, Otway, and Betterton; noble authors: Dorset, Rochester, and Killigrew, many young poets, and struggling actors. She was an omnivorous reader in both French and English, a brilliant talker in an age of wits, and an amateur of music. For eighteen years she had been living at high pressure. Plays, poems, novels, translations, paraphrases appeared in quick succession; her name on a book cover guaranteed a ready sale, a play by her was sure of a hearing; yet in the height of her vogue she was never free from care, and anxiety about money shadowed her triumphs. In a letter to Jacob Tonson, her publisher, written just before the appearance of "A Voyage to the Isle of Love" (1684), and other poems, she says: "As for ye verses of mine I shou'd really have thought 'em worth thirty pound and I hope you will find it worth 25 £ . . . Alas! I would not lose my time in such low gettings . . . but I have been without getting so long yt I am just on ye poynt of breaking. I want extreamly or I would not urge this." Another note of August 1, in 1685, shows Aphra in debt to a certain Mr. Baggs for the sum of "six pound." With all her success and ability the wolf was always at her door.

There were probably several reasons for Aphra's impecuniousness. She lived among needy folk, she was warm-hearted and open-handed, among her familiars were minor poets and unpopular dramatists who were not ashamed to ask and receive help from their more prosperous confrères, and who even when not hungry were perennially thirsty. Anxiety, constant mental tension, sedentary habits, and overwork began to tell on Aphra's health three years before her death, without lessening her industry. A scurrilous attack (for Aphra's popularity, not her character, made her enemies among the unsuccessful), describes her as ill and weak, suffering with sciatica; "her limbs distortured and nerves shrunk up with pain." The same year (1687), in her letter of condolence to Waller's daughter-in-law, Aphra speaks of herself as "very ill, and dying this twelve months," and apologizes for her writing "with a Lame hand scarce able to hold a pen." The poor crippled hand did hold it valiantly until the last, fending off the wolf, conquering languor, depression, and a torturing complication of ills. Her last work was a "Pindaric" (March, 1689) to Dr. Burnet, who had asked for news of her health. The poem breathes a noble resignation; Aphra sees with sad clairvoyance that her cause is forever ruined, her King's reign is over, her friends are in disgrace, or worse, hurrying to make their peace with the new sovereigns. Yet in spite of her personal loss she is large-minded enough to perceive what England has gained by the defeat of her own party, and salutes in Dr. Burnet the historian of the new order:

"Tho' I the Wondrous Change deplore,
 That makes me Useless and Forlorn,
 Yet I the great Design adore,
 Tho' Ruined in the Universal Turn.
 Nor can my Indigence and lost Repose,
 Those Meagre Furies that surround me close,
 Convert my Sense and Reason more
 To this Unpresidented Enterprise,
 Than that a Man so Great, so Learned, so Wise,
 The Brave Atchievement Owns and Nobly Justifies."

"Loyalty commands with Pious Force" Aphra to "like the Excluded Prophet stand," and only watch the "Chosen possess the Promised Land."

This was her evensong. She died in harness, pen in hand. "Too satiate with life to strive with death," she literally entered into rest on April 16, 1689, and was buried in Westminster Abbey under a slab of black marble with two wretched verses engraved on it:

"Here lies a Proof that Wit can never be
Defence enough against Mortality,"

by a gentleman (John Hoyle) who was credited, by the envious, with the authorship of some of Aphra's own poems. The Unknown remarks that the lameness of these votive lines is a sufficient refutation of this unworthy suspicion.

A finer tribute might have been paid to the writer of the first modern novel, to one who was as versatile and diligent as she was gifted, and in whom the oppressed found a champion and the wretched a friend.

AÏSSÉ

> "I'll tell thee, Celio.
> He who far off beholds another dancing,
> Even one who dances best, and all the time
> Hears not the music that he dances to,
> Thinks him a madman, apprehending not
> The law that rules his else eccentric action.
> So he that's in himself insensible
> Of love's sweet influence, misjudges him
> Who moves according to love's melody:
> And knowing not that all these sighs and tears,
> Ejaculations, and impatiences,
> Are necessary changes of a measure,
> Which the divine musician plays, may call
> The lover crazy; which he would not do
> Did he within his own heart hear the tune
> Play'd by the great musician of the world."
>
> —*Calderon, "The Painter of His Own Dishonor": Fitz-Gerald's Translation.*

Never, God is my witness, never have I sought anything in thee but thyself: I have sought thee, not thy gifts. I have not looked to the marriage bond or dowry: I have not yearned to satisfy my own will and desire, but thine, as well thou knowest. The name of wife may be holier and more honored but the name of friend—nay, mistress or concubine if thou wilt suffer it—has always been the sweeter to me. For in thus abasing myself for thee, I should win more favor from thee, and do less injury to thy greatness. . . . God is my witness that if Augustus, the emperor of the whole world, were to honor me with the thought of wedlock, and yield me the empire of the universe, I should deem it more precious and more honorable to be thy mistress than to be the empress of a Cæsar.

—*Letter I of Heloise to Abelard.*

AÏSSÉ

I

IN 1717 what was euphemistically termed the heart of the French Regent was unoccupied despite the efforts of many intrepid ladies who had vainly tried to storm that battered but well-defended citadel. And yet it was necessary for the success of certain enterprises of Councillor Dubois's that the Regent's attention should be diverted from affairs political. Those weak short-sighted eyes of his were supplemented by a most penetrating inner vision when he occasionally turned it upon questions of state; nor could orgy dim, nor even intoxication entirely obfuscate it. But a passion might blind it—for a time—at least until the coveted red hat was firmly placed on Dubois's shabby little flaxen wig. Where frank assault had failed the miner and the sapper might succeed, thought the would-be cardinal, and his familiar, the unfrocked nun, Claudine de Tencin. Subterranean ways were familiar to them both, and had proved royal avenues to fortune.

The weasel-faced Dubois was a notable example of the triumph of mole-like methods. Ex-tutor and ex-tout of the Regent, half valet, half confidential adviser, had he not after a lifetime of burrowing, emerged into the light, even into that proverbially fierce light that beats upon a throne? Was he not the master of his master, the obscure motive power in French politics? Had he not just secured the peace of Europe by the Triple Alliance, while at the same time by counselling the easy policy of inaction he paralyzed the generous reforms of the Regent? And his Egeria, Madame de Tencin, the dowerless demoiselle whom custom and her impoverished family had condemned to the cloister, was she not a refutation of the fact that the shortest distance from one point to another is a straight line? Had she not dominated fate by tact, dissimulation, and dexterous manipulation of human weaknesses; utilizing even her own detected disorders as a means of aggrandizement, and leaving her convent not as a disgraced nun but as a pensioned canoness? Later drawn to Paris she became the adviser of her brother the Cardinal de Tencin, and like a sleek, graceful beast of prey, crouched in wait for a no less noble quarry than Philippe d'Orléans himself. He was an ingloriously easy conquest she thought at first, but when under her caressing playfulness, her smooth flatteries, he felt the steel claws tangling his policy, clutching at his schemes, he, usually so courteous, so debonair, drove her snarling and cringing from his presence.

Failing the lion she accepted the jackal, and Dubois consoled her for the Regent's rebuff. For

Dubois, unlike d'Orléans, "from whom," said St. Simon, "women got little money and never a secret," was a devout believer in their influence. They formed no mean part of his secret police, and helped to spin the dusky webs of intrigue which extended from the royal bedchamber at the Escurial to the King's cabinet in London, from the perambulating cabin of the Great Peter to the Papal anteroom in Rome. The Spanish Queen's nurse, the wrinkled Dulcinea of the old Pope Innocent XIII, the Fillon's venal nymphs were on his pension list, and earned the money that he wrung from a bankrupt France which could not pay her troops.

But what was gained by all this back-stairs intrigue if the Regent persisted in his liberal policy? There would be no cardinal's hat for a minister whose nominal master ceased persecuting Protestants, unchained Huguenot gentlemen from the oars of the royal galleys, and opened libraries to the public. Rome could not draw her sacred circle around the servant of a prince who found his model of kingcraft in the half-heretic Henry IV. Therefore, in order that the rosy aureole should surround Dubois's brow, the Regent's attention should be distracted from such minor matters. The famous suppers of the Palais Royal were beginning to pall. Dissipation was growing dull; to pass the time d'Orléans and the *roués* were cooking their own dishes, but the host yawned over even the Spanish omelet which he made to perfection. Then came the champagne and soon afterwards the slumber of boredom, for, with due apologies to Terence, Ceres and Bacchus without Venus are but frosty affairs. But where was the new Venus to be found? Not among the tumbled beauties of the court. Mesdames de Parabère, de Sabran, d'Averne, d'Argentan were the roses of yester-years. The actresses Desmares and Grandval were cast-off puppets; even the wonderful dancing doll, Florence of the Opera, had ceased to please. The pretty English girls, seductive agents of the Pretender, had been bowed out of the presence by one who saw the hook quite as plainly as the bait. The task of leading him by the nose was no easy one even for such adroit players upon human frailty as the future cardinal and the ex-nun.

D'Orléans was a bewildering, composite creature; devoured by curiosity to know and to feel all things, he was the spirit of the eighteenth century made flesh, the incarnation of its aspirations, its aims, its weaknesses. Never was there a more industrious or more accomplished prince. He was a good cook and a brave soldier, gathering bays at Neerwinden and Steinkerke, and meriting a triumph in Spain. He was an excellent chemist, and sacrificed to the Muses, studying painting with Coypel, and making a fine collection of pictures, distinguished by an eclectic taste. He wrote the music of the opera of "*Panthée*," and engraved a series of illustrations for the "Daphnis and Chloe," of Longus. He was a friend of letters, pensioned Voltaire, and printed "*Télémaque*" at his own expense. He was an encyclopædia of information, useful and otherwise. He spoke with ease, clearness, warmth, and at times even with eloquence; and with history, court gossip, science, the fine and industrial arts, he appeared equally familiar. He was impious and benevolent; he believed in the devil though he denied the existence of God. This scoffer at things divine, this mocker at priests and kings, who laughed at the old tarnished Olympus of Louis XIV, was the benefactor of the poor to whom he opened the doors of the University of Paris and of the Royal Library. To relieve the rural population from the burden of feeding and lodging his soldiers he built hundreds of barracks all over France, while to amuse the Parisians he founded the masked balls of the opera. He was an inconstant, but never a cruel or brutal lover. He was a profligate but an artistic one; in the midst of a carouse, Mademoiselle Duclos would be asked to declaim the verses of Molière or Racine, or the Regent himself would sing an air of Lulli. The orgies of the Palais Royal, flavored with art and wit, were feasts of reason compared to the barbaric bacchanals of Peter the Great, or the drinking bouts of Augustus of Poland, or the dull, gross "feeds" of the English court. But one could not always appeal from Philippe drunk to Philippe sober. The

Regent's mind was firm but his character was weak. He loved pleasure too well to sacrifice it to an idea. Thus the many reforms he projected: the equal division of taxes, the publication of an account of the expenditure of public moneys, the proclamation of liberty of thought, remained on paper until nearly the close of the century. But he desired them, and familiarized the minds of his subjects with them; burdened as he was by the awful heritage of Louis XIV, surely goodness and mercy followed him in many of his days as ruler.

Dubois could certainly count on the kindness of one whose first visit after attaining power had been to Madame de Maintenon, to assure his archenemy who had vainly plotted to deprive him of his life and then of his rights to the crown, that the pension allowed her by the late King should still be paid. But Dubois's hopes of ecclesiastical dignity were menaced by the passion for justice of one who had bridled the Jesuits, and stood between the Protestants and their persecutors. An innovator who had promptly cast aside the old, rusty thunderbolt of Louis XIV, and made the Parlement a mouthpiece for the expression of public opinion, was a menace to other forms of tyranny. To serve a prince tolerant in matters religious, liberal in matters political, would not advance the prospects of a would-be father of the church. Fortunately the weakness of the *Roi Galant* might be exploited in his disciple, but where was the required plaything, the Circe in leading strings, warranted to advance the interests of orthodoxy and Dubois?

To answer this question he sat long in council with Madame de Tencin. Many were named and all refused; Dubois grew impatient; the resourceful canoness seemed almost at a loss before she found the desired answer. Aïssé! Ah! here indeed was a duly qualified aspirant to those smirched honors. An Oriental princess, a Circassian slave, an accomplished Parisian at once! Better still, a pretty, wistful girl, with a background of romance and mystery, in a pathetic situation, most appealing to the kind heart of the Regent. Could a spoiled, fastidious prince ask for more? And the young creature was so helpless, so penniless, so poor in friends in spite of her apparently brilliant social position, so utterly dependent on the sister of Madame de Tencin, and therefore under the thumb of that dexterous lady herself, that it really seemed as though the Lord, or rather some less beneficent power, had delivered her into an unscrupulous hand. Surely she could but prove as wax under the modelling tool when properly approached and instructed. So the council broke up, and the duumvirs separated well pleased; Dubois to write to his agents at the Roman court, and Madame to visit her sister Madame de Ferriol, the guardian of Aïssé.

II

During the last years of the seventeenth century Messire Charles de Ferriol, Baron d'Argental, was French ambassador at the Porte. He was an original person, more of a *mousquetaire* than a courtier; a fire-eater who insisted on wearing his sword even in the Sultan's presence and a brave and loyal friend who had given asylum in his own house to the Dutch ambassador, when Holland's prudent allies, the English, refused him refuge in their embassy.

Ferriol found Oriental manners much to his taste. The military code suited his stern temper, and the slave-dealers supplied him with material for an agreeably varied domestic life. It was of one of these *jellabs* that in 1698 he bought a winning little girl of four years. To create interest, and probably to justify the price (fifteen hundred livres) asked for her, the merchant assured Ferriol that she had been stolen from a palace and was the daughter of a prince, which statement was unsustained by any proof. The child was probably one of a lot carried off in a Turkish descent on a Circassian village. The ambassador, whether moved by pity or desirous of providing a nurse for his old age (in 1698 he was already fifty-one years old), sent his purchase to Paris to the house of his brother, who occupied a high position in the magistracy. It was Madame de Ferriol, a young, light-minded and light-mannered person who took charge of the little Haïdée or Aïssé, as the new French family, softening the harsher Arab syllables, preferred to call her. Like most of the children of the nobility, she was immediately bundled off to a convent. This convent of *Les Nouvelles Catholiques* was one to which youthful heretics, taken from their parents, were sent to be cured by argument and exhortation, or if these bland means failed, by starvation and the whip, of the errors of Protestantism. Recurrence to such measures to oblige the baby Mohammedan to abjure the faith of Islam was probably unnecessary. The instruction in this retreat was largely confined to religious matters, one may infer, for some years later when "*Demoiselle Charlotte Haïdée*" stood godmother to Madame de Ferriol's youngest son, she was unable to sign her name to the baptismal certificate. Music and dancing, a fair knowledge of etiquette and genealogy, needlework and church history— very much the kind of education she would have received in a seraglio of her native land, she brought back with her when she returned to the Hôtel Ferriol in the rue Neuve St.-Augustin where her real education began.

Madame de Ferriol's liaison with the Maréchal d'Uxelles made her a power in certain circles where she shone moon-like; her sister, Madame de Tencin, was already the mentor of Richelieu, and a dispenser of favors; de Ferriol himself as a magistrate enjoyed a position of less dubious authority and their *salon* was frequented by a brilliant and witty circle of intellectual and even celebrated people eminently fitted to form the mind and manners of a girl who possessed the precocious intelligence and the desire to please of the Oriental. Even dulness would have acquired burnish from constant contact with such minds as those of the young Voltaire, Fontenelle, or Montesquieu; a semblance of wit from such women as Mesdames de Lambert and du Deffand, a high degree of social culture from Lady Bolingbroke and St. Aulaire.

The portionless girl did not lack admirers. The effeminate Duke de Gesvres, in his early youth, before he occupied the uneasy position of King's friend, and carried his knotting and worsted work to Versailles, sighed for her, and the Prince de Bournonville made no secret of his devotion. But the young Circassian showed an insensibility and a discretion rare indeed in one born to the *yashmak*, and though M. de Ferriol had been sufficiently alarmed at the duke's attentions to write Aïssé a letter in which he brutally reminded her that she was his property, when he returned to Paris in 1711, a premature dotard, weak in body and infirm in mind, he found his beneficiary heart-free. Until his death (in 1722) Aïssé cared for him with a filial devotion which must have often been subjected to severe tension, as a stormy youth, a self-indulgent maturity, and a despotic temper are not the elements from which an amiable and venerable old age is derived. Among the old gentleman's delusions was the conviction that his past career deserved the recompense of a cardinalate, and though his pretensions were not more ill-founded than those of many clerical aspirants to the red hat, they were a source of alarm and mortification to his kinsfolk. In his will he partially rewarded the care of his devoted slave, who had passed her youth in his service, by leaving her a life-annuity of four thousand livres, and a considerable sum of money which was to be paid by his heirs, the Ferriols. Madame de Ferriol, selfish and avaricious, mourned so constantly over the tax on her heritage made by this legacy that Aïssé more generously than prudently tore up the deed and threw it into the fire. This act was a significant one and may stand as an example of the relations of the two women. On the side of the great lady constant exactions, on the part of her ward continual sacrifices; a grumbling and peevish middle age had followed Madame de Ferriol's dissipated youth, and her whole household were alternately depressed and irritated by her constant ill-humor. Her miserliness restricted her hospitality, bared her table, cooled her hearth. The men of the family could easily escape these domestic discomforts and this forbidding atmosphere of discontent, but on a proud and sensitive young spirit they fell like a cold, numbing mist, blotting out the sunshine of life.

To a girl so ill-circumstanced, sick-nurse to a crazy, tyrannical invalid, and companion to an imperious, ill-tempered ex-beauty, would not the favor of the Regent come like a messenger of deliverance? He, the easy-going, amiable prince, would be a gentler master than any the young slave had known. Thus reasoned Madame de Parabère, once Lady Paramount of the Regent's shifting seraglio, desirous of retaining some influence by choosing her own successor. Poor Aïssé was persecuted with advice and argument by her three counsellors, Mesdames Ferriol, Tencin, and Parabère; the last presented her to the Regent on whom her rose-bloom, and gazelle eyes, as well as the sad little romance of her life, promptly produced the effect desired. The Prince was not only pleased but sought to please, and the novice whose fragile defenses had already been adroitly sapped, was exposed to the manœuvres of an accomplished heart-breaker.

The slave, however, possessed a free soul. Either by appealing to the generosity of the Regent, who always respected a woman who respected herself, or by threatening to betray Madame de Ferriol's designs to the old Ambassador, who had lucid moments, and a title and fortune to leave to his nephews, she escaped the snare—though she earned the hatred of the baffled Tencin which pursued her all the rest of her life.

III

The cast handkerchief of d'Orléans, even though she had flicked it from her lap, had a fateful influence on Aïsse. It brought her to the notice of the Regent's circle, of the elegant *roués* who fluttered about the Duchesse de Berri, and frequented the salon of Madame du Deffand. It added lustre to the alien charm of the girl's personality and gave her unfamiliar beauty the seal of royal approval. The report of high favor disdained awakened the curiosity of the young pleasure-seekers who crowded the court at St. Cloud. Among them, leader in madcap frolics, a favorite of the reckless coterie, was the Chevalier Blaise Marie d'Aydie. He was well connected and allied to two celebrities, a cousin of Rions, the professed lover and secretly wedded husband of the Duchesse de Berri, and nephew of the old poet, the Marquis de Saint-Aulaire, who after a long career spent in the pursuit of more facile ladies had, at the age of sixty, wooed the Muse with signal success. With such friends at court and in the city, a handsome person and a winning manner, the Chevalier, as he was universally called, soon achieved a degree of social prestige that would have spoiled a nature less sound and delicately poised than his. He did become a courtier and a trifler for a time, but the aberrations of his young manhood, while undoubtedly diminishing his moral energy, and somewhat enfeebling a character more amiable than heroic, left his heart uncorrupted. Like so many of the sons of poor noblemen, he was an ecclesiastic and a soldier. His parents were blessed with many children and little property. They palliated the worldly disadvantages consequent on the rather cruel fertility of their union by consigning three daughters to a convent and putting three sons into holy orders. The much-lauded fecundity of marriage in the past condemned to death the superfluous children it called into being: Pagan parents by the exposure and abandonment of newly born infants, the Christian family by burying its undesired progeny in the living grave of the cloister.

Blaise d'Aydie, however, hurried into the devout life irrespective of his inclinations and entirely lacking vocation for it, wore his habit with secular jauntiness. Although a "tonsured clerk of the diocese of Périgueux, and an unprofessed knight of the order of St. John of Jerusalem," his monastic vows were purely professional, and in no wise a hinderance either to his social triumphs, or his affairs of the heart. The mighty order of the Knights Hospitallers, with its long list of Paladins and glorious record of unceasing struggle with the paynim invader, now that it was no longer devoted to the succor of "poor Latin pilgrims," provided sinecures for younger sons. The duties were few, the prayers short, the black mantle with its Maltese cross becoming. The stipend was small, but adequate for a bachelor with wealthy connections in an age of open houses, and the many quarterings the order required, rendered the position of the Chevalier akin to that of a high-born canoness in modern German society. Yet in a larger sense the Chevalier was shackled by his vows. He was a non-productive member of society; he could neither work nor marry; he was condemned to poverty, celibacy, and obedience to the Draconian though unwritten code of his social order. That he was mentally unfettered by prejudice, that his narrow means and limited opportunities had neither cramped his mind nor restricted his sympathies, Voltaire, Fontenelle, Montesquieu, D'Alembert bear witness. That marvel of mental lucidity, the blind Madame du Deffand, wrote of him in one of those pen-portraits which were a popular but dangerous exercise of wit, penetration, and too often of malice, in the eighteenth century. From this subtle analysis of the character of the man who became the arbiter of Aïssé's destiny, the nature of her fate may be divined.

"The mind of Monsieur le Chevalier d'Aydie," wrote Madame du Deffand, "is ardent, firm, vigorous, and possesses the force and truth which spring from sincere feeling. It was said of Monsieur Fontenelle that in place of a heart he had a second brain; one might believe that the head of the Chevalier contains a second heart. He proves the truth of Rousseau's saying that it is in the heart that the mind resides.

"The ideas of the Chevalier are never weakened, attenuated, or chilled by oversubtlety. With him everything is spontaneous. He often becomes more moved while speaking, sometimes he hesitates in the choice of the term most fitting to convey his thought, and the effort imparts more vigor and energy to his words. He never borrows the ideas or expressions of another; what he sees and says he sees and says for the first time. His definitions are apt, strong, and vivid. In fine, the Chevalier demonstrates that the language of feeling and of passion is true and sublime eloquence, *but the heart does not always possess the capacity to feel.* It has moments of repose, then it seems as though the Chevalier had ceased to be. Enveloped in gloom, no longer the same man, one might well believe that ruled by a Genius, he is possessed and abandoned by it according to its caprices.

"Though the Chevalier thinks and acts through feeling, nevertheless he is not perhaps the most impassioned, or the most tender of men. He is moved by too many things to be strongly affected by any one thing. His emotional sensibility is, so to speak, distributed among the different faculties of his soul, and this felicitous distribution perhaps protects his heart, and assures it a freedom which is as sweet as it is strong because it is as removed from indifference as from tenderness. Meanwhile he believes that he loves, but does he not deceive himself? He is fired by the virtues he finds in his friends, he grows warm in speaking of what he owes to them; but he leaves them easily and we are tempted to believe that no one person is necessary to his happiness. In a word, the Chevalier is more emotional than tender. . . . *The freer the heart is the more easily is it moved.*

"The judgment of the Chevalier is enlightened and penetrating; his taste sure; he cannot remain a passive spectator of the follies and blunders of humanity. That which offends honesty and truth becomes his private quarrel. Without mercy for vices, and without indulgence for absurdities, he is the terror of fools and evil-doers. . . . The Chevalier is too often moved and perturbed to possess an even temper. Pensive without sadness, misanthropical without shyness, always true and natural in all his changing moods, he pleases even by his faults, and we should be very sorry were he more perfect."

Such was the verdict of a fully matriculated student of mankind whose knowledge of the masculine heart had been dearly purchased. It was at Madame du Deffand's house that Aïssé met the Chevalier. If she had seen as clearly as her clairvoyant hostess, would her story have been a different one? Perhaps not. The same mischievous deity who many years later was to veil the mind's eye of the sagacious Marquise, and transform her into the humble adorer of Horace Walpole, was present, an unseen guest, at the girl's first interview with d'Aydie.

She succumbed to the charm of one whose virtues and graces were his own, and whose defects and shortcomings were those of his breeding and environment, all too soon to note the absence of energy in his character. And who, save perhaps Richardson's heroines, ever loved by book?

The Chevalier, who unconsciously served as model to Voltaire for his Sire de Couci in the romance of "*Adelaide du Guesclin*," a noble portrait of a loyal and chivalrous patrician, was also a representative *gentilhomme* of the eighteenth century. Educated by the Jesuits; polished by early and constant attrition with an urbane and witty social circle; open-minded, almost tremulously responsive to the appeal of the new philosophy, to the humanitarian ideals of his illustrious friends, mentally enfranchised from the mediæval prejudices of his caste, he was fundamentally wanting in initiative. He was satisfied with intellectual freedom merely, and lacked the moral force to place himself in practical opposition to the conventions of his age.

The edge which democratic institutions, at least in their infancy, impart to character, he did not possess. How often one meets to-day in London or Rome or Paris young men of the type of the Chevalier; well bred, cultivated, enthusiastic; with a sincere love and reverence for beautiful and noble things of which they talk well without affectation or false shame, who remain ineffective through absence of active energy, content to think straightly, and to talk brilliantly without attempting to precipitate thought and theory into action and practice. They are the remoter results of the same causes which were in operation in the eighteenth century. Then education, not only instruction but the whole scheme of education, was in the hands of ecclesiastics, one might almost say of the Jesuits. The character of their teaching emasculated the moral vigor, and enfeebled the will, of even those who in afterlife revolted against it—witness the tortuous diplomacy and untruthfulness of the youthful Voltaire. Unfortunately the evil effects of a false system are not confined to those who remain attached to it; the fiercest opponents of the Jesuits were their own ex-pupils, who in their opposition unconsciously retained the very methods they denounced, and bore unmistakable evidences of the pressure to which they had been subjected.

The Chevalier had ceased to believe in the creed of his old masters, but he had not learned to believe in himself, and the teachers who had been unable to stifle original thought in him had weakened his capacity to translate speculation into action. In any practical matter he had no more initiative than Aïssé herself. But he was brave, brilliant, at home in court and camp and study, and deeply, reverently in love. Not for the first time, but in a new way. "Every woman fashions in her own image the love tokens that are offered her," wrote George Eliot, and the sentiments inspired by a creature as generous and unworldly as the young Circassian were assuredly different in degree and in kind from the feeling evoked by the turbulent Duchesse de Berri or the free-ranging ladies of her court.

IV

There was at first no question of marriage between Aïssé and the Chevalier. She was a dowerless orphan without family or position, companion and protégée of Madame de Ferriol; he was a *gentilhomme* with all that the term implied in an age which was still feudal in its reverence for noble blood, no matter how diluted or corrupted that honored ichor might have become. It is difficult to estimate in a world where the giant wave of democracy has swept over the strongest breakwaters of caste, the sharp line which was drawn between him who possessed titled ancestors, and her who did not, or had at best only a picturesque tradition of princely parentage. The knees and backs of the *bourgeoisie* were still oversupple in the presence of the pettiest aristocrat. Michelet mars his otherwise just appreciation of "*Manon Lescaut*" by sneering at the Chevalier des Grieux's "*étalage de sa petite gentilhommerie,*" and the difference it caused in the attitude of society, the law and the Church towards the two culprits. Since, however, the possession of that "*petite gentilhommerie*" was the reason for the favor shown to the cheating, card-sharping noble and the lack of it entailed the punishment meted out to his fellow-swindler, the woman of the people, it does not seem unnaturally complacent in des Grieux to refer to it. There was still another barrier between the young people, their poverty. Aïssé had no portion, only the small sum left her by Monsieur de Ferriol, insufficient for her needs, and if the Chevalier had renounced his vows, a tedious and costly proceeding, he would have been obliged to sacrifice his slender income.

At first the lovers seemed oblivious of obstacles; they loved, and apparently took no thought for insuring by any external bond or symbol the permanence of their attachment. Aïssé, so indifferent to the brilliant conquests of her early youth, so scornful of the Regent's proffered left hand, possessed no defenses against the promptings of her heart. Like Byron's Haidée of the Ionian isle, she

"Spoke not of scruples, ask'd no vows,"

for with a royal love of giving she had so little to bestow that the same munificent impulse which had urged her to throw a fortune into the fire now impelled her to cast herself on her lover's generosity. Not consciously perhaps, for Aïssé was not only young, oppressed, lonely; she was in spite of her Parisian breeding an Oriental woman. We cannot deny our blood and our race. Love was her natural element, born with her, in her,

"—so intense,
It was her very being—not a sense."

What was there in her education, or environment, to rein impulse or uphold a wavering ideal? In the convent a set of formulæ had been learned by rote which had as much relation to the duties of life as though they had been written on parchment or graven on metal and hung on the girl's neck, like the amulets of her native land. Never was the divorce between morality and the practice of religion more marked than during the Regency, when such spiritual lights as Dubois and de Tencin determined the faith of Christendom.

Nor was public opinion a restraining influence during the license which followed the hypocrisy imposed on society by the expiatory piety of Louis XIV. The nobles frolicked and caroused like boys escaping from the magister's ferule. The relaxation of discipline imposed from the outside, without "the consent of the governed," produced, in the higher classes at least, a moral anarchy which in many individuals co-existed with generous sentiments, and a disinterested philanthropy; for cynical or audacious immorality is often the direct result of intellectual enlightenment when the theological tenets on which ethics had been founded are undermined or destroyed. Until morality is permanently re-established on a basis of natural law and social obligations, an ideal for the conduct of life is at the mercy of the individual.

Michelet, who disclosed to modern eyes the true character of an epoch long obscured by ecclesiastical prejudice, said of the Regency that it was an illumination and a revelation. In the process of revelation many masks were twitched off, many veils torn away. In the universal rending of draperies and thrusting of torches into dark places short work was made of decorum. The screens and curtains of Madame de Maintenon's autumnal reign were sometimes decent as well as discreet, and wholesale destruction of them left human frailties stark and bare. Much was gained by the stripping of shams, but something was lost in the warfare against hypocrisy. In their revolt from the barbarous piety which had made France desolate, men denied the existence of true devotion. In their horror of Tartufe, they enthroned the *roué*. The old King had fasted, therefore the Regent got drunk. Madame de Maintenon was prudish and wore soberhued clothes, hence for the Duchesse de Berri and her following jests could not be too Rabelaisian or brocades too gorgeous. Louis XIV had veiled his weaknesses with stately observances; therefore his successor discarded all reserve. Cant and falsehood are far-reaching and there is no moral *cordon sanitaire* to limit their effects.

Public opinion then was no guardian angel to the tempted, and the conduct of the friends and intimates of the Ferriols was of a nature to make poor Aïssé's disinterested lapse from virtue almost meritorious by contrast. Indeed the attachment of the Chevalier and the Circassian was regarded as a touching idyl by their more worldly associates, who could appreciate the beauty of a sentiment which they could not share, and even enjoy a certain complacency from the consciousness of a capacity to esteem it. Madame de Créquy summed up the opinion of her circle in a letter to the Vicomtesse de Nanthia: "In delicate natures the needs of the heart are paramount, and how little are they satisfied. They are the sunken rocks which shipwreck virtue. They wrecked Mademoiselle Aïssé. She was young, captivating, susceptible, and unoccupied. She met a charming man who adored her. This man was full of wit and fire; in a word, he was a Gaul brought up in Athens; he possessed the loyalty of the former, the graces of the Athenian. She was weak; one would be so for much less. The most virtuous woman is often she who has not found her conqueror."

Such was the indulgent verdict of one who in an age of easy victories had remained unvanquished, and it represented the attitude of society towards the *liaison* fairly well. Aïssé, like Julie de Lespinasse, had no family, therefore no duties towards one. She was not responsible for her behavior to the head of a noble house; she was not an agent to sustain its honor or upbuild its fortunes. Hence, as the irregularity of her conduct hurt no interests and injured no one but herself, it was readily condoned. Of a larger ideal of duty, of any moral obligation to society, neither of the lovers had any idea. That the sacrifice of the happiness of the individual is often necessary to secure the well-being of a collectivity of individuals, or the stability of an institution, is a consideration which has seldom divided people madly in love with each other.

The Chevalier and Aïssé thought but little, we may be sure, of their duties to the public; all it exacted of them was a certain decorum, an apparent observance of the proprieties which was not more than self-respect spontaneously imposed. In spite of the outbreak against Louis XIV's pompousness, ceremony was still honored in certain circles. Intimacy did not imply familiarity. A lover of ten years' standing would never have been guilty of the indelicacy of leaning on his *inamorata's* chair-back. Morals were loosely worn, but manners were straight-laced. Perhaps, too, in an epicurean society punctilio in public heightened the allurement of abandon in tête-à-tête.

When, however, man and woman taste the sweetness of stolen waters in secret it is generally the woman who pays the score. Aïssé was not to go scot-free. If the lovers at first had thought only of themselves they were soon called upon to extend the circle of their sympathies. Aïssé, poor in many things, was rich in friends; of one of them, Lady Bolingbroke, she made a confidante.

This amiable woman, a niece of Madame de Maintenon, was first married when almost a child to the Marquis de la Villette. Widowed while still young, she remarried in 1720. Her second husband was the brilliant Lord Bolingbroke, the eloquent orator and shifty statesman, whose unsuccessful efforts to eat at two mangers, to smile upon Hanover and beckon to Stuart synchronously, resulted in impeachment and a hurried departure for France. There, seeking to combine the rôles of Petronius and Seneca, the man of pleasure and the philosophizing ex-politician, he lived in elegant retirement until 1723, when a heavy bribe to the Duchess of Kendal secured a mitigation of his sentence, and permission to return to his native land.

Kind Lady Bolingbroke, extending the indulgence which her famous aunt, Madame de Maintenon, showed only to aristocratic sinners, invited Aïssé to accompany her to England, and to pass the summer there. Permission was obtained and Aïssé left the Hôtel Ferriol in her friend's company. Then, still aided by Lady Bolingbroke, she hid herself in an obscure quarter of Paris, where (May, 1724) her child was born. In September Lady Bolingbroke returned from England and took the little Célénie Leblond, as Aïssé's daughter was christened, to Sens. There in the convent of Notre Dame, in charge of the abbess who was a daughter of the Marquis de la Villette, the baby was left under the name of Miss Black; she was called a niece of Lord Bolingbroke's, and was supposed to be English.

The dispossessed mother went back to the Ferriols, a shade paler, a trifle more pensive, with a new

AÏSSÉ

wistfulness in her eyes and a new hunger in her heart. Her languor and melancholy did not remain unobserved by her keen-eyed friends. But bah! it was not to be wondered at! England was a very sad country; small marvel that the Oriental rose should have blanched and drooped after so long a sojourn in its fog. Something of it had dampened her spirits, or perhaps she had brought back a touch of the spleen, that eminently British ill. She made no complaints nor confidences, and took up her daily round of duties and her usual diversions, outwardly unchanged, as though her heart were still in her own breast instead of in that cradle at Sens.

She did not lack distractions; life was sometimes hard at the Ferriols, it was never dull. The two sons, Antoine, comte de Pont de Veyle, and Charles Augustin, comte d'Argental, had reached young manhood and brought more than an echo of gayety to their father's house. The elder, whose health was delicate, had a position at court, that of reader to the King, and was expected to succeed his uncle as ambassador to the Porte. He was the most amiable of men, a social favorite, even his censorious mother could find no fault with him, but to Aïssé he was less dear than his impulsive, petulant younger brother. Perhaps the cause of her preference, and of Pont de Veyle's unruffled sweetness, was divined by that seeress of *salons*, Madame du Deffand. In her sightless old age Pont de Veyle, a life-long friend, continued to pay her a daily visit. One day as they sat over the fire together, she snug in her *tonneau,* he lost in a huge armchair, she asked him suddenly: "Pont de Veyle?" "Madame." "Where are you?" "By your chimney-corner." "You must know that there are few friendships as old as ours." "That is true, Madame." "It is fifty years old." "Yes, over fifty." "And during this long space of time not a cloud, not the shadow of a misunderstanding." "That is what I have always admired about it." "But Pont de Veyle, was not that because we have always been quite indifferent to each other?" "That may be, Madame."

The ardor and enthusiasms which his elder brother lacked d'Argental was overrich in; *"très joli garçon"* in spite of the smallpox, witty, generous, a squire of dames, devoted to the new philosophy and its exponents, he was the romantic element in the family. As he was Voltaire's "guardian angel," the executor of Adrienne Lecouvreur's will and the literary collaborator of Madame de Tencin when she ceased living romances and took to writing them, it may be assumed that he was welcomed in many different coteries. Aïssé sometimes speaks of him as dwelling in "the enchanted isle," but though the act of adoration seemed a necessity of his nature, the image and the shrine were often changed. His fantasies only added to the social relations of the Ferriols, which were sustained almost entirely by the younger people.

Their father had grown "dreadfully deaf and greedy"; the once judicious Président du Parlement had withered into a fanatical follower of Molinos, a strident promulgator of Quietism. Madame de Ferriol, in addition to her avarice, possessed a peculiarly irritating form of obstinacy; she was at once wavering and disputatious, undecided, yet always of the opposite opinion to that of her interlocutor. Indolent in mind and body, her energy expended itself in a perverse contrariness to any plan or proposition until it was abandoned by its wearied advocate; then she adopted it ardently as a subject for further discussion. Corpulence and rheumatism had transformed the siren to a harpy. Though her beauty had long since become a matter of ancient history, and the Maréchal d'Uxelles's passion had waned as her circumference increased, she still kept up the comedy of influencing and advising him until he bowed himself out of court. Aïssé and the household paid dearly for his retirement. Short commons and long scoldings were the portion of all who owned madame's sway save only two privileged beings: Clément, the surly lap-dog, and a morose old footman, misnamed Champagne.

But in spite of monsieur's pugnacious piety and madame's grumbling, there was always something doing with the Ferriols. There was constant attendance at the theatres, where Lecouvreur and Quinault were playing, and where the new comedies were literary events; and there was the opera with three-act ballets and wonderful new scenery and stage machines which France borrowed gladly from Italy, though she scorned Italian music. There were suppers where great nobles and greater writers met on equal terms. There were cards, quadrille or ombre, promenades in the statue-lined alleys of the Tuileries garden, where all fashionable Paris met towards sunset, and gay little parties were made up for a *medianoche* at the Porcherons, or to drink *ratafia* on the Neuilly bridge. Above all, there were visits. Everybody was always making or receiving them. French life meant social life even to the peasants, those blackened, tattered scare-crows that La Bruyère saw scratching the ground, and its sociability increased as it rose in rank. Visiting was one of the "offices" of existence. It began in the morning as soon as curtains were drawn and chocolate was served, and continued all through the day and evening until the small hours. People made visits everywhere; at the opera in their boxes, in their carriages during the afternoon drive on the boulevards, and during service at church. When Pomme, a popular physician, prescribed long baths of three and four hours' duration for certain nervous troubles, fashion was horrified at the prospect of such prolonged solitude. Fortunately a mixture of powdered almonds and perfumes rendered the water opaque, and combining hygiene and decorum one could receive in one's tub. The young mother propped up her aching head on laced pillows and received. The widow sat in funereal state in her cypress-hung chamber to receive. Even to the tomb visits were formally made at least once a year, and every event, domestic or public, joyful or mournful, was the occasion for a reception. The Ferriols naturally saw much distinguished company and it was, socially considered, a very great world in which Aïssé played her somewhat effaced rôle. Among the many visitors of the house, brought probably by the Bolingbrokes (with whom she was connected by marriage), was a certain Madame Calandrini, *née* Pelissary. This lady, the wife of the Resident of the Republic of Geneva, was a little out of place in the Bolingbroke circle. She was a new type of woman to the Circassian. Aïssé had seen much of perfunctory piety. She had heard Molinism and Jansenism exhaustingly discussed; she had listened to bewildering explanations of the exact meaning of the bull *Unigenitus*, she knew intimately several bishops, and at least one "mother of the Church," as flippant Paris nicknamed Madame de Tencin, but she had never before met a truly devout person. To her, religion as an inspiration to a pure life, as a censor of conduct, was a novel conception. To Madame Calandrini, piety implied righteousness; a Catholic in creed, she was a Puritan in spirit. Although she would have repudiated them both with equal horror, she was at one with antique stoics and the new *phil-*

osophes in her belief that virtue lies in action. Her faith was an armor, not the convenient *déshabillé* so lightly worn by many of her fellow-believers, for though Madame Calandrini was a Frenchwoman, her religious ideal had been formed by an influence more powerful than any her own Church could then command: that of Geneva.

To-day Geneva, the pretty, prim town cherished of the cheap "tripper," a paradise of jewellers and hotel-keepers, has again become a holy place for the lover of human fraternity. Ever since the Reformation the free city has grandly filled a double rôle, that of champion and hostess of a persecuted people. Geneva as a well of pure doctrine, as the Annunciation angel, awakening the drugged conscience of Europe, has been magnificently eulogized, but her milder virtues also deserve celebration. The practice of the temporal works of mercy seems a civic duty to her citizens, and the modern Genevese are as nobly hospitable to the victims of German brutality as their forefathers were to the sufferers of the Dragonnades.

When after the revocation of the Edict of Nantes Louis XIV tore open the arteries of France and drove the Huguenots into exile, the Protestant nations opened their hearts and homes to them. Most munificent where all were generous was the burgher Republic. This small commonwealth of sixteen thousand souls for more than ten years clothed and fed four thousand fugitives, and received and comforted many more. And though those refugees were the most laborious and inventive of French subjects, though they built up the industrial prosperity of the countries which welcomed them, yet they had been so despoiled and hunted down, so wounded and tortured, that they came as naked and bleeding suppliants to the savior city. For years Geneva was not only a sanctuary but a hospice, and it was at the price of constant sacrifices that the Republic maintained its charities; it called upon every citizen for daily self-denial, it asked a dole from each burgess, and never was the love of neighbor more confidently counted on or more nobly responsive. The Genevese acquired the habit of abnegation, and with it that discipline of the will and the members which implies a martial attitude of the soul. A people cannot be inured to voluntary privations, trained to systematic unselfishness without such exercise leaving profound traces on national character. A standard of conduct evolved from such conditions will be tinged with asceticism, it will prize self-government, it will exact clean living, it will demand a certain correspondence between precept and act. And the existence of a moral code, so securely based and so sincerely accepted, imposed a higher ideal on the truly devout of other creeds who came in contact with it. The stricter rule indirectly strengthened the moral discipline of an elder religion more tolerant of human frailty, more indulgent to the brute and the child in man. The

Genevese Catholic was a Protestant in manners, his moral code was sterner, his self-control was greater, than that of his French *coreligionnaire.* The presence of virtue evokes virtue, and the rose is not fragrant for herself alone but for those who dwell in her sweet society. Thus Madame Calandrini, though a child of the Church, was a daughter of the Republic, and wore her faith with a difference. In an age of casuistry and lax concessions, she was as straightforward and rigorous as a Calvinist. From her Aïssé learned the vital significance of duty, and the love of virtue was awakened in a heart framed for its shrine.

V

That the conscience of an Oriental woman, living in a pleasure-loving Parisian *milieu,* should be aroused because many years before a cityful of Protestant burgesses had played the Good Samaritan, is only another instance of the far shining of even a remote good deed in a naughty world. Aïssé stood in bitter need of some such comfortable light, for a groping inquietude was then master of her soul's household. Not that she lacked illumination of a kind. Through suffering enlightenment glared on her. She was learning that the ordering of the social world, even when its code seems complacently lenient, is made for those who obey its mandates, not for those who evade them; that family joys are the guerdon of submission to conventions, and no provision is made for domesticity outside the law. In how many ways were these truisms pressed in upon her! She was "wolf's head," beyond the pale, she and her baby. What anxious tenderness, what vain reaching out of mother-love may be inferred from a few short sentences which, like half-suppressed sobs, occasionally interrupt the pleasant flow of her written chat! Ah! if she and her child were together! What shaft of scorn could reach her heart shielded by that dear body on her breast? The thought brought with it a regret that stabbed, a longing that turned her faint; in the depths of her soul something infinitely tender and pitiful seemed gasping and bleeding. Only the palms of motherhood were hers, not its crown. For if a secret *liaison* bestows moments of transport, hours of blissful confidence to weigh against the lingering torments of separation, clandestine maternity spells agony only. Aïssé's sufferings would have been counted as adequate expiation for her fault by the most austere censor. The miracle of motherhood, the instant decentralization of the *ego*, had been followed by the loss of the dearest part of the newly revealed self. The heart dilated with a new mysterious joy was so soon contracted with a novel anguish of frustration! To the orphan and the exile her child meant kinsfolk and family; to her, robbed of a past, it brought a future, and the cruelty of circumstance bereaved her of it.

Custom in France (until late in the eighteenth century) separated the baby from its mother during the years it has most need of her, but Aïssé was not a Frenchwoman, she was an Oriental, to whom motherhood is the justification of a woman's existence; her race-inheritance intensified her sufferings. What tumult of the rebellious will, what revolt of instinct against convention her calmness cloaked while she played trictrac with Madame de Ferriol, or counterfeited interest in monsieur's diatribes. The woman's imagination, most vivid when exercised on things unseen, must have haled her nightly through a hell of torturing possibilities. Her child might be neglected, forgotten for one fatal minute! It might be ill—dying even, among those holy maidens whom the poor, despoiled mother hated at times with a fierce, jealous hatred. Grim forebodings tightened her chest, and beat upon her heart in hours of darkness and solitude. Messengers from Sens brought her a fever of hope and terror in their mails with the desired and yet dreaded letters—letters received in dizzy suspense, opened with such cold, shaking hands, devoured with such greedy eyes. Even good news brought but scant comfort. The sisters, knowing her anxiety, were deceiving her perhaps. Who knew what might be happening even while she read? Ah! those nuns! Was an eternity of felicity not enough for them that they should hear her baby's first word, chronicle its first step, while for its mother the cold record of

AÏSSÉ

such sweet wonders must suffice? Her whole being clamored for her little one, her flesh ached for her child as though a physical tie still bound them. For a few blissful months she had held happiness in her arms, and now memory cheated her yearning, recalling the tender warmth of the wee creature nestling against her side, the flower-soft touch of the waxen hand, the silken down of the tiny head pressed against her cheek.

This anguish of longing was almost mute; it moans in half a dozen piteous sentences in Aïssé's letters. To her lover she was probably mercifully reticent. Why distress him with the recital of sufferings he was impotent to remedy? Was not his own heart heavy enough? Black care was peering over his shoulder also, for the Chevalier was not taking his new responsibilities lightly, and was planning for the little one's future. The suppression of self, without which parenthood is a mere expansion of the animal existence, had already begun in a sensitive nature. The daily renunciation of some small pleasure, the heroic little economies by which the poor Frenchman dowers his daughters and establishes his sons, were already familiar to Célénie's father. The Chevalier's was one of those rare spirits to whom a sense of obligation is grateful instead of irksome; he loved Aïssé as much for the sacrifices she had made for him as though he had made them for her. He was a lover with whom it was not imprudent to be quite disinterested. Aïssé's sorrows fixed his affections as coquettish manœuvres would have riveted a baser sentiment in a man of coarser fibre. Every proof of attachment that tact and delicacy in the service of love could suggest was offered her, and in defiance of circumstances in his presence she still was happy. That was seldom, however, for his duties at Versailles, where he was *garde du corps du roi*, and his visits to his family in Périgord kept him away from Paris much of the year. His absences were purgatorial seasons for Aïssé. His health was delicate, and, clever as he was, he had never learned to care for it, even after it became precious to some one else.

It was probably during one of these long separations of the lovers that Madame Calandrini became Aïssé's friend and mother confessor. Two natures so eminently sincere inevitably attracted each other in an artificial *milieu*. Of Madame Calandrini little is known. Her replies to Aïssé's letters were probably destroyed. They may come to light some day, however, like so many lost documents, and oblige us to modify our judgment of the lady and her opinions. There is at present no reason to doubt that "she was a good friend for this world and the next," as Madame de Créquy said; that, though born in Paris, she was Genevese to her marrow, and that she soon obtained an extraordinary ascendancy over the younger woman. She was middle-aged and the mother of married daughters when she made Aïssé's acquaintance. It is only in the Circassian's letters to her that the reflection of this expatriated Puritan is mirrored. What she thought, *i. e.*, what she was, as the early eighteenth century believed with Descartes, must be taken on trust, *foi d'Aïssé*, and as reported by a partial observer.

The devoted friendships of many well-known women were a characteristic feature of social life in the past. Modern conditions with their tendency to modify sex-differences, and by constant daily intercourse to promote more platonic relations between men and women, are not so favorable to these long attachments. At a time when man was by courtesy a pursuer, by custom a master, and by nature often a despot, these friendships were rather touching alliances of weaknesses. They were generally suspiciously regarded as leagues for mutual assistance, or as pretexts for a pretty pose. The wits, and especially the playwrights, laughed at them a little—as they did at everything—but even the sentimentality which the disciples of Rousseau brought to the cultus of friendship was but an exaggeration of a genuine sentiment. There was little affectation or aiming at effect in the tender affection which united many noted ladies, since it was not sundered either by absence, or family cares, or differences of opinion, or the dissipation of a complicated social life. The antique altar of friendship was perhaps rather frivolously decorated by its feminine votaries, and emotion sought expression through the arts, as was natural in a form-loving people. But the erection of temples to *Amicitia*, and the manufacture of Sèvres groups of two young persons lovingly entwined, labelled "*L'Amitié*," discreetly watched over by a small dog symbolizing "*Fidélité*," does not necessarily prove that the sentiment was unreal because it happened to be fashionable. Nor was the custom of wearing portrait miniatures and hair bracelets incompatible with the existence of sincere feeling. Madame de Lamballe, the most sentimental of Marie Antoinette's bevy of friends, gave her life for the Queen.

During the Regency the manifestations of an affectionate comradeship were not spectacular. Women were intimate without feeling obliged to wear the same colors, or to address each other in terms which friendship filched from Love's quiver. By persons as austerely frank as Madame Calandrini, and as sweetly candid as Aïssé, the deftly-turned compliments and sugary endearments of certain oft-quoted correspondences would have been deemed excessive. There is no dearth of tenderness in Aïssé's letters, but when she enters the realm of emotion she uses the simplest phrases, as though she felt that the heart which she bared to her friend was best seen through a transparent medium. Between two people so interested in the realities of life, the factitious graces of a *précieux* style would be as ill timed as the bridling and mincing of one of Marivaux's coquettes in a scene of genuine passion.

An exchange of letters between the two friends

began in the autumn of 1726, when Madame Calandrini was on her way back to Geneva and Aïssé was in Paris; it ended in 1733 with a farewell written on a death-bed. Twenty-five years afterwards Madame de Rieu, granddaughter of Madame Calandrini sent this correspondence to Voltaire, who, always susceptible to pathos and nobility, read it with emotion, and praised it warmly. Aïssé's letters either in manuscript or in a copy were passed from one friend to another, until 1787, when, most of the persons mentioned in them having died, they were published with Voltaire's notes. D'Argental after they appeared questioned their authenticity, prompted by filial respect for his mother's memory. But his protest was a mere formality, and rated at its true value by his friends and those (they were many) of the letters. The little volume gradually found a place among the memoirs and autobiographies and confessions which have drawn the men and women of the eighteenth century within the radius of our sympathies. Aïssé's letters are important additions to those documents. To the student of history they offer a collection of *genre* pictures of the early years of Louis XV's reign; to the lover of literature, they contain a series of character sketches: vivid glimpses of famous *salonnières*, and of writers who directed the thought of Europe. The reader of delicate taste and sensitized imagination discovers in them something far more precious, the story of the evolution of a soul.

"*C'est un livre presque dévot,*" a pious lady wrote

of it, and it may be classed among those records of spiritual experiences which are loved by saint and sceptic alike, so human are they and so universal is their appeal. To open "*Le Mie Prigioni,*" or "*Le Lépreux de la Cité d'Aoste,*" is like entering a wayside oratory on a crowded, dusty highroad. Without, the tumult and the glare—within, dusk and coolness, and the faint fragrance of incense. True, there are pity-moving images of suffering and sorrowing folk in these quiet places, but their pain was an oblation, their sorrow was so sweetly borne, that the peace which followed them seems to fall gently on our own spirits, and we feel that it is good to have been sad in such blessed company.

Though she equalled Pellico and de Maistre in poignancy of feeling, and elevation of aim, as a writer Aïssé did not possess the consummate ease and purity of their style. One precious element she shared with them, perfect limpidity. To this cardinal literary virtue she added a quality which seemed the birthright of the women of her time, a pliant facility in the use of language, an apparent spontaneity in expression that lend to the written word the vitality of the spoken one. Life itself seemed to flow and sparkle under pens careless of grammar, licentious in spelling, yet through the flexible medium so adroitly handled, under the general "*ton de la parfaitement bonne compagnie,*" personality flashed out like a striking face beneath a filmy veil. Had the famous dictum run, "style is the woman," it

AÏSSÉ 329

might have been felicitously applied to the work of these ladies. Aïssé's letters, though inferior to those of Madame du Deffand in precision and penetration, to those of Madame de Staal-Delaunay in verve and piquancy, are so simple in expression, so informed with feeling, so evidently at first hand, that they achieve style by abandoning all pretensions to it. They are not written for a circle of wits, to be handed about from one literary friend to another, and they are free from self-consciousness in consequence. Theirs is the true epistolary form: an improvisation dashed down with a racing pen; a chat on paper, a monologue necessarily, but one in which the presence of the unseen auditor is constantly felt. Aïssé's object is communication, and she seeks the most direct means of attaining it. She is alone in her room with her friend, in undress, unlaced, under no bond to be brilliant or profound. She lets herself go. Her "pen trots, the bridle on its neck," and is not constrained to riding-school paces. Through the crystalline clearness of her pellucid style objects are perceived undistorted, in their true relations, and are seen as from an open window.

Unfortunately, she omitted to add her own portrait to the series of pictures, though a generalized likeness of her may be constructed from engravings and allusions. She was none of your fine women, but a very slim person, always too thin for the rather Olympian ideal of the Regency; her expressive features were too large for her face, her head out of proportion to her narrow shoulders. Her delicate chest was that of an immature girl, and her half-sleeves left uncovered her "poor flat arms," under their laces. The charm of this fragile creature lay in her coloring, in the pearly sweetness of her rare smile, in the sombre fire of her eyes, and above all in what her contemporaries, who set vivacity and mobility far above beauty of line and mass, called physiognomy: a transparency, an illumination of the face from within, as though the body shared and expressed thought and emotion. The bloom of an exquisite skin, delicate in tint and texture as fine porcelain, cannot be expressed in black and white, and the engraved portrait of Aïssé which heads her letters does but scant justice to her sensitive, spirited face. The eyes, however, even in the worn plates reveal an exotic origin; they are the liquid, lustrous eyes of the East, shaded and lengthened by a sweep of black lashes, and weighted down by heavy brows; eyes which in a collection of contemporary portraits strike one as strangely as would the wail of the rebab heard above the tinkle of the spinet. With such jewels in her head and the coloring of a Dresden china shepherdess, no woman could fail in charm, but Aïssé possessed a more potent attraction than beauty, the mysterious glamour which envelops those who die in their prime; an allurement at once pathetic and piquant as though the life currents ran in fuller tide before they ebbed forever. Who can define the subtle indications, airy as the stir of unfolding wings by which the psyche betrays its approaching flight? A touch of languor, capricious gayety, teeth of translucent pearl, a skin that seems to radiate light, a purple stain under the fever-bright eyes, slender shoulders inclined forward like shut pinions—happy are they who have not watched these danger-signals and divined what they portend! Something of this fragile grace may have been preserved by the portrait in pastel which Aïssé describes in one of her letters.

It was then the custom to ornament the centre of carved wall panels, the overdoors and overmantels with portraits treated decoratively after the manner of Lely or Nattier. The costume of the time lent itself admirably to such arrangement. Though the choice of subjects sometimes caused heart-burnings among rival toasts, as for instance in the English court where Kneller painted a series of beauties chosen by Queen Mary for her rooms, the practice continued to be popular through the eighteenth century. Aïssé alludes incidentally to this pretty fashion. "I have had myself painted in pastel, or rather M. de Ferriol, who has a charming room, has had six beautiful ladies painted (and I am among them, not as beautiful most assuredly, but as a friend), Mesdames de Noailles, de Parabère, Madame la Duchesse de Lesdiguières, Madame de Montbrun, and a copy of a portrait of Mademoiselle de Villefranche at the age of fifteen years. They are all of the same size and mine resembles me perfectly. I have decided to ask for a copy of it, and if the painter thinks that it would be better to make it after nature, I will have him come here; it is only an affair of three hours. One leans on the table on which the painter works, one is amused by seeing him paint, and consequently the attitude is not constrained. As soon as I have this copy or the original I will send it to you. When you see it I beg you to believe that it is praying to Heaven for you, because they wished to have it with the eyes raised, and a blue veil like a vestal or a novice."

What has become of this portrait, which was "*parfaitement ressemblant*"? Sainte-Beuve in his sympathetic study of Aïssé referred to one which hung in a bedroom in the country house of her great-grandson the Marquis de Bonneval. The Chevalier d'Aydie in 1741 sent a picture of her mother to Célénie with the words: "M. de Brisseuil, who returns to Périgord in the month of January, has promised me to take the portrait of your mother with him. You will see her face, why could not one paint the qualities of her soul as well!" Meanwhile until these portraits are more accessible fancy must soften and amplify the hard, meagre little engraving to the more genial semblance of an arch and animated person.

The Aïssé of the letters is not the prim and busked fine lady of the official portrait. When the last hand had been played and the last coach had trundled away after the late supper, she hurried to her room, threw off her harness (for the heavy brocade robe, with its cumbrous hoop-petticoat, its long, tightly laced bodice was a veritable armor), slipped on a bed-gown, kicked off her high-heeled slippers, and sat down to her writing-table for a cosey chat with her friend. It is difficult to associate the idea of black care with a pink-and-white person in a short, flowered petticoat and a beribboned corset, or to realize that a brilliant figure suggesting nothing more serious than one of Lancret's lenient beauties should be saddened by a mother's anxieties, or an unhappy lover's griefs.

And the background was as apparently frivolous as the *déshabillé*. Aïssé shared her contemporaries' *culte de la chambre*, half bedroom, half boudoir, which they decorated and draped and upholstered and sometimes painted themselves. Even the most indolent embroidered a screen, or worked a set of chairs or of curtains in tapestry-stitch. The most economical loosened her purse-strings to renovate or embellish her room, and Aïssé spared a hundred pistoles to arrange hers. It would doubtless seem rather bleak and bare to modern eyes, but height and space were essential to an older and less crowded world. "My furniture is simple but made by the best workmen," wrote Aïssé at a time when the cabinetmaker, if not an artist, was at least a well-taught artisan, and the industrial arts were vivified by a new impulse. The andirons and candelabra, the locks, and window fastenings, and the metal ornaments on this simple furniture were chiselled like goldsmith's work, for taste then manifested itself not in a profusion of details, but in a perfection of finish in details. There was probably a Persian rug or two on the polished floor, and the light from the lofty French windows was sifted through curtains of embroidered muslin. Doubtless there were engravings on the delicately tinted wall-panels when they were not covered with an "Indian paper," splashed with a fantastic medley of gorgeous flowers, and outlandish temples, and brilliant birds in the utterly irresponsible and entirely decorative manner of the Oriental. Over the chimney-shelf the mirror panelled into the wall was divided into small sections, for in spite of Colbert's new manufactories, looking-glasses were still costly. The fireplace, once large enough for a whole witch's Sabbath to fly up the chimney, had shrunk to more modest dimensions. It was usually surrounded by screens, big and little, in tapestry, in embroidery, and in *découpage*, the new fashion, which in winter made a *niche*, a room within the larger room where the owners of domed ceilings and palatial spaciousness kept themselves from freezing. It was an innovator in all things, Voltaire, who at Cirey warmed his apartment with a furnace concealed in the wall behind a statue of Love. Few followed his example and ladies in low-cut bodices and the thinnest of slippers continued to sit well into the fire, "*blotties derrière les paravents comme un oiseau sous la feuillée,*" as Michelet prettily phrased this enforced hibernation. On the narrow shelf over the chimneypiece was room for a small collection of porcelain; tall jars, a nodding mandarin, and a perfume-burner filled with dried and spiced rose-leaves exhaling a delicate aromatic odor. Frenchwomen shared the weakness of Addison's readers for china, and it formed the most acceptable of gifts. "'*Vous avez de bien belles porcelaines et entre autres cette jatte*', *me dit La Mésangère, qui vint l'autre jour,*" Aïssé wrote her friend; and again, apropos of her room, "there is nothing magnificent in it except the porringer (*la jatte*) you gave me."

Besides the draped bed in its alcove, the armchairs and stools, and a console, there would be for the writing-desk, the work-case, and the toilet utensils three or four little jewels of tables. Madame du Châtelet required no less than six for her paraphernalia, but she was an exacting and complicated person. On them were set out those "necessary superfluities," as Voltaire named the dainty trifles on which the goldsmiths and jewellers of the "woman's century" lavished such delicate workmanship, and such fertile invention. Not only was the "woman's world," as the Latins ungallantly termed the arsenal of the toilet, embellished, but the writing-table also, where from the seal to the ink-pot each object was a tiny artistic creation, and especially the workcase (the untranslatable *étui* or *nécessaire*). Pretty hands were industrious hands in this frivolous society. The airiest coquette was ballasted with a work-bag, which contained besides the rouge-pot, the sweetmeat-case, the snuff-box, the song of the season, the latest lampoon, the newest tale, a bit of work, and the delicate tools of the needlewoman. These were enclosed in a sheath, wrought in some precious substance, chiselled, enamelled, or jewelled, and shaped like Cupid's quiver. Surely "sage Minerva's needle" was never more coquettishly housed. The accommodating sack would also hold, if its owner had the least of pretensions to elegance, a shuttle in *vernis Martin* or mother-of-pearl for knotting, a kind of edging that for years occupied all feminine fingers, from those of Madame Adelaide, whom Nattier painted *navette* in hand, to those of the nuns who brought their knotting to the convent parlor on reception days. It was the grace of the process rather than the beauty of the product which commended this somewhat ostentatious industry. Knotting was done everywhere, even at the theatre, where "during the play, the ladies one after another take a gold shuttle from an embroidered bag, and begin to knot with a busy air, looking only at the spectators."

The *navette* with the snuff-box were the contributions of the eighteenth century to a list of pretty playthings for grown folk. Snuff, forerunner of the cigarette, was the *péché mignon* of Aïssé and her friends. Nor was there a semblance of secrecy about taking it; it was not a stolen delight like a sip of *ratafia*. There was a right and a wrong way of snuffing; an awkward, a provincial, and a supremely elegant manner of taking and offering a pinch, of using the handkerchief, and dusting the laces after it. Aïssé's was an "admirable snuffbox in green jasper of a charming form, mounted in gold by a most skilful jeweller," a gift from Madame de Parabère.

The Lar of this pretty hermitage was Patie, Aïssé's dog, whose shrine, miniature pagoda, or Greek temple probably occupied a warm corner near the hearth. One cannot picture a lady without this engaging parasite, little hound or fluffy spaniel, who inspired a *passionette* in his mistress during his life, and an elegy or two after his death. The education, the diversion, and the care of the lap-dog provided the engravers with subjects for several charming compositions; he was modelled by Clodion, painted by Fragonard, graven on gems, and his name has often come down to us coupled with that of his adoring possessor. Patie was loved more temperately than Madame d'Epinay's Pouf or Marie Lecszinska's *bichon*, but he was Aïssé's only pet, as she had neither monkey, parrot, squirrel, nor black boy to divert her affection from him.

There were few books lying about a woman's room when the eighteenth century was young.

They were still valuable; the *précieuse* kept them carefully in her cabinet. Even at Cirey they were lent one by one, and rather grudgingly to guests, Madame de Graffigny complained. Books of devotion, plays, and a novel or two might be found on a console, or under a pillow, but the little corner shelves with a dozen or two of favorite volumes, kept close at hand like the miniature of a lover, indicate a further stage of literary culture. In her whole correspondence Aïssé mentions only two books, "Gulliver's Travels" and "*Manon Lescaut.*"

This absence of things literary affords matter for conjecture; it casts a novel sidelight on the youth of some celebrated *salonnières* and awakens doubts in an open mind. Aïssé was an intelligent person, of delicate health, naturally inclined to tranquil pleasures, the stuff of which readers are made, living in what has been universally conceded to be the most intellectual society in France. She was the constant companion of two brilliant young men who were considered ornaments of that society. She was the confidante of Madame du Deffand, a "*débauchée d'esprit,*" one of, or perhaps the most gifted of, the women who passed their lives surrounded by men of letters. Aïssé was also the friend of an accomplished man, whose mind and acquirements were sufficiently distinguished to win the regard and esteem of famous writers and thinkers.

Yet, if we should judge her from her written words, for Aïssé the realm of the intellect was a *terra incognita.* Was she as insensitive to the new ideas which were quickening the minds of the men with whom she was in daily contact, as though she had seen life only through a gilded lattice in her own land? Can one judge of her real mental attitude and interest from her letters? In a correspondence is it not the receiver as well as the writer who imparts the general tone, and influences the treatment and selection of topics? It should not be forgotten that Aïssé was writing to a serious-minded, devout person in whose estimation the new literature was given over to the devil. The *philosophes* had greatly enlarged the domain of the Evil One, already (ever since the middle ages) lord of nature and science, by adding letters to his kingdom. The pious were permitted to weep over "*Manon Lescaut*," but they were forbidden to laugh over the "*Lettres Persanes.*" This may possibly be the reason why Aïssé writes of Prévost's book and does not mention Montesquieu's, which constrained even the most lightminded of its readers to meditation on the existing order of things political. Again the closing of the cemetery of St. Médard, where prodigies unauthorized by the Church took place, and on whose barred gates some wit hung the lines:

> "*De par le roi défense à Dieu*
> *De faire miracle en ce lieu,*"

is chronicled. The closing of the Entresol Club, a reunion where men of letters, officials, and diplomatists met to discuss social and political questions, is not mentioned, though Aïssé's friend, Lord Bolingbroke, was one of its prominent members; but that might have been because the deism professed by the leading spirits of the Entresol was anathema to Madame Calandrini. But even when ample allowance is made for the prejudices of her correspondent, the general tone of the letters is emphatically not that of a reader. The women whose ideas and theories of life were formed or at least influenced by books were born later in the century. Aïssé's last letter was written in 1733, and few of the works which moulded thought were produced until after that date. Even Voltaire's "*Lettres Anglaises*" were not published until 1734, and the "*Esprit des Lois*" appeared fourteen years later. Rousseau, of course, appealed to the next generation, and the Encyclopedists were many of them boys in Aïssé's day. Even the sway of the *salons* did not begin until some years afterwards. Mesdames de Prie and de Parabère had none. Madame du Deffand and Madame de Tencin were still young adventuresses, too generally discredited by the disorders of their youth to wield the social sceptre which they won in the fulness of years and worldly wisdom. Sceaux, presided over by the flighty and imperious Duchesse du Maine, was a court, not a *salon;* the manners there were mediæval; there was none of the free speech and intellectual equality of the real republics of letters. The Marquise de Lambert, who died in the same year with Aïssé, had inherited the tradition and the lofty ideals of the Hôtel Rambouillet, but her *salon* in the Palais Mazarin, beautifully decorated and painted by Watteau, was rather too academic in tone to represent the freer, gayer meeting-place of wits and thinkers with which we associate the untranslatable French word. Though the suppers were brilliant and the presence of Adrienne Lecouvreur enlivened the solemnity of Madame Dacier's discussions on Homer; though Fontenelle, most worldly of wise men, or perhaps most wise of worldlings, was mindful to decorate his scientific *conférences* with the flowers of sentiment, there was always something official about this *salon*, which was truly "the vestibule of the Academy."

Aïssé then was born too soon in a world too young to gather the fully expanded flowers of French intellectual life. She was a spectator of only the beginnings of the great change. But the ferment of springtime was in the veins of the century, the intellectual atmosphere was germinant with new ideas, floating amorphous as yet. Something of the vernal season remains in Aïssé's slender contribution to French literature; the spontaneity, the vivacity of youthful creatures, the poetic charm, the freshness of early flowers. Reflection, criticism, analysis are a later fruitage of the mind. They abound in the memoirs and correspondences of the friends of Aïssé's youth, to whom a more ample share of life was granted. The Circassian had no such breadth and keenness of mental vision as Madame du Deffand possessed, for instance, but the dryness which accompanied it, the cynicism which followed an entirely detached point of view, were unknown to her. Remorse, sorrow, apprehension overshadowed her life sometimes, but *ennui* never rendered it insipid.

Tiny ripples from the stormy waves which swept over France purl through the letters. Aïssé got her news at first hand from Pont de Veyle and the Chevalier, who were constantly at Versailles. "The Queen has twin daughters (Mesdames Henriette and Adelaide); what a pity there is not a dauphin among them!" wrote Aïssé, echoing the regret of the people. Madame de Prie, the voracious Madame de Prie who had been devouring France, is exiled to her estates, and Monsieur le Duc, her purveyor, is to reform and be married. Later there is a description of the new fourteen-year-old duchess, and her naïve remarks at court. The King has gladdened his easily gratified subjects by a remark on the history of Henry IV which he had just finished reading; when asked what he thought of it, Louis XV answered that Henry's love of his people pleased him more than anything else. "*Dieu veuille qu'il le pense et qu'il le suive*," adds Aïssé.

The Indians in Louisiana have risen and murdered the colonists, who could have been saved had they but heeded the warning of a squaw who betrayed the natives' plot to her white lover, a French soldier. Aïssé writes: "They say the English stirred up the savages against us, and we are very much puzzled to know how to treat them. This has made stocks fall and has caused many alarms. I have had only a slight one, as I am but little interested, owning only half a share; but my friends have more and that is enough to render me anxious. I have spoken of it to a well-informed person, who assures me that one should not sell."

Public affairs are considered from a decidedly practical point of view; the money question is paramount in this cultivated, aristocratic society. Speculation had tempted all Frenchmen since Law had performed the modern miracle of turning paper into gold, and Aïssé, desirous of making a little venture, had by selling her diamond buckles raised eighteen hundred livres to buy three shares for "you know who" (*la petite*). "I had no doubt that the dividend would be a large one. The shares were at six hundred and fifty livres. Just as I was ready to buy them Madame de Ferriol wanted a thousand francs. I lent them to her, counting on her promise to return them in two days. That was six months ago and the shares have risen to eleven hundred and fifty livres; they are now at a thousand. You can judge for yourself; I should have made a thousand *écus* by selling them, and could have paid some of my debts. Thus my fortunes drift with the stream. I have paid some trifles with the six hundred livres that I have left. One must console oneself for the losses of fortune. Far better people than I am are much more to be pitied. This is a cruel consolation when such people are our friends."

The "good" Cardinal Fleury is filling the state coffers, emptied by Monsieur le Duc, by taxing the small incomes, and Aïssé and her friends suffer from the "*visa*." Her pittance is reduced, in spite of a letter at once pathetic and diplomatic, intended to loosen the minister's grip on her purse. Guilty and innocent are mulcted alike—Madame de Tencin as well as Madame Calandrini.

There are rumors of war, and war itself throws its grim shadow across Aïssé's pages, but it is always regarded as a pincher of wallets rather than as a sunderer of companions. The great enemy of these helpless spenders is poverty. It is curious to read so much of wanting money, winning it, losing it, lending and borrowing it, raising and begging it, and never a word of earning it. Poor, charming, careless, wasteful folk whose grandchildren faced exile and poverty gayly armed only with a fiddle or a French grammar, but, more fortunate than the grasshopper of fable, earned a scant living by teaching the industrious to dance.

Aïssé glides lightly over thin ice in referring to the Council of Embrun which Cardinal de Tencin assembled to quash the Jansenists and incidentally his own opponents. This council, a scandal to the devout, and a laughing-stock to the unbelievers, included among its members such beacons of the faith as the Cardinal Bishop of Rohan, renowned for the delicacy of his skin, his face-poultices, and his baths of asses' milk; and the Bishops of Laon and Soissons, who were qualified to play Nero to Rohan's Poppæa, and whose proceedings won for the Council the sobriquet of "the brigands of Embrun."

"I do not speak of the Council to you, for though I was born under the eyes of its *chief* [de Tencin], I have never wished to hear it mentioned; meantime if you are curious about it I will send you all the documents. Truly I don't advise you to have this curiosity, as it will cost you much *ennui*. With the exception of a letter of the twelve bishops [a protest against the action of the Council], which is fine, all the rest is pitiable. I quote Madame Cornuel who said that as there were no heroes for valets-de-chambre, there were no fathers of the church among one's contemporaries. *What I see gives me awful doubts about the past.* Don't let us speak more of this business. I have said stupid things enough about it already."

Thus the discreet Aïssé; she was more communicative with her court gossip, and this book, "*presque dévot,*" is occasionally something of a *chronique scandaleuse*. Madame de Parabère leaves M. le Premier to take a new lover, Monsieur d'Alincourt; an unattractive person of whom her friends disapprove. She is not more fortunate in pleasing them when after Monsieur d'Alincourt's desertion she chooses, from a crowd of aspirants, Monsieur de Mothe Houdancourt to replace him. Madame du Deffand after a rupture with a too exacting lover sighed for the peace and security of domestic life. Her amiable husband was invited to return to his migratory penates; he accepted the invitation, and its conditions, viz., that a novitiate of three months should precede his public reappearance as head of the household. For six weeks the forbearing marquis was a welcome guest, and dined and supped with the wittiest woman and the cleverest talker in Paris. But the novelty of her friend's approval, and of the flirtation matrimonial soon grew stale. Madame's mood changed; she made no complaint, failed in no perfunctory courtesy, but her usually sprightly face assumed an expression of utter dejection; her silence and melancholy informed the husband-on-trial that his candidature was unpopular, and he ceased his visits, leaving the volatile lady "the fable of the town," Aïssé adds, who was friend and confidante of the women whose mutations she recorded.

The tragic death of Adrienne Lecouvreur, a Decameronesque adventure in a *petite maison* of the Prince de Carignan, an elaborate practical joke played on a famous surgeon, the copy of a naïf letter from an officer of the Invalides asking for a wife, the cabals of the opera-singers Le Maure, La Antier, La Pélissier, news of all sorts and of all the different social worlds is despatched to the sedate friend in that respectable but rather humdrum Geneva, because she "must be amused a little." Truly, for a book of devotion—but then in the eighteenth century devotion had a long leash.

The appearance of a new publication is rarely noticed. "I shall send you at the first opportunity a book which is very fashionable here, '*Le Voyage de Gulliver*,' it is translated from the English. The author is the Doctor Swift. The book is very amusing; it contains much wit, imagination, and delicate pleasantry." Delicate! Oh, Aïssé "*Manon Lescaut*," which was first published during the Regency under another name, does not fare so well. "There is a new book here entitled: '*Mémoires d'un homme de qualité retiré du monde*.' It is not worth much, nevertheless one reads its hundred and ninety pages crying all the time." Perhaps the Abbé Prévost would not have been displeased with such depreciation of his novel.

There is more generous mention of the theatre and the opera, which were not only temples of the Muses but salons of conversation in a social age, and to which their habitués carried their lap-dogs and cushions, their work-bags and foot-warmers as well as the score or the libretto. A box was a boudoir, very much as it is still in Italy, and the pit was a rather mixed drawing-room. The prevalent passion for the theatre is curiously illustrated by Aïssé's anecdote of a famous Jansenist. This learned theologian, who was a canon of Notre Dame and a veteran antagonist of the Molinists, after having resisted temptation for a lifetime, succumbed at the age of seventy to the desire to see a comedy. He had often told his friends that he should not die without witnessing something of which he heard people constantly talking. Of course this remark was considered a pleasantry. He had preserved his grandmother's wardrobe in spite of his lackey's remonstrances, to which he always replied that he might need it some day. That day finally came, and to the dismay of the old servant the canon called for the clothes to wear as a disguise to the theatre. In vain the lackey urged that such an antiquated dress would draw all eyes to its wearer, that his master would do better to go in his own costume as the house was full of priests. The canon was fixed in his project. He feared that his scholars would recognize him, and argued that as he was old, no one would be surprised to see him in an old-fashioned costume. He therefore dressed himself in the archaic cornet and scant petticoats, went to the theatre and took a seat in the pit. One can imagine the attention such a masquerader would naturally attract. His neighbors began to make remarks, and the disturbance spread. Armand, the actor, who was playing Harlequin saw the canon, went down to the pit, looked him over, and then very civilly asked him to leave as the audience was laughing at him, and a scandal was imminent. The poor old gentleman thanked the actor and tried to comply, but lost his way and was stopped by the guard who, not unnaturally, believed him to be a rogue in disguise, arrested him and brought him before the chief of police. This inexorable official declined to listen to the reverend doctor's explanations, was unmoved by his tears, and probably for the first time in his life, refused the bribe that the now demoralized canon offered him. Partisan feeling, for the chief was a devoted Molinist, inspired this act of virtue, and urged him to make the affair a public one. The elderly votary of the drama was exiled to a village some sixty leagues from Paris, and the Jansenists humiliated in the person of their champion.

Aïssé's sympathies were with the tempted doctor, though her constant theatre-going was rather the result of custom than of personal predilection. She wept over "*Regulus*" at the "Comédie," and she recorded the prodigious success of Destouches's play, "*Le philosophe marié*," for which "boxes are sold eleven nights in advance." She writes that the opera of "*Proserpine*" is too sad; "*Pyrame et Thisbé*" is interesting on account of the Greek scenery, and "*Bellérophon*" is enlivened by an unforeseen catastrophe. "The other day when the dragon appeared on the stage something went wrong with the machinery, the stomach of the animal opened, and the little naked boy was seen, which made the pit laugh."

Not very valuable criticism this; more vivid, if not more interesting, are the miniature pictures of contemporary life. Here is a bit which suggests a painting of Watteau or Pater. The lofty pale-tinted *salon* of the Ferriols, with its gray-green tapestries, its long windows opening on the century-old trees of the park; Madame de Ferriol in a new taffeta gown taking her coffee, Clément the pet dog by her side, and patient Aïssé in attendance. Enter an unexpected visitor, Madame de Rieu *en négligé*, unrouged, but rosy and fresh as a nymph. Madame de Ferriol tries to rise, the caller to prevent her from observing this ceremony, a difficult one for the cumbrous ex-beauty. The greedy pet, whose education had been deplorably neglected, seizes the unguarded coffee-cup and upsets it over his mistress's new gown; the petticoat is spotted, the neckerchief soiled. Loud-voiced despair of Madame de Ferriol, flushed embarrassment of Madame de Rieu, and inward laughter of Aïssé. During the commotion arrives the Abbé d'Aydie, the brother of the Chevalier, just at the right moment to receive the *coup de foudre* from the sweet confusion and dewy freshness of Madame de Rieu.

We are with the Duc de Gesvres in Saint-Ouen. The effeminate young man is ill after the failure of his weak little conspiracy to cut the King loose from Fleury's leading strings. The Duc was more expert with the needle than with the sword, and had gained the royal ear while teaching Louis XV tapestry stitch. "Ours is the most valiant of kings," jeered Paris on this historic occasion, "*nul autre n'a jammais commencé quatre sièges à la fois.*" The Duc receives in bed, a bed draped with lace and ribbons, covered with a flower-strewn counterpane; on one side is his knotting, on the other a *découpage;* twenty attendants surround him, in a green livery of his own designing, while his father and brother welcome a crowd of courtiers.

Here is a sketch of life in a country house in Burgundy: "In the morning after mass, the archbishop shuts himself up with a Jesuit until after dinner-time. After dinner a game of quadrille, filled with rapacity and bitterness over five *sous* that are never paid; every day company from town, not interesting and with whom we must be as ceremonious as though they were the king's officers. Towards evening every one goes for a stroll except the mistress of the house and myself; we remain at home, the one reading, the other knitting or cutting out pictures. After the walk there is an ear-splitting concert. We sup wretchedly, we have neither good fish nor good friends."

The pretty frivolity of the epoch flutters over these pages on glittering wings. There are playful allusions to current fashions, the craze of the moment, *découpage*, that vandalism of a polite age. "We are here in the height of a new passion for cutting up colored engravings, just as we were last year for cup-and-ball. Every lady, great and small, is cutting away. These cuttings are pasted on sheets of pasteboard and then varnished. We make wall panels, screens, and fire boards of them. There are books of engravings which cost up to a hundred livres, and women who are mad enough to cut up engravings worth a hundred livres a-piece. If this fashion continues they will cut up Raphaels."

There are half-mocking references to new gowns which were biennial events with Aïssé; the *toile peinte*, or the brocaded taffeta generous Madame de Parabère leaves on her toilette-table. Aïssé's few luxuries were precious to her as she owed them to the affection of her friends; she and her correspondent evidently held as an article of faith that "*les petits cadeaux entretiennent les grandes amitiés*," and there were constant exchanges of little gifts. Madame Calandrini works an armchair in tapestry stitch for Aïssé, which only the favored are allowed to use, or Aïssé sends to Geneva a little snuff-box in flame-colored tortoise-shell, "from which one day I permitted myself to take a pinch that you may say when you do so that it has been used by the person who loves you more than any one else in the world."

There are tidings of Patie, the dog; dear Patie who knew the Chevalier's messengers and always waited for them at the door; Patie who is lost, and lost forever apparently, for there is no further mention of him. There is news of Sophie, the faithful maid who after Aïssé's death became a nun.

A curious interest is awakened by the appearance of this once familiar figure, the waiting woman, the humble confidante, a type of feminine creature now rare as the apteryx. What virtues were hers, what loyalty, what devotion to an erring or capricious mistress, to whom she gave her wages as freely as her unheeded counsels, for whom she disinterestedly lied and schemed, and from whom she bore neglect and ingratitude with the patient reverence of the savage for his unresponsive fetich. Formed by feudal traditions, her service was as stanch as that of the man-at-arms, and more intelligent. To the audacity of the page whom she replaced when mediæval merged into modern customs, and the *châtelaine* became the court-lady, she often added a lively wit and much fertility of resource. Iris was not a more adroit messenger. She could slip a love-letter into her kerchief under the very eye of the most vigilant guardian, as easily as she could set a tucker or shift a patch. Can one imagine what the playwright or the novelist would have done without her? Her lady's understudy always, she often held the centre of the stage in the social drama. In the comedy of intrigue, she was a very hard-worked person; the ingénue whose love was star-crossed needed her as much as the reckless coquette, and she was as indispensable to Miss Western as to Millamant. Fancy *"Tartufe"* without Dorine, or the *"Malade Imaginaire"* bereft of Toinon.

Sophie was a simpler and more innocent being

than those pert, beribboned minxes who lace the long bodice, or hand a love-letter with the morning chocolate in delicate, yellowed engravings, or the powdered soubrettes who plot so dexterously behind the footlights. Sophie was not of their sisterhood; she was one of Chardin's womenfolk; those graceful girls who, in their austere gray gowns and modest high-crossed neckerchiefs *en paquet sur la poitrine*, seem more akin to the gravely sweet attendant maidens of Ghirlandajo than to the saucy coquettes of Beaumarchais and Baudoin.

It was Sophie who was intrusted with the most delicate commissions, who went to Sens when Aïssé was unable to do so, and who brought back news of "the little one" to her eager mother. Célénie is the pearl of daughters; everything about her prevents her mother from repenting of her birth, and Aïssé fears that the poor tot will weep more over it than she has. Célénie grows prettier day by day; she is adored by the whole convent for her reasonableness, her goodness, and her courage; only the other day she had four teeth pulled without a single scream. She was praised for it, and replied: "What good would crying out have done? Did they not have to be pulled?" She is the pet of all the good sisters, whose only weakness is a tendency to spoil young and helpless creatures, and is as docile and amiable as Ver-vert, the famous parrot of the Convent of Nevers, her illustrious contemporary. "She is very affectionate; the poor little one already feels, I think, the need she has of being so. The Chevalier is in despair at no longer being able to see her; he loves her desperately. . . . We are trying to get together a dowry for her in case she should not wish to become a nun. The Chevalier has already invested two thousand *écus* for her."

Sometimes Aïssé could go herself to visit her treasure, and then what joy was hers. A little clouded doubtless by the sad necessity for dissimulation, for to Célénie Aïssé was only a friend of Madame de Bolingbroke who was good enough to interest herself in the English orphan. Poor Aïssé could not wear her crown, she could not press her child to her hungry heart, but must kiss her decorously on the brow, she could not hear the dearest word in the world from those fresh lips. But the voice of blood pleaded for her in her daughter's veins, and without knowing why her girl was drawn to Aïssé. With what elation she writes to her friend: "The poor little one loves me *à la folie*. She was so overjoyed to see me that she almost fainted. You can imagine what I felt, when I saw her. . . . She told me a hundred times that the day of my arrival was a happy one for her; she couldn't leave me; nevertheless, when I sent her away she went very sweetly. She listened to my advice, and seemed determined to profit by it. She did not try to excuse herself for her faults as children do. Ah, me! the poor little thing when I left her was so overcome with grief that I did not dare to look at her, she affected me so much; she could not speak. I carried the abbess off with me to see

Madame de Bolingbroke, who was at Rheims where she had been very ill. The whole convent was in tears over the departure of the abbess, and the poor little one said: 'As to myself, mesdames, I am as sorry as the others to see you go away, but I believe it is necessary and that Madame de Bolingbroke will be glad to see you, and that the sight of you will do her good; that is what consoles me a little for your going.' Then the poor little one choked. She sat down feeling too overcome to stand, kissed me, and added: 'This is an awful contretemps, my dear friend; otherwise you might have remained here longer. I have neither father nor mother; be my mother, I beg you; I love you as much as though you were.' You can judge for yourself, dear lady, what confusion this speech brought upon me, but I behaved very well. I remained two weeks, and had an attack of rheumatism there; my whole body was benumbed by it. For two days she did not leave me. She remained at my bedside five consecutive hours without wishing to leave me; she read aloud to amuse me, or she chatted with me. If I dozed for a moment or two, she hardly dared to breathe for fear of waking me. A person of thirty could not have been more sensible and attentive. Mademoiselle de Noailles asked her to play with her; she begged Mademoiselle to excuse her as she did not want to leave me. In fine, Madame, I am persuaded that if she had the happiness of being known to you, you would love her dearly."

AÏSSÉ

Aïssé begged Madame Calandrini's good-will for her daughter rather timidly; the puritans of both creeds were rather apt to visit the sins of the erring mothers on their offspring; the attitude of the mediæval bishop who naïvely named his illegitimate children Vulpecula and Latro, doing vicarious penance through these poor innocents, was not entirely obsolete. Aïssé was also singularly restrained in expression of emotion. She felt a modest hesitation in unveiling her heart. She seemed to fear the tone of insincerity which emphasis and stress might impart; with impeccable good taste she unconsciously, as feeling deepened, simplified her language; like a true gentlewoman, she lowered her voice when profoundly moved. A certain quality of self-command, not stoical but springing partly from consideration for her friend, partly from self-respect, imposed a fine reserve on her up-wellings of personal emotion. If at times she abused the understatement, and attenuated rather than accentuated touching situations, it was because she feared to cast aside the high-bred self-control of which she stood in continual need. She was still a slave; she was a mother who dared not say "my child," a lover with no rights over her beloved, a proud and delicate-minded woman in a false position; it was dangerous for her to let herself go, and when she seemed cold or flippant she was perhaps most moved.

For anecdotes, news, and gossip were but the

tripping accompaniment to a motive of regret that dominates the correspondence, a tone of pervasive sadness, now subdued to a gentle melancholy, now falling into a lament; the despair of the illicit love that owns no future, that can evoke no vision of ultimate union to lighten the burden of present separation, to people the solitude of the heart. Aïssé's plight was that of Dante's damned folk who possessed desire without hope. Her sprightliness is the result partly of kindly courtesy, the wish not to weary or distress her friend with her sorrows and perplexities, partly of the belief of the Latin peoples that courage without cheerfulness is courage of a poor sort.

VI

This gentle valor never abandoned Aïssé in the long duel between the two women, for a duel literally to the death it was: Madame Calandrini fighting to save her friend's soul, to separate her from her lover, to lead her through renunciation and repentance back to righteousness; Aïssé battling for her love, justifying it, pleading for it. Has not the Chevalier besought her to marry him? She is no light o' love, she is a wife in all but name. Theirs is a *liaison* with a difference, it remains a *liaison* because Aïssé refuses to sacrifice his fortune and his future by allowing him to become her husband. "His passion is the most extraordinary in the world! He sees me once every three months. I do nothing to please him, I have too much delicacy to abuse the ascendency I have in his heart, and no matter how happy it would make me to marry him, I must love the Chevalier for himself. Consider, Madame, how such a step would be regarded by the public, if he should marry an unknown person who has no resources but from the family of Madame de Ferriol. No, I love his honor too much, and I am also too proud to let him commit such a blunder. How mortified I should be to hear the remarks that would be made about it! Could I flatter myself that the Chevalier would always feel as he does now towards me? He would repent most assuredly of having yielded to a mad passion and I should not be able to survive the grief of having caused his unhappiness, and of losing his love. He makes the most tender, the most extravagant, the most passionate projects in the world, . . . that if I wish to marry him I am the mistress of our fates; if not, he believes that we could, as we are both unimportant people, spend the rest of our lives together; that he would settle the greater part of his property on me, that he is displeased with his relatives, with the exception of his brother, to whom he can give enough honestly to content him, and in order to make it easier for me to accept his plan, he says that we could each will our property to the one who survives the other. I joked about my old petticoats, which are the only heritage that I could leave him, and our talk ended with a jest. . . . You ask me for news of my heart. It is quite happy, Madame, except in one particular. . . . But God is master of all; I hope in him. The attachment, the consideration, the affection [of the Chevalier] are stronger than ever, and likewise esteem and gratitude on my part —something more—if I dare to say it. Alas! I am just as you left me, tormented by the thought you know of, which you have developed in me. I shall never have the courage to entertain it; my reason, your counsels, heavenly grace, are less strong than my passion."

Again, when she has been ill, Aïssé writes of the Chevalier: "He shows the same affection, the same fears of losing me. I do not abuse his tenderness. It seems to be a natural human impulse to profit by the weakness of others. I do not know how to use such arts; I know only one: to make life so sweet to him I love that he will find nothing preferable to it. I wish to retain him only by the sweetness of living with me. . . . I make him so contented that his only ambition is to pass his life in the same way. Perhaps that may lead to what we desire so much. The nature of his property is a terrible obstacle to it. God will look upon us with pity perhaps; sometimes I have impulses that are difficult to combat. . . . Alas! Why were you not Madame de Ferriol? You would have taught me to know virtue. But enough of this. Meantime I am as regards love the most fortunate person in the world."

AÏSSÉ

As time goes on and they become more intimate, Madame Calandrini presses Aïssé more closely. How can one who loves virtue live in mortal sin? What are Aïssé's protestations worth if she refuses to follow the right course when the hand of affection points it out for her? Is her constantly expressed love for her friend of any value, if she continues to wring that friend's heart by her misconduct? To these reproaches Aïssé replies: "I am pouting over your last letter. You accuse me most unjustly of not loving you, and you add that when one loves one adopts the sentiments and the way of thinking of one's friends. Alas! Madame, unhappily I met you much too late. I repeat what I have said to you a hundred times. From the very moment that I knew you I felt the greatest friendship for you, the greatest confidence in you. It is a real pleasure to me to open my heart to you. I have not blushed to confide all my weaknesses to you; you only have created a soul in me; it was born to be virtuous. Without bigotry, knowing the world, not hating it, and accordingly understanding how to forgive, taking circumstances into consideration, you learned to know my faults without ceasing to esteem me. I seemed to you to be an object of pity, one who was guilty almost unknowingly. Happily, it is to the *délicatesses mêmes* of a passion that I owe the desire to know virtue. I am full of faults but I respect and love virtues. Do not take from me the least of that merit. How obliged I am to you to love some one who practises so ill the counsels you have given her, and who follows your good example still less well. But my love is strong; everything justifies it to me. It seems to me that I should be ungrateful, and that I ought to preserve the affection of the Chevalier for the dear little one. She is the tie that binds fast our love. Often this tie makes me regard it as a duty. If you are just, believe then that it is not possible for me to love you more than I love you. No, you do not doubt it. I feel the tenderest friendship for you. I love you as my mother, my sister, my daughter, every one whom one ought to love. My affection includes all the sentiments of esteem, admiration, and gratitude; nothing can efface from my heart a friend as worthy as yourself. Do not then tell me any more things that afflict me."

When Aïssé returned from a long visit to her austere friend these afflicting things had apparently been much discussed, and Aïssé's guard had been beaten down; her defense grew feebler and she began to waver and shift her ground. "Alas! Madame, I recall constantly our talk in your study; I make efforts that are killing me. All that I can promise you is to spare no pains that one of those things should happen. But, Madame, it will perhaps cost me my life. How happy are those who have virtue enough to surmount such weaknesses! for really one needs an infinite deal of it to resist him whom one finds lovable, and whom unfortunately one has not resisted always. Cut down a violent passion, the tenderest and most well-founded affection! Add gratitude to all that! It is frightful! Death is not worse. Meantime you desire me to try to do so. I will, but I doubt whether I can with honor or with safety to my life. I fear to return to Paris, I fear everything that draws me to the Chevalier, and I am unhappy away from him. I don't know what I desire. Why is not my love lawful? Why is it not innocent?"

It was perhaps during this first effort of poor Aïssé to detach herself from her lover that the neglected Chevalier wrote her the following letter, which was found by M. Ravanel among the papers of Madame de Créquy, to whom it may have been given by the Vicomtesse de Nanthia, Aïssé's daughter:

"You ill-treat me, my queen. I do not know the reason why nor can I guess your pretext for doing so, but apparently you need neither the one nor the other. Caprice in truth disdains reasons and is a law unto itself. Besides, perhaps you have decided to put my patience and my dependence on you to the proof from time to time. Well! are you not satisfied with me? Three letters have I written you without your having deigned to answer me. I despatched a special messenger for news of you; you sent him back, saying dryly that you were in good health. You must confess that one needs perseverance to take the initiative again and to make advances. I fully realize the pitifulness of my conduct; but I love you, and to what cannot love reduce us? Allow me to observe that for your own honor you should treat me with more respect. You will make me so ridiculous that my attachment to you will no longer be a compliment to you. Leave to me in your own interest some semblance of good sense and freedom. People have always believed (and doubtless quite justly) that it was by a very enlightened choice that I love you more than my life, and that the source of my felicity existed in your character rather than in mine. But if you become unreasonable and capricious, the idea that we have of an Aïssé who is always just, tender, sweet, and even-tempered will disappear. I shall probably not love you less (my passion is a part of my soul and I can only lose it by ceasing to live), but you will be less amiable in the eyes of others, and that would be a pity. Leave the world an example of a woman more lovable than any other, who loved with fidelity, and who knew how to make herself beloved quite artlessly. What have I done to you, my queen? Tell me, if you can. Nothing, truly. I swear that I have not ceased for one moment to be entirely yours; you have not a hair on your head which does not inspire in me more affection and feeling than all the women in the world, and I authorize you to tell this and to read it to whom you will."

Alas! for renunciatory resolutions! The Chevalier comes to Paris from Marly ill with fever and asthma, and the sight of her lover's sufferings, his need of her, melt in a twinkling Aïssé's reluctant rigors. But his tenderness and devotion justify her weakness. "Love has made me divide my heart, Madame, but if I did not find in the object of it the virtues that I love in you, this love would not endure. You have made me fastidious in such matters. I confess, to the shame of love, that it would cease if it were not founded on esteem."

A little later Aïssé writes: "The Chevalier is better. I wish that there were no struggle between my reason and my heart, and that I could enjoy utterly the pleasure that I feel in seeing him, but, alas! nevermore. My body succumbs to the agitation of my spirits, . . . my health is terribly shaken. . . . I have confessed all my weaknesses to you; they are great, but I could never love where I could not respect. If my reason is unable to vanquish my passion, my heart could not be seduced but by goodness or by what had the appearance of it. I own that you cannot tear a violent passion out of my heart, but be assured that I feel all my obligations to you, and that I shall never change the tender feelings which I have devoted to you. . . . I pass over my remorse in silence; it is born of my reason, but my love stifles it. Some rays of hope of an ending, a conclusion of all this, tempt me to err still, but it is not in my power to renounce them. Adieu, Madame, I can no more. This is a long letter for a person as weak as I am."

Thus Aïssé turned in a constantly narrowing circle, striving to still the reproaches of her newly awakened conscience, to hold fast to her lover, and to content her friend. So she faltered and drifted, she renounced and yielded, she rebelled and appealed. Her moral sense, captive to artificial standards, was imprisoned between narrow walls. The wings of her spirit were not strong enough to lift her above them, and her intellect was not vigorous enough to overleap them. Her mind accepted the rule of convention while her heart defied it. A stronger character would have braved the future and married her lover; a more ascetic nature would have renounced the joy of his presence, but shrined his image in her heart; the average woman of Aïssé's time would have been sufficiently tender of appearances to permit herself a little private indulgence in the realm of the affections. But Aïssé, poor Andromeda in the fetters of convention, did not find a Perseus in the Chevalier. He loved her faithfully, devotedly, but his love seems almost too high-bred, too restrained, too reasonable. It lacks resource and initiative. It is too ready to acknowledge everybody else's claims on her, Madame de Ferriol's, Madame Calandrini's; it is hardly exclusive enough. Passion should not courtesy to observance, nor wait on scruples. The Chevalier, noble and tender as he is, seems a little pale, somewhat lacking in accent, like a delicate, faded miniature. Aïssé's sacrifice, the fragile barriers her self-denying love built between her and happiness, would have crumbled before the brunt of a virile will; a direct and, above all, a sustained attack would have carried her slight defenses ill-manned by a traitorous heart. One longs for a little rude, masculine common sense to thrust aside these flimsy obstacles, a more persistent, more tenacious lover, who would have said and repeated to a generous woman distraught between love and duty, not "*you* are the mistress of our fates," but "*j'en suis le maître.*"

Madame Calandrini advocated renunciation, she did not advise marriage. Perhaps, knowing Aïssé's passion for self-sacrifice, she wisely urged her in the direction of her natural inclination. For Aïssé's woes, penance, not rehabilitation, was her friend's remedy, the soul's salvation, not the heart's desire. The changes effected by the *philosophes* in the ideal of duty are piquantly illustrated by the differing points of view of Madame Calandrini and of Madame de Créquy. Both ladies were devout, each after her own fashion, both were austere in their lives and moral standards, but from 1727 to 1787 a new idea was shaking the rigid old codes into new crystallizations: the right of the individual to happiness— the individual, not the family, or the order.

The Marquise, after reading the letters, wrote Aïssé's daughter: "It is quite true that the Chevalier wished to marry Mademoiselle Aïssé, and that she told my uncle (the Bailli de Froulai) 'I am too much his friend to suffer it.' *She was wrong.* The

Chevalier was esteemed in every way; he would have had places, governorships, pensions; he would have made a position for her also. An Oriental princess, full of virtues, would have turned all heads." Thus pronounced a pious lady who heartily disapproved of the new philosophy, and yet whose ideas of the conduct of life had been greatly modified by it.

It is almost impossible to sound the social gulf which divided Aïssé from her lover. Society was then a very tightly knit and highly organized body, and the family, especially the noble family, was a jealous god to whom countless individuals were sacrificed. Revolt against our lightly worn conventions is ingloriously easy, but formerly to defy social laws was to invite martyrdom. And the question of money was an all-important one in an unproductive class. A knight of Malta could renounce his vows and marry, but he remained a poor younger son, as his revenue from the Church went with them. He might hope for a small sum from the King whose soldier he was, and through a death or two in his own family he might come into a modest fortune. Perhaps these possibilities were the "rays of hope" to which Aïssé alluded. What she sought to demonstrate was, however, that a disinterested passion associated with self-abnegation was a *moral* emotion; that a feeling which clasped hands with unselfishness, with humility, with aspiration, could not be inherently evil; it might be illicit, it was not vicious. She dimly apprehended the great difference between ethical and social laws, and felt, though she could not reason it out even to herself, and far less to her friend, that a love whose very essence was sacrifice ranked among the sanctities, not among the sins. She was too untrained in the casuistry of the heart, too weak in dialectics either to convince Madame Calandrini, or to detect the flaw in her own logic. She knew that her love had quickened noble strivings and revealed a loftier standard of duty than she had known before it unsealed the eyes of her soul. She was conscious that her great passion had called forth in her new enthusiasms, new capacities, a more long-suffering patience, a firmer fortitude, a more complete detachment from the pettinesses of life. But she could not translate these convictions into arguments, so she repeated helplessly, that *les délicatesses mêmes d'une passion* had taught her to revere goodness.

Meantime the conflict between her concept of duty and her love shattered her health and shook her gentle courage. Sleepless nights filled with anxious questionings, with sad or terrifying thoughts, the morbid introspection which is the twin brother of insomnia, were followed by listless days each with its burden of petty annoyances, which worn nerves rendered hard to bear. For if an abiding sorrow diminishes the importance of smaller cares and worries, it also weakens the capacity for resistance to them. In the wake of insomnia followed lassitude, indigestion, rheumatism, and finally tuberculosis. "Men have died . . . but not for love," laughed Rosalind. Not directly for love, perhaps, but from the wasting of vital force, the gradual lessening of physical energy that are the result of anguish of mind or desolation of heart. Hope, that eternal cozener, was lacking to Aïssé; for she knew that the obstacle to her felicity was in her own will and that by her own act she had elected to suffer. This element of sacrifice had ennobled her love and justified it in her own eyes, but with broken health and racked nerves doubts assailed her. Step by step she gave way, hard pushed by her zealous friend, who either failed to realize that love and life were synonymous to Aïssé, and that to abjure the one was to abandon the other, or rated the salvation of the soul as of infinitely more importance than the wellbeing of the poor, frail body. Thus with the clearest of consciences the good lady broke Aïssé on the wheel, never doubting that she was serving her sinning friend's best interests. In the opinion of this wellintentioned executioner, human love possessed in itself no inherent quality of holiness, therefore to renounce all worldly advantage for it was merely a form of delectable self-indulgence; it was buying what was most desirable in life at a very high price; it was a choice of what was dearest to a person who was indifferent to other prizes; such easy abnegation merited no admiration and inspired no respect. Love, indeed, unblessed by the Church was mortal sin, and to pick and choose duties, to decide that we shall obey certain laws and set others aside, was contrary to the very spirit of Christianity. Aïssé's desperate clinging to her lover was sinful self-will, and therefore this Mother Inquisitor felt no scruples in stretching her on the rack. Reading the last letters is like watching the writhings of some gentle animal in the prolonged agonies of vivisection. Gasps of anguish, sharp cries of pain break through the smooth order of the sentences. "I cannot tell you how much the sacrifice I am making costs me. It is killing me. . . . If the Chevalier does not keep his promise to me, I shall see him no more. I have no doubt that these resolutions will shorten my life. Never has love been so overmastering, and I can add that his is as strong. Adieu, Madame; be persuaded that if Aïssé lives she will make herself worthy of a friendship of which she understands the value."

"If Aïssé lives." She knew that after her recantation, life would become meaningless to her. Her worldly friends shared her conviction, and redoubled their kind offices. Madame de Tencin, who ever since Aïssé had refused to collaborate with her in the subjugation of the Regent, had been an implacable enemy, sought a reconciliation. Madame de Parabère neglected her admirers to spend whole days and nights in the sick-room. Madame du Deffand renounced suppers and conversations to watch at Aïssé's bedside. Monsieur de Voltaire sent her a flask of ratafia with some languishing verses, strange lines for a dying woman:

> "*Va porter dans son sang la plus subtile flamme;*
> *Changer en désirs ardents la glace de son cœur;*
> *Et qu'elle sente la chaleur*
> *Du feu qui brûle dans mon âme!*"

Sophie is devotion in person, and the Chevalier "believes that by force of generosity he can buy back my life. He gives something to everybody in the house, even to my cow for which he bought some hay. He gives to one money for the apprenticeship of his child, to another something to buy capes and ribbons with, to everyone he meets, and to every one who appears. It approaches madness. When I asked him what good it does he answered: 'It will oblige all those who are around you to take care of you.' As to the faithful Sophie, 'he would carry her in his heart.' His anxieties and distress are so sincere and so pathetic that they bring tears to the eyes of those who witness them."

If ever a man deserved pitying tears it was the Chevalier. He sat on helpless and mute while the woman he loved was dying, not only to the world, but to him. He knew that to secure peace for her last hours—hours which would be hideous if the offices of the Church were denied to her—she must renounce him. She must promise to repent of their love as though it had been a degrading and shameful vice; she must give bonds that she would never again think of him as her lover, never again look at him save with the eyes of regret. He was an unbeliever, and the rites she craved, the spiritual comfort she longed for, were void of significance to him. But so completely had love vanquished self-love that not a plaint escaped him, and he submitted to be exiled from her heart without a reproach, occupied only with the desire to smooth the dark way for her, to consecrate himself to her service while she still could be served.

VII

It was, however, only *in extremis* that the tortured woman turned renegade to love. The continual pressure so ruthlessly applied, increasing weakness, the detachment that is the concomitant of a wasting illness, the belief that death was at her side rendered renouncement possible to her. As a first step in the steep upward path, Aïssé wrote to the Chevalier the words that would separate them, words she could not trust herself to speak. Her letter has disappeared, but a copy of his reply to it was sent to Madame Calandrini. In it the suppression of self is absolute. A lover's breaking heart was never more sternly leashed. The solemn hour has struck when hope is gone, and the fond wishes and proud ambitions for the beloved have dwindled to one piteous prayer: "An easy passing, O Lord!" The letter is a salutation to one about to die. Hence the subdued tenderness it breathes. Passion is transposed into the minor key of affection. Even the pleading for a place in the laboring heart that will soon cease beating is not insistent. There should be no perturbing emotion, no moving appeal to quicken the difficult breath, to flutter the faint pulse. Grief and despair wear the mask of tranquillity in a death-chamber; the most sincere become mummers there, and self-control, self-effacement, sacred duties.

"Your letter, my dear Aïssé, touches me far more than it afflicts me. It has an accent of truth, and an aroma of virtue which I cannot resist. I complain of nothing since your promise to love me always. I confess that your principles are not mine, but thank Heaven, I am still further removed from proselytizing, and I find it most right that each one should guide his conduct by the light of his own conscience. Be tranquil, be happy, my dear Aïssé, no matter by what means. I can bear anything that does not drive me from your heart. You will see by my behaviour that I deserve your kindness. Alas! Why should you not love me still when it is your sincerity, the purity of your soul, and your goodness that bind me to you. I have told you so a thousand times, and you will see that I did not deceive you, but is it fair that you should wait until acts have proved it to you? Do you not know me well enough to have in me the confidence that truth always inspires in people who are capable of feeling it? From this instant, dear Aïssé, be convinced that I love you as tenderly as possible, as purely as you can desire; believe, above all, that I am farther than you yourself are from ever seeking any other ties. I find that nothing is wanting to my happiness as long as you permit me to see you, and to flatter myself that you regard me as the man of the whole world who is most attached to you. I shall see you tomorrow, and it is I who shall give you this letter. I preferred to write rather than to speak to you, because I could not talk of this matter with you, without loss of self-control. I am still too much moved, but I have no wish to be anything but what you desire I should be, and as to the decision you have reached, it is enough to assure you of my submission, and the constancy of my attachment under any conditions that you choose to impose upon it, without letting you see the tears which I cannot help shedding but which I disavow since you assure me that you will always be my friend. I dare to believe it, my dear Aïssé, not only because I know you are sincere, but also because I am persuaded that it is impossible that an attachment as tender, as faithful, as unselfish as mine, should not make the impression that it ought on a heart like yours."

Having formally renounced her lover, Aïssé wrote to her mentor: "At last, Madame, rejoice over your good works. I give myself up to my Creator. I am trying to free myself from my love, and I have resolved to abandon my errors. If you lose the person in the world who is most attached to you, reflect that you have labored to make her happy in another world. Goodbye, dear friend; love me and pray for the repose of my soul either in this world or in the other."

The stumbling-block of a Chevalier removed from her path, Aïssé took the next step on the road to Heaven: confession. Madame du Deffand smuggled in the Père Boursault while Madame de Parabère took Madame de Ferriol for a long drive, as she was an ardent Molinist and would have forced her own confessor upon Aïssé. "The Père Boursault is a man of intellect, much knowledge of the world and of the human heart, he is discreet and does not pride himself on being a fashionable director." It surely did not require much knowledge of the human heart to realize that Aïssé's transgressions were caused by love and self-forgetfulness, and the wise Jansenist had probably little difficulty in bringing the wandering lamb back to the fold again. A tender shepherd of souls he seems to have been, dwelling on the omniscient comprehension of the Infinite Mercy rather than the rigors of the Law or the torments of Hell. So with Roland in Roncesvaux, Aïssé "made the *amende honorable* to God" and entered into peace.

Like the navigator of the pathless air, who as he rises from the grosser vapors to purer ether sees the earth sink beneath him, the soul uplifted on the wings of prayer and aspiration looks down on a world that seems falling into space. Is there a psychological delusion that in the realm of the spirit corresponds to the optical illusion of the aeronaut? Is it that the soul really soars into a higher region, or that life, with waning physical powers, merely recedes? Whatever the cause may be, anything that sustains or elevates the spirit, that gently enfranchises it from earthly cares, and softly unclasps the clinging fingers from what they hold too fast for peace, is blessed. Aïssé's last letter to her friend is inspired by this beatific detachment, this blissful absorption in the thought of the Infinite Goodness. "I cannot talk long with you today, but I will tell you that which will crown your wishes. I have, thank God, done what I wrote you of. I am perfectly content. My tranquillity is only too great, for I feel that I am not sufficiently penitent for my errors, but I am firmly resolved not to yield to them again even if God should not soon take me to himself. I no longer wish for life except to perform my duties and to act in a manner that may merit the mercy of the Good Father. Eight days ago Father Boursault heard my confession. The step which I have taken has given my soul a calmness that I should not have had, had I remained in my sins. With the prospect of a speedy death I should have had remorse which would have made me very unhappy in these last moments. I am in such a state of weakness that I cannot leave my bed. . . . My doctor is astonishingly attentive to me; he is truly my friend; poor Sophie takes wonderful care of my body and my soul; she set me such a good example that she almost forced me to become better; she didn't preach to me; her example and her silence were more eloquent than all the sermons in the world. She is grieved to the very depths of her heart. She will never want for anything when she has lost me; all my friends love her, and will take care of her. I hope she will not need it, as I have the consolation of leaving her daily bread. I do not mention the Chevalier; he is in despair to see me so ill. A passion as strong, more delicacy, more feeling, more nobility and generosity have never been seen before. I am not anxious about the poor little one; she has a friend and a protector who loves her tenderly. Goodbye, dear Madame, I have no more strength to write. It is still infinitely sweet to me to think of you, but I cannot indulge myself in this delight without becoming too much affected, my dear friend. The life I led has been very wretched. Have I ever had a joyful moment? I could not be alone, I feared to think. From the moment that I began to open my eyes to my transgressions, remorse never abandoned me. Why should I be affrighted by the departure of my soul since I am persuaded that God is All-good, and that the moment when I shall enjoy happiness will be that when I leave this miserable body."

Formerly people died in a more leisurely fashion than is customary to-day; there were salutations, and parting words, and solemn good-bys before the last journey. To-day, as we travel faster and with less preparation, we have learned to die quickly and with the same absence of form and phrases that we perform most of the acts of our lives. We cannot wait—even on the Lord. Perhaps it is because there are so many who say "*adieu*," and so few who say "*au revoir*," that in life and art death-bed scenes and speeches have been abridged. More accurate knowledge of realities has not resulted in increased enjoyment of them, and though the joy of living may not have lessened in our wiser times, the joy of dying has, and consequently there is less loitering over it.

Aïssé lingered a little; her light flickered long enough before it was extinguished to illumine softly the dark vestibule to the tomb. She had served a long apprenticeship in trusting and loving, so belief and adoration came easy to her, and she left a sweet heritage, a fragrant example of patient resignation, and faith in the loving clemency of the All-Father. "I am still persuaded," said Parlamante, "that man will never love God perfectly until he has perfectly loved some creature of His in this world."

ROSALBA CARRIERA

"This remarkable woman carried pastel to such a degree of perfection that it has been justly said of her that no master has surpassed, and few artists have equalled her."
—Vianelli.

"Quelque chose de vaporeux, de volatil, d'à peine fixé: c'est son art; . . . dans cette écriture lumineuse et féminine, qui semble inventée exprès pour les coquetteries de son temps, elle dit—avec quelle adresse!—la société efféminée du moment, le monde lustré et poudré de Venise."
—Philippe Monnier.

ROSALBA CARRIERA

I

IN these days of impersonal philanthropy and public "service," the extension of sympathy in certain directions has been accompanied by a notable shrinkage in others. The woes of the well-to-do have ceased to excite commiseration. The most touching recital of the griefs of the opulent or the nobly born fail to move pity in the gentlest breast, and it is to be feared that the care-free modern parent will smile rather than sigh over the worries and anxieties of Rinaldo d'Este, Duke of Modena and Reggio, in the year of grace 1721.

His contemporaries were not so hard-hearted. If his cross was a heavy one, he was not expected to bear it alone. Not one of his kinsfolk, and he was related to half Europe, the crowned and coroneted Europe that counted, went free. Grandmothers, cousins, aunts lent a more or less willing hand to lighten his burden or to thrust it on to others' shoulders. At the first blush the duke might be considered a fortunate person. His little duchy was a fertile garden, his subjects were docile and industrious, his favorites were not immoderately rapacious. His somewhat complicated family life was fairly peaceful; and in spite of his turbulent French daughter-in-law, his heir presumptive was too bullied and cowed to give umbrage to a suspicious and jealous parent. The duke's firm grasp on the moneybags, as well as on the reins of domestic discipline, had secured him a handsome hoard for emergencies, and he had adroitly managed to avoid the imbroglios which had impoverished so many small states. His picture-gallery was famous, his villas and palaces, even if somewhat neglected, were beautiful—and yet he was a perplexed and troubled potentate.

> "*Dans une famille,*
> (*Je le dis tout bas*),
> *Une jeune fille*
> *C'est un embarras.*
> *Quand i' n'y en a q'une*
> *Certes, c'est affreux,*
> *Mais quelle infortune*
> *Quand i' y en a deux!*"

sings Boléro in "*Giroflé Giroflà*," confidently counting on the applause and heartfelt sympathy of every father of girls in his audience. Duke Rinaldo's case was more pitiful, his *embarras* was tripled in the very pretty persons of their Serene Highnesses Benedetta Ernestina Maria d'Este, Amalia Giuseppina d'Este, and Enrichetta Anna Sofia d'Este, daughters of Duke Rinaldo, and his wife Charlotte Félicité of Brunswick.

Abstractly considered, these disturbers of paternal peace were void of offense. They were pious and gently bred, and their captious sister-in-law, the

Regent's daughter, vouched for their amiability; as to their good looks there was no doubt. Too deep-chested and upstanding for our modern standard of beauty, their heads well set on long, round throats, were lovely, for the sweet red and white, the radiant freshness of youth masked their defects, and if the rather heavy chins were Teutonic, all Italian were the velvety eyes, the straight, delicately pencilled brows, and the low arched foreheads, on which the abundant hair encroached. The princesses then were good girls and pretty girls, but they were *girls* to be provided with establishments, dowers, and husbands—hence the duke's cares.

> "Day, night, late, early,
> At home, abroad, alone, in company,
> Waking or sleeping, still my care hath been
> To have her matched,"

scolded Juliet's father, and he had only one girl, and was no duke. Multiply Capulet's difficulties by a hundred and you have some idea of his Highness's task.

Eligible princes came very high, suitable consorts were shy and few for ladies with thrifty sires and small portions. To the all-important question of money was added that of religion. Protestantism further narrowed matrimonial opportunities, and many a harassed parent, burdened with female olive-branches, cursed Luther's heresy with a fervor not inspired by religious zeal.

Modena was too near Rome for its duke to follow the example of the far-sighted German suzerain who, to forestall future difficulties, brought up his daughters without any creed whatever. So in the scarcity of nubile princes the beauties of Este bade fair to wither ungathered on the parent stem, with as little comfort to themselves as to that somewhat thorny and reluctant prop. To avert this calamity the ducal family pondered, planned, and prayed. The orisons of all the professionally religious persons in Modena, and there were many, were requested, the good offices of Court favorites were besought, backstairs diplomacy was pressed into service, and ambassadors were kept busy. Nets were spread and traps were set for every noble quarry. The most tireless hunter of them all was the princesses' grandmother, the Duchess of Brunswick; "faint yet pursuing," ignoring smaller game, she kept steadily on the track of her prey, the Dukes of Brunswick and of Burgundy. To *partis* like these, rich enough to buy beauty, fine eyes might appeal more strongly than "*les beaux yeux de la cassette*" of some plainer princess.

Wise Grandmamma Brunswick, considering ways and means with Rangoni, Modenese ambassador at the French Court, eagerly adopted his suggestion that after she had drawn the attention of the two dukes' mothers to the princesses' virtues and charms, their portraits should be sent to Paris where they could not fail to excite a general interest that with skilful management might become a particular one. Perhaps Rangoni remembered how Holbein's picture of Anne of Cleves bewitched Henry VIII, perhaps he thought only of turning the Parisian craze of the moment to his master's profit. In any case, warmly seconded by the Duchess of Brunswick, on March 19, 1721, he wrote Duke Rinaldo that "the famous Rosalba" was in Paris painting all the great personages of the Court, "and if from her hand I could have here the portraits of our Serene Highnesses the renown of her brush would excite the curiosity of the most distinguished persons, but the beauty of the subjects would more justly awaken admiration."

This suggestion was rather tardily adopted by the duke who suspected that the prices of so fashionable a painter would be a costly item in his carefully balanced budget, but it was heartily approved by his home-keeping duchess, by the princesses' secretary, a learned nun, by Selvatico, Rinaldo's grotesque, tyrannical favorite, and by the ducal confessors, directors, and spiritual advisers of the dreary little Court of Modena.

Who was this artist? Who was the last resort of distressed beauty, the painter-paladin who, brush in hand and palette on thumb, was called on to deliver the captive princesses from their "perpetual prison," as a less resigned princess called it. Who was "the famous Rosalba"? It is easy enough to "locate" Rosalba Carriera, the Venetian painter in miniature and pastel, but it is difficult to account for her conquest of Europe, to understand how a lowly born, poor, plain, honest little Cinderella became a princess of art without a fairy godmother. Her fame has been as evanescent as the fragile beauty of much of her work, which has faded away before the eyes of the eager seeker like fairy gold. It was often called the work of the fays, for in the eighteenth century, positive and sceptical as it was, the fairies still lingered in Venice, Paul de Musset would have us believe in his "Life" of Carlo Gozzi. Unhappy Gozzi, who dared to utilize them for dramatic material in his *"Fiabe,"* that drove Goldoni's real folks and scenes of every-day life from the Venetian theatre, had desecrated the enchanted ground of fairyland. His greedy fingers had rudely handled airy shapes composed of dew and gossamer, and the rainbow dust of butterflies' wings. He had dragged into the glare of the tallow dips of San Samuele's stage to be laughed at by gondoliers and shopkeepers and fisher-folk, aerial beings who should be dimly seen only by moonlight, in the faint glow of a dying fire, or the warm shadows of brief southern twilights. He bruised these delicate essences by rough contact with the old boisterous masks Harlequin, Pantaloon, Brighella, and their ilk, by impact with Venetian scullions and newsboys.

Gozzi had, in his so-called fairy-plays, disenchanted this magic realm. De Musset therefore saw in the constant mishaps, accidents, contretemps, and mystifications that befell the unlucky Carlo, the vengeance of these offended sprites. De Musset was, however, if not a poet himself, a poet's brother, and assumed the bard's immemorial privilege of irresponsibility in handling facts. He was pleased to find in Gozzi a precursor of the Romantic movement, a forerunner of Beckford and La Motte Fouqué, and to present him and his adventures humorously and fancifully in the spirit of Romanticism, a Puck-like literary prank.

If Rosalba's biographer were tempted to take so Hoffmannish and fantastic a view of Rosalba's extraordinary career, she might easily be considered the godchild if not of the fairies, who seem obsolete in the Venice of Tiepolo and Longhi, yet of those thoroughly up-to-date sprites, the sylphs, who were the elves of rococo, the fays of the prosaic age of Voltaire and Pope, of Queen Anne, and the French Regent. They flit airily through Marmontel's "Moral Tales," they are the gods *and* the machines in "The Rape of the Lock," they were the tormentors and the consolers of the Rosicrucians. It would be so easy to account for Rosalba's innate distinction, her patrician quality, her rare good fortune, and extraordinary success by imputing it to the guardian sylphs. If she had been chosen by these gentle spirits devoted to the service of the young and lovely of the late "fair sex" to preserve as in a magic mirror the last incarnation of Venetian beauty, she could not have been more fitly endowed. Gifts of the sylphs might have been her daintiness, her passion for pretty things, for birds and flowers, her steady, clever head; her gentle heart framed for family tendernesses and pieties but cool to love as that of any Undine, and her quick, deft fingers—"*véritable doigts de fée*," as they were often called. If we could only accept the theory of the sylphs' guardianship how naturally we could account for that grace which charmed her sitters: the touch of Correggiosity in her silvery tones, and enchanting lighting, the innocence and serenity of her youthful heads, the seductive suavity that envelops her work like a spell which blinded fellow painters, acute critics, and rigorous Academicians to its defects and weaknesses. It was as if she had been borne in a dream by her attendant sylphs, like Prudhon's sleeping Psyche, into the fairyland of the magician of Parma. Correggio should have been indulgent to sprites and their wards, for his own angels and *putti* and cherubim seem to have been summoned from Oberon's realm to soar and float and sail on tossing carrier-clouds across the frescoed heavens of his domes.

Siora Rosalba would have smiled at such fantastic nonsense, as she doubtless did at the eccentricities of her friends, the Gozzis, Carlo and Gaspare. She would have thought, though she was too modest to say so, that her fairy godmothers were her talent and her will; she might have added her plainness and her poverty. For Rosalba who so loved beauty, and made it her business to beautify other people, had but a small share of comeliness herself. Consequently life was immensely simplified for her. Beauty is a drawback to achievement in certain arts and professions. Its possession complicates the worker's problems, it is a handicap in careers where personal appearance is not a factor. Like all precious possessions, beauty demands care and consumes time and strength; it is always a preoccupation, sometimes even an occupation; its possessor is constantly tempted to lean too heavily on it, and to count on it as a substitute for something else—hard work for instance. In Rosalba's case plainness and poverty were spurs to her ambition, and were active agents in the development of talent and character.

II

Rosalba's talent may have been hereditary, for her paternal grandfather was a painter; her character was assuredly a direct inheritance from her father, Andrea Carriera of Chioggia. Like Duke Rinaldo, he was the father of three daughters. Unlike the duke, he was a poor man earning a small salary as steward of the Procurator Bon, and though later he may have occupied more important positions in the service of the Republic, his means were always straitened, and the future of his three girls probably preoccupied him. To provide for it he dowered them handsomely with an education more solid and brilliant than that of most great ladies. How it was managed with Andrea's scanty resources is not known, but Rosalba, Giovanna, and Angela studied Latin, French, and Italian literature, and became accomplished musicians, Giovanna a fine singer, and Rosalba a proficient with the violin and the harpsichord. Their mother, Alba Foresti, the daughter of a Venetian wood-seller, was a lace-maker, and her work may have eked out the family income. Rosalba, who was born in 1675, when hardly more than a baby, by drawing pictures in her lesson-books, early chose her walk in life. Giuseppe Diamantini, and later his disciple Balestra, were her first masters, and she followed the usual course of Italian art study *in bottega*, doing the humble tasks and the toilsome drudgery that has fallen to the lot of the painter's apprentice ever since Buffalmacco set colored cubes for Cimabue. It was eminently practical, this art education, designed to provide the student with a means of livelihood. It ignored the fostering of personality, and was unconcerned about temperament, solely intent as it was on developing the *means* of *expressing* personality, and of providing a *vehicle* for the *manifestation* of temperament. If the teaching was rather inflexible and exacting, by declining to accept intentions in lieu of performance, and concentrating effort on the mastery of technic, it disciplined the will, cultivated the habit of industry, and furnished the young artist with the practice and the tools of his trade. Rosalba had been painting in oil for some time, and was already earning by copying pictures, an art industry that has flourished in Italy ever since she has had old masters to copy, when the great demand for it tempted her to study miniature painting, probably in 1698. Restricted as was this field, there was in it opportunity for originality in choice of subject, and in treatment. Rosalba was well equipped; under Balestra she had been painting life-size heads constantly, and by her studio-training had acquired the ease and freedom of execution characteristic of the Venetian school. Probably Felice Ramelli, a canon of the Lateran, an old friend of her father's, and a kind adviser and counsellor of Rosalba, was her master in miniature painting. She showed singular aptitude, and in 1704, before she reached her thirtieth year, was classed among the well-known miniaturists. Some of her orders were amusingly characteristic of a period which considered painting as a craft (*arte*). Antonio Orsetti of Lucca wished to exchange two pairs of gloves, and two perfumed sachets embroidered by nuns, for his own portrait on ivory, and Conte Caldana, while thanking her for a Madonna just received, asks her to find him a young painter who can copy landscapes and historical subjects to decorate a hall in Caldana's castle. For twenty ducats a year, his board, and outings with his patron on holidays, the artist is to work as hard as he can; and when guests are entertained to act as waiter and boatman! One wonders if Rosalba was able to find a youth at once so gifted and so amiable.

The immense popularity of snuff-boxes afforded unlimited opportunity for miniature painting. Costly boxes, not for tobacco only, were in the hands of all people of fashion, and jewels, enamels, and precious stones were lavished in decorating these tiny receptacles for snuff, sweetmeats, patches, and scents. Finally, to add to their value, small paintings were set on or inside the lids; sometimes there was a double cover, and by pressing a spring the outer one flew back disclosing a hidden portrait, a contrivance suggestive of romance. And the miniature in its jewelled setting was not only an indispensable property in every love-drama, it was an obligatory marriage gift, and a symbol of royal favor. The presentation of *boîtes aux portraits* of reigning sovereigns to diplomats, envoys, and courtiers was a part of ceremonial usage at Court. There were everywhere these "pictures in little," in bracelets and brooches, in boudoirs and oratories; they found a place on every toilet-table, and even nestled in the powdered curls of the elaborate coiffure, and when the century waxed sentimental every "delicate female," if not every "man of feeling," was obliged to carry about a collection of miniatures, not only of relatives and friends, but even of defunct patched, the signora finishes her toilet, and be-pearled and brocaded passes to her harpsichord to the study of a new toccata by Galuppi or an aria of Scarlatti. There were no books in the Venetian *mundus muliebris*, but a-plenty of violas, violins, and MS. music. But the eighteenth-century Venetian is not a home body like her grandmother, and Rosalba shows her ready for mass in the half-alluring, half-repelling *zendàdo*, or dressed for a walk in the Piazza with a pert tricorn on her unpowdered hair, or in kerchief and shepherdess's hat with a bunch of field flowers at her breast, and a basket of fruit on her arm after a stroll through garden or orchard.

Longhi, in his portrayal of Venetian high life, had but to amplify the theme, to set the scenery and add the other actors; the *cavaliere e la dama*, especially *la dama*, the type of the Venetian, of the enchantresses of Rousseau, the pretty rakes of Casanova, the engaging great ladies of Des Brosses, was found and fixed by Rosalba. Her portraiture of mature men was less successful; boys with their mothers still in them, youths softened almost into femininity by curled and powdered periwigs, by the folds of satins and laces, were within her scope. Princelings like the beautiful, grave little Louis XV, the pretty, sulky-looking grandson of Augustus the Strong, the proud, stiff child covered with stars and ribbons and orders, Duke, later Cardinal, of York, are characterized and individual as indeed are the portraits of Metastasio, the mischievous-looking young noble of the Dresden Gallery, and the subtle Procurator di San Marco, weighed down by his huge wig and voluminous draperies. Still life and flowers are painted with a careful brush—these indeed might be the work of complaisant sylphs; and delineated with equal diligence and fidelity is the fauna of this little world: the goldfinch perched on a taper finger, the parrot leaning forward from the back of his mistress's chair to listen to her playing or to tweak her fichu, doves nestled in girls' arms, a rabbit at home in a satin lap, a pug dog or a monkey couched in silks and laces. Pets, flowers, and hands were extras, in Rosalba's tariff of prices, and she earned her money when she painted them.

III

Rosalba's sitters were of all ranks and nationalities. During the whole course of the eighteenth century Venice was a cosmopolis, an oasis of peace and order in a distracted Europe. The officers of the continental armies found there not only an asylum but elegance and amusement as well. Like the Paris of Daudet's "*Rois en Exile*," Venice was a refuge for deposed monarchs and rulers temporarily out of work; it was a favorite station of the foreign traveller, a Corinth of pleasure-seekers, and a sanctuary for adventurers of all kinds, from Longo to John Law. The English were already marking

Venice for their own æsthetically, and English officials, tourists, and amateurs were notable patrons of the latest Italian art—that of Rosalba, Longhi, Canaletto, and Guardi. Rosalba's young fame attracted the attention of Cole, an English art-lover and an amateur artist in pastel. She painted his portrait in miniature, and later encouraged by his enthusiasm and practical advice, took up the study of pastel, profiting by the leisure of a *villeggiatura* to essay portraiture in this facile and ingratiating medium in which Rosalba discovered an even greater brilliancy and *morbidezza* than in *gouache:* the same color, flower-like or gem-like, plus a velvety surface that caressed while it captivated the eye. From *gouache* (*guazzo*), opaque water-color, to pastel was but a step, as *gouache* becomes pastel when gum or glue has given it solidity and hardened it. The old masters employed these colored chalks in their sketches and cartoons; a few traces of it remain in those of Leonardo, Mantegna, Correggio, Barrucio, and Guido Reni. The use of pastel, however, was limited, and wisely, too, perhaps in view of its fragility, to preparatory sketches and to slight retouches in fresco-painting; Mignard in his "Paradise" on the dome of Val-de-Grâce depended on this fugitive medium for certain effects of color and perspective with disastrous results, after the dampness had done its usual work.

The pastel portrait was more stable. Nanteuil, the great engraver, had popularized it, Lebrun,

Vivien, and the Italian Tempesta had developed its resources, and in Florence Giovanna Fratellini, the miniature painter, was already pleasing amateurs with her pastel portraits when Rosalba tried her novice hand on them with immediate and brilliant results. The modulated harmonies of the older school were dulled by the freshness, brilliancy, and transparency of her color; the *sfumatura*, the *chiaroscuro* la Carriera loved lent a mirage-like effect to her figures, veiled their weaknesses of drawing and lack of modelling. Their bright, soft color so seduced the eye that pastels became a passion all through the eighteenth century, and a successful rival to Rosalba's own miniatures. Fortunately, for even with help Rosalba was finding miniature painting tiring to her eyes, in pastel the strain was less severe, and the freer handling and larger size of the figures made the portraits seem more important. In a couple of years the vogue of Rosalba's pastels rivalled that of her miniatures, she was hailed as "*la prima pittrice d'Italia*," and her name crossed the Alps. She was evidently naturally deft in her use of the colored crayons, for one of her first essays, a girl's head that she sent to Bologna, was greatly esteemed. In answer to an admirer who in a burst of enthusiasm exclaimed, "How fortunate will be the artist who marries Rosalba!" Lo Spagnuolo, the painter, replied, "To match her properly we should have to bring Guido Reni back to life," which was more of a eulogy in 1703 than it would be to-day.

It was, however, a miniature that Rosalba sent to Rome when, thanks to the canvassing of Mr. Cole and Carlo Maratta's praises of her work, she was elected to membership in the Academy of San Luca (1705). The miniature on ivory represented a girl in white with a dove in her hand, a difficult and delicate color study. In Maratta's handwriting on the frame we can still read: "*La presente miniatura è stata fatta dall'insigne miniatrice Rosalba Carriera, veneziana, sopra lastra di perfetto avorio, il colore del quale è servita di mezzatinta con stupore dell'arte.*"

Rosalba was busy painting English travellers when she received the news of her election, for Cole's friends, fired by his enthusiasm, made pilgrimages to Venice to sit for their portraits. Those who could not come to the artist sent her commissions for pictures of mythological or sacred subjects. One David Roberts begged her to paint a sleeping Venus for him on ivory, "as nude as her conscience would permit." The English were not Rosalba's only foreign patrons; the war of the Spanish succession brought as many diplomats as soldiers to Venice, and almost as many potentates as diplomats. Among them were admirers and purchasers of Rosalba's work; her arch-patron, however, was the hero of a hundred fights and twice as many gallant adventures, Augustus II, the Strong, Elector of Saxony, and King of Poland. This battered Prince Charming fell in love with Rosalba's talent. He was as devoted to pretty things as to pretty women, and capitulated at once to the attractions of her nymphs and fine ladies, and as Augustus the Strong, sire of Maurice de Saxe, great-great-grandfather of George Sand, did not love or admire tepidly, we owe the only collection of Rosalba's work, that of the Dresden Gallery, to his *grande passion*. He was phenomenally faithful all his life, and handed on his infatuation to his son and grandson. At one time, through the crown prince, he tried to monopolize Rosalba's pictures, and secure her output for a number of years. Yet discreet Rosalba never included the Court of Dresden in her triumphal progresses, for Augustus was a heart—as well as a city—taker; he was one of the handsomest as well as the strongest men of his time, and many strenuous years had but seasoned and mellowed him. When he went awooing, the critical little Princess Wilhelmina, daughter of the King of Prussia, sister of Frederick the Great, found him attractive though he was fifty-eight years old, had a harem, three hundred and fifty-four natural children (he brought several of them with him to present to his betrothed, as specimens probably), and an open wound in his foot, though he stood on it valiantly when etiquette demanded. "He was rather broken for his age," but "his port and mien" were majestic as well as jovial, the princess recorded, evidently much impressed by her overripe suitor. He said many kind things to her, and perhaps during his stay she had enough to eat. This may be a rash supposition, for when her father, Frederick William, who habitually half-starved his family, gave Augustus II a banquet nine hours long, the Queen and the royal children were thriftily excluded from the board. Perhaps Wilhelmina, shabby, hungry, and half-frozen, inured to harsh words and blows from her royal sire, had heard of the Gargantuan good cheer of Augustus's Court, and the hope of being well-fed biassed her judgment; in any case, she was sorry when politics prevented the match.

Augustus's envoy to Rosalba was his only legitimate son, the crown prince, who visited Venice in 1712-15-17. Rosalba painted him several times, once in oil, periwigged and red-coated; he was a very pretty boy, and a constant visitor to Rosalba's studio during his sojourns in Venice; he had not, however, inherited his father's geniality, and the French Duchesse de Berri thought him dull and ill-bred when she was commissioned by Louis XIV to do the honors of Marly. He was mute when they climbed the hill together, and his governor had to shout to him several times to give his hand to the *duchesse*, which he finally did in silence. When they reached the summit she said jestingly: "This would be a good place to play blind man's buff." The prince opened his mouth for the first time to say rather eagerly, "I will play willingly," and spent the rest of the afternoon doing so without paying the slightest attention to his hostess. Yet Rosalba, whom "good fortune permitted to know him, and to know him well," considered him "one of the most generous, kind, and pious princes that have ever lived." The boy who was shy and stupid with the vivacious Duchesse de Berri, probably was less timid and dumb with his simple-mannered hostesses and their pets. Each of his Venetian visits meant sales and orders for Rosalba and her sisters, and after he assumed the cares of state, which he wore as lightly as his Court finery, he sent the Comte de Brühl, his worthy prime minister, the statesman of so many wigs and so few brains, owner of three hundred snuff-boxes with canes and costumes to match them, to purchase for him. In Rosalba's studio the crown prince had found himself in noble as well as good company. Roaming royalty was eager to be painted, to carry home its own portrait with the Greek vases, Roman coins, Maltese lap-dogs, MS. music, chapelmasters, antique marbles carefully repaired, Bolognese-school pictures of sentimental saints, and lusty, sprawling martyrs—the junk and the treasure that an inexhaustible Italy offered her enamored invaders.

Maximilian II of Bavaria, a refugee in Venice after Hochstadt (1704), ordered not only his own portrait of Rosalba but those of several Venetian ladies. His example was followed by Christian Louis, of Mecklenberg, and by Charles VI, Elector

Palatine; they found Rosalba's studio an attractive spot, and Mecklenberg, who played the viola well enough for a prince probably but badly for a Venetian, often tried his hostess's patience by begging her to accompany him on the violin. In 1709 Rosalba received another illustrious visitor, the Count of Oldenburg, otherwise Frederick IV, King of Norway and Denmark, who promptly followed the example of his predecessors, sat for his portrait, and ordered those of twelve fair Venetians. Some of them refused to form part of the royal collection, but they were the exceptions; pretty ladies, like nice customs, generally courtesy to great Kings. Who were they, these pretty ladies, and where are their portraits? Some of them have melted away like "*les neiges d'antan*," others remain faded like the roses of yesteryear. The list of names evokes memories of dead glories: Cornaro, Correr, Foscari, Zenobia, the Maria Labia, much admired by Des Brosses; the *Procuratessa* Lucrezia Mocenigo, "*la Mocenigo delle perle*" as she was called from the big pearls that were family heirlooms, which she always wore, and Isabella Pisani, whose portrait so pleased the painter of it that Rosalba kept it always in her own room. Catarina Barbarigo, with a three-cornered hat cocked saucily on her dark curls, Camilla Minelli, la Recanati, still bloom like pale-tinted flowers, frost-touched, in the Dresden Gallery.

There was work for a year or two ahead at least,

and Rosalba's studio bade fair to become a *bottega*, when, as always in time of stress, one of her assistants failed; Angela, the prettiest, tallest, liveliest of the three sisters married. Her choice was a happy one, highly approved by her family, who gained an affectionate son and a helpful brother in the painter Antonio Pellegrini. He was one of those prodigies of the Italian decadence, a *Fa Presto*, who covered numberless ells of walls and ceilings with huge, gesticulating, well-fed figures, not too ill-drawn, not badly composed, not disagreeable in color, but utterly void of significance, originality, or invention. Pellegrini and his fellows filled his vast spaces from the overflowing horn of plenty of the great Italian masters. With such examples he could not go absolutely wrong, his work was never offensively bad, it was only tiresome, as even a far better imitation than his of a fine model is fated to be; but, like many hard-working and ambitious painters, he had not discovered that greatness is not attained by drinking from a large glass, even when that beaker was once the property of the illustrious. If Pellegrini lacked talent, he possessed industry, enormous facility, perfect health, with its attendant good spirits, a love of enterprise and adventure. Into the quiet little household he came like a fresh breeze from the Lido; Andrea Carriera was in ill health, and Pellegrini was a revelation of the ideal eternal masculine, of its energy, geniality, and initiative, to the busy women of his new family. He was adored by them all, even by his wife, whom he never ceased to amuse, and who called him her *burattino* for his ceaseless activity and his rollicking humor. The wedding fluttered the dove-cot, work was laid aside *pro tem* for toil over clothes and sweetmeats. Canon Ramelli wrote his regrets that he could not contribute his specialty, an omelet with sausages, to the wedding feast, but promised one for the first baptism. Malamani describes a pleasant evening at home in *casa Carriera*. Andrea reading by the lamp, the amiable, industrious mamma bent over her embroidery, Rosalba at the harpsichord, the young couple chatting, and Giovanna dozing in her armchair. No wonder she was sleepy, for Giovanna, or Zuaneta as Venice softened her name, or Neneta in the caressing domestic diminutive, had risen at dawn, gone to early mass, to market, and then to visit her poor people. On her return home she had ordered dinner, made up the family accounts, mended the household linen, cut out costumes for a masquerade, and perhaps rubbed in a background or copied a drapery for Rosalba. Poor Neneta had surely earned the right to nap in peace, but not in the family circle; she moans, nods, makes faces, and opens her eyes with a sudden start to find them all laughing at her; she slips away to the kitchen to drink some strong coffee, and returns resolved to keep awake. Of course she is soon asleep again, and Pellegrini seizes the opportunity to draw her usually pretty, delicate face, now grimacing and distorted by uneasy slumber. A loud burst of laughter greets his finished caricature and awakens his model, who expostulates, abuses the drawing, upbraids the artist, and ends by laughing heartily with the others.

The jovial Pellegrini soon carried Angela off to England and Rosalba and Neneta were left with too much work to allow them time to miss her and her *burattino*. The procession of visitors to the studio continued. More noteworthy even than royalties were the scholars and collectors and literati who came to the little house between the Mula and the Venier palaces; among them was the generous Mæcenas, Pierre Crozat, called in Paris "*Crozat le pauvre*," because he possessed only a few millions and to distinguish him from his rich brother Antoine, the founder of the colony of Louisiana. Pierre, however, was as generous and open-handed as though he were "*Crozat le riche*." His were also what St. Francis called "the riches of the spirit"; he was the patron, or rather the friend and comrade of artists and savants. Mariette and Caylus were his gossips, Watteau his commensal, and when the painter Lafosse died in the service of Crozat, his widow and grandniece became part of his patron's household, who, not content with domesticating the arts, extended his hospitality to their followers. Crozat was not only the richest, most enthusiastic, most enlightened collector in Europe, whose gallery and antiquities were known and envied by all connoisseurs, he was also desirous of popularizing his treasures and of placing them at the disposal of artlovers and students. He had come to Italy to augment his collections of drawings of old masters, and of coins and medals. The former had been commenced at the instigation of Mariette, and the opportunity was vast; for the drawings of the great masters were not prized by those who valued and, in many instances, overvalued their pictures, and generally had remained in the artists' families, among other old papers.

Crozat fell under the spell of Rosalba's crayons and her engaging personality. He did not admire calmly, but, with something of the *furia francese* Italians had learned to expect from Frenchmen, proposed that Rosalba should come to Paris at once as his guest, she and her whole family. An apartment in his house should be at her disposition, a studio made ready, a carriage placed at her commands; fame and fortune awaited her, all Paris would strive to be painted by her, and just across the Channel was England, a country of gold, where more could be earned in one year than in a decade elsewhere.

When to these tempting offers, repeated in writing after Crozat's return to Paris, were added the enthusiastic descriptions of a young Italian noble to whom Rosalba had given a letter of introduction to Crozat, and who had been most hospitably received by him, the painter's hesitations vanished. The splendors of Crozat's palaces, his agreeable household, his magnificent entertainments, his hosts of distinguished friends, his bountiful and tactful hospitality! Young Recanati could talk of nothing else, and the quiet household was fired by his enthusiasm and began to consider seriously a journey to France, no slight undertaking for an invalid, an old lady, and two women who had never left Venetian soil. An order for the decoration of the ceiling in the great hall of the Royal Bank in Paris, given to Pellegrini by John Law, decided the matter.

Law had visited Rosalba's studio in 1716, when he was a refugee from English justice. His offense was a venial one, judged by contemporary codes—killing his adversary in a duel. After his escape from prison he wandered about the Continent seeking his fortune, and finding it at the gaming-tables of Geneva, Venice, and Genoa. He was a handsome man, the son of a rich Edinburgh jeweller and banker, who left him a large fortune, soon gambled away, and the recently acquired title of Baron of Lauriston. Law was well educated, had pursued scientific studies, was a born mathematician, and owed many of his successes at pharaon and basset to his capacity for "lightning calculations." He became deeply interested in the methods of the famous bank of Amsterdam, of whose credit system he perceived at once the many advantages in economy, facility, and safety, and conceived the idea of extending it universally.

Law, who has often been represented, or rather misrepresented as a mere adventurer, was in reality an ancestor of our financiers, and many of his ideas have been applied in the modern banking system. He first tested and proved the potentialities of credit, and if the abuse of it was largely the cause of Law's disastrous failure in France, the universal fever of speculation in all classes, and the brutal greed of the great nobles whom he was forced finally to gorge with gold also counted for much. When the phantasmagoria of riches faded away, the sane and practical elements in the system remained, a handful of precious metal at the bottom of the crucible, after the enchanter and the vision had vanished.

Law after his sojourn in Amsterdam returned to Scotland, hoping to apply the principles he had discovered in Holland, but he was young and inexperienced, his canny country folk were incredulous; rebuffed, he applied to the Regent, hospitable to novelties, but the old Louis XIV would not hear a word from "a Huguenot." Law repulsed by the King, revenged himself on the nobles, winning such huge sums from them that he was ordered to leave Paris within twenty-four hours. He took up his wandering life again, expounding his theories to various royalties with no success, meanwhile placing a fortune of two millions of francs in France. After the death of Louis XIV he drifted back to

Paris, welcomed by the Regent, whose easy confidence he had already won. France was deep in debt; the wars of Louis XIV had left her almost bankrupt, with her population diminished, her industry languishing, and her soil impoverished. The Regent had dabbled in alchemy, and vainly sought the philosopher's stone; he listened eagerly to the wizard who promised to change paper into gold, and was an easy convert to Law's famous "System." After various successful *coups* he was made a Catholic and *Comptrôleur général des finances*, and enabled to work out his theories on a colossal scale. The debts of the state were paid in paper money issued by the new Royal Bank and these notes were supposed to represent the value of land in Louisiana, Mississippi (which many believed to be an island), and Senegal. The Royal Bank which had taken possession of the rich *Compagnie des Indes*, founded by Colbert, at first prospered famously, and an immense quantity of its paper was soon put in circulation to meet the public demand. We have become familiar with extraordinary exhibitions of greed and credulity, provoked by "frenzied finance," but this was France's first attack of speculation fever, and she soon became delirious. Law was the idol of Paris, the proudest nobles crowded his offices, the greatest ladies struggled for his favors. One of them, desiring to make his acquaintance, ordered her coachman to overturn her carriage in front of his house.

She was obeyed, the financier came to the rescue, and the lady confessed that she had taken these desperate means to meet him. Madame Palatine says that when the Regent was looking for a duchess to accompany his daughter to Modena, a courtier told him: "You can take your choice at Madame Law's house; all the duchesses are there."

At the height of his popularity (1719), wishing to decorate the great hall of the bank, Law remembered Pellegrini, whom he had met in London while the artist was painting in St. Paul's, and made a contract with him to begin work in Paris the following spring. It was a small caravan therefore that left Venice in March (1720) for the great adventure of a journey to France: the three Carrieras (Andrea had died after four months' illness the previous April, 1719), Pellegrini, Angela, and the family friend, Conte Antonio Maria Zanetti.

Zanetti belonged to the race of artist-connoisseurs who have been, ever since the Renaissance, the treasurers of Italy's artistic wealth. Born in Venice in 1680, a few years younger than Rosalba, he had made her acquaintance in their student days, an acquaintance that rapidly bloomed into a devoted and enduring friendship. After he finished his art studies in the Academy of Bologna, he spent two years in travel, and was recalled to Venice by the death of his father and the necessity of earning a livelihood. For many years he divided his time between his ledgers and his engraving. Most of the large fortune he acquired was spent on his collections, and he lived very frugally in his great palace, piling up treasures: antique gems, drawings, pictures, and engravings. A French traveller, Clément, laments the numbing cold of the stately rooms in January, where "according to the custom of the country no fire was ever lighted." The shivering visitor, forerunner of the modern tourist who is soon *frappé* in Italian galleries, had admired cameos for two hours in a polar temperature when he besought Zanetti to have pity on him as he was freezing. "Do you know what he did?" wrote Clément; "this is not a joke; he had some fire brought to me on a plate! I almost swallowed the coals!"

Zanetti was an engraver as well as a collector. During his sojourn in England in 1720–1 he discovered in the Arundel collection and purchased the drawings of Parmigiano, stolen, Vasari tells us, from that master two hundred years before, by a dishonest pupil. Zanetti revived the wood engraving with four blocks, invented by Ugo da Carpi, which was reputed a lost art, and so highly prized in England that Zanetti was encouraged to essay it, and after many experiments he published facsimiles of his Parmigiano drawings engraved in this manner (1743). The revival of Carpi's processes, though too expensive and difficult to become popular, added greatly to Zanetti's reputation. He was an indefatigable worker, yet his business, his art studies, and experiments, his travels, his constant entertainment of distinguished strangers—for every savant and artist who came to Venice visited the host and the collections of *casa Zanetti*—all these multifarious occupations never prevented his visits to Rosalba's studio, or his letters to her during his tours. He was also included in Crozat's generous invitation, so it was natural that this old and tried friend should join the travellers. Journeys were long and often tedious, there was time to spare for cosey talks, for evening stories around the inn fireside; the more society the better, for privations and hardships born in common were more easily endured, and the companionship of a cultivated man of the world, who was also an artist, was appreciated by ladies errant.

Rosalba when she left Venice in quest of new fortunes was in the forty-sixth year of her age, and the seventeenth of her vogue as a fashionable portrait-painter. She was a member of two famous Italian academies, those of Rome and Bologna; she was a European celebrity, respected even by those who did not admire her work, envied by mediocre painters, often overestimated by her abler fellow craftsmen. Pure in her life and honorable in her business relations, she was at once *honnête femme et honnête homme*.

As an artist her success had been constant. Her sitters and patrons became and remained her friends; if her work aroused admiration her character retained it, and she cultivated her friendships carefully; letters, messages, and gifts sweetened and strengthened her social relations. Like most successful portrait-painters she was something of a diplomat, and undoubtedly owed much of her popularity to her tact; but she was too fundamentally sincere to be a courtier, and her correspondence bears witness to her frankness at crucial moments. If she was an unusually attractive person, and there is every reason to believe that she was, her appeal was to the mind and heart. She was not pretty, but in Italy as well as in France "*le charme prime la beauté*," and of charm Rosalba had enough and to spare. To-day we should consider her fine-looking, rather handsome; but her type of face, thoughtful, intelligent, full of character, differed so essentially from the standard of her time that her marked departure from it was accounted plainness. The contrast between her own appearance and that of her sitters, of her portraits of herself and her ideal heads edged the essential difference of type. Time has its revenges, and to-day we prefer Rosalba's pastel of herself as "Winter" to many of her beauties and fine ladies. But when the eighteenth century was young, reflection or decision was as marring a defect in a woman's face as a squint or a scar, and gravity was as much disliked as flippancy was prized. When the Emperor Charles VI said after Rosalba was presented to him: "*Bertoli mio, questa tua pittrice sarà valente ma molto brutta!*" he was probably astonished at the contrast between the animated, gypsy face of the painter and the porcelain-smooth, conventional prettiness of her Muses and Seasons. Her plainness had so many mitigating circumstances, that it might more reasonably be called comeliness, "item: two gray eyes," clear and keen; "item: two lips indifferent red," perhaps, but sensitive, and delicately sinuous, a slightly aquiline nose, a well-turned, wilful, deeply cleft chin, with a rounded but beautifully clean-cut line from it to the ear. Her forearm and hand were lovely, especially the latter, with its long, taper, deft fingers, and her neck and shoulders were plump and dimpled. She was short, and in her maturity rather thick-set, like most women of unusual vital force; and of course she desired to be tall, and propped herself up on high heels. She loved to wear fine and delicate clothes as well as to paint them, and all the portraits of herself are tastefully costumed. The earliest of these, painted after 1701, of which the original is lost, and only the engraving in color of Bartolozzi remains, might be the Rosaura or Mirandolina of a Goldoni play; it is the typical young Venetian girl, vivacious and coquettish with her striped corsage, a delicate gold chain threaded here and there with pearls on her neck, a fan in her hand, and the black silk *zendà* covering her head, falling on her shoulders, and tied at the waist. A later portrait painted by Bombelli for the Academy of San Luca, in Rome, is older, darker, and much more grave;

in it Rosalba holds a nosegay of flowers to her bosom, and seems sadly reflecting on their fragility. Another portrait, in the Hall of the Painters in the Uffizi, of Rosalba with a drawing of her sister Giovanna in one hand, and a crayon-holder in the other, has been so barbarously restored that it has no iconographic value.

The best painted and characterized portrait of Rosalba is the pastel of 1731, one of the "Four Seasons," ordered by Charles VI. The painter, then fifty-six years old, in a blue gown with a Polish cap and mantle of white fur flecked with black, is the "Winter" of the series. Winter truly, but with its glow and sparkle, its crisp snow-white, its cold sky-blues, and its garnered fruits. The faint touches of time on Rosalba's face, the little lines between the brows and about the mouth, delicate as frost breath on a window-pane; the slight flattening of the well-rounded cheek, the subtle modelling of life and experience on human clay Rosalba could indicate in a portrait of herself without fear or reproach. Young still is the low, broad brow, the short Italian oval of the face, clear and penetrating the blue-gray eyes that had looked on so much vanity and remained candid. And just as in this high-hearted, hard-working daughter of the people there was always the love of elegance and luxury, so even in these exquisite and austere harmonies of blues, grays, and whites there is the Venetian touch of gold and pearl, in the Oriental embroidery of the fur-trimmed cap, and in the moon-tinted jewels in Rosalba's ears. What Venetian was ever painted without her pearls! Diana could as easily renounce her bow, or St. Catherine her wheel.

Rosalba also drew her own psychoportrait, as we barbarously term it, in her journals, notes, and letters. This mass of papers, with a drawing-book containing sixty-seven pen-and-pencil sketches, piously preserved in their old house in Chioggia by Angela and Giovanna Pedrotti, Rosalba's heirs, was presented by them to Don Giovanni Vianelli, canon of the Cathedral of Chioggia, thirty-odd years after Rosalba's death.

From this collection of documents Vianelli selected for publication (Venice, 1793) Rosalba's journal written during her stay in Paris (1720-21). He was a careless, and from a historical point of view an unscrupulous editor, confusing dates, distorting names, and obscuring the meaning of the original by his jumbled entries and fragments of correspondence. His real object in publishing the journal was to advertise the collection of autograph letters that he had received with it; his plan proved successful, and he sold all the MSS. soon afterwards to the collector Clementino Tomitano for his famous library at Oderzo. There they were classified, annotated, and bound in five volumes, four filled with the letters of Rosalba's correspondents, the fifth containing her own notes, minutes for letters, appointments, receipts, diaries, reflections, sonnets, verses, and several lively and picturesque letters of Giovanna Carriera to her mother. From the library at Oderzo these volumes passed into the hands of the well-known dealer in incunabula and MSS., Guglielmo Libri, then into those of Lord Ashburnham, who buried them in his huge collection at Battle Hastings.

In 1865 Alfred Sensier published a French translation of Rosalba's Paris journal accompanied by notes, letters, her will in Italian and French and some unpublished documents relating to the artists and art amateurs of the period. The notes on the Parisians and the Paris of the Regency were scholarly and illuminating, the letters were those already published by Vianelli or Bottari, and the translation of the journal was very faulty, and sometimes misleading. Rosalba's record of her sittings, appointments, sightseeing, and visits were hastily jotted down during a year of great activity, of unremitting work and social dissipation. These rough notes can hardly be called a journal, but were rather memoranda for future reference. In her haste the painter often fell into vernacular Venetian, and so disguised the names of her illustrious sitters by her Italian pronunciation and phonetic spelling that Sensier's corrections and biographical sketches are truly enlightening, while his publication of Rosalba's will, discrediting the popular legend regarding her old age, was a precious addition to her biography.

Sensier had sought long and vainly for the Rosalban MSS. hidden in the Ashburnham library and reputed lost; it was not until after the death of Lord Ashburnham that they were bought by the Italian Government, and were assigned finally (1881) to the Laurentian Library in Florence. In 1899 the "*Gallerie Nazionali Italiane*" published a certain number of the letters, the most valuable historically and artistically, selected by Rosalba's latest biographer, Vittorio Malamani. They introduce us to a strong yet winning personality, surrounded by an interesting group of cultivated, amiable people, who are also musicians, poets, and painters, well-bred folk who consort with princes and millionaires without losing their self-respect, and become friends but never favorites of the great. A glimpse is afforded of that quiet, laborious, comfortable life of the Venetian *borghesi*, that *mezzoceto* and lesser nobility from which so many artists sprang; Goldoni who transported it to the stage, Longhi who illustrated it, Guardi and Canaletto and Bellotto who found in its marvellous setting inspiration and subject; the Gozzis who never strayed far from it either in satire or fairy-tale. They seem curiously *bourgeois*, these children of Apollo, industrious, tranquil-minded people, simple in their habits, frugal in their living. They are commercial and Philistine from an up-to-date art student's point of view, unconscious of the possession of genius, manifesting no signs of temperament except in their work. They are tamely conventional in their habits (the Gozzis excepted), these innovators in the arts, and seekers after novelty only in material and technic. A quiet, domestic, busy life was the ideal of these humdrum folk, seasoned with delicate pleasures; a concert *al fresco*, a day in the groves and gardens of the mainland, playing at sonnet-making on winter evenings, a stroll *in Piazza* among the masks and the dancers, a christening, or a wedding-dinner. Venice herself was a feast in the days of royal and ducal progresses, of magnificent church festivals, and of public holidays. To perpetuate some aspect of this spectacle, instead of merely surrendering soul and senses to the environing magic, artists needed a steady head and a disciplined will. There were sirens on every side, tempting them to waste of time and strength and substance. Fortune enticed them with hopes of sudden gain in the Ridotto, the tinkle of Folly's bells was always close at their ear, yet they remained attentive spectators only of the carnival of Venice, watching the gorgeous pageant as it flowed past their studio windows, sensitive to its beauty, penetrated by its charm, but as alien to its idleness and frivolity as to the judgments and decrees of the mysterious Three. Tiepolo, the greatest, indeed the only great Venetian of the decadent century, though he had a wife who risked his earnings at gaming, was the most indefatigable worker of them all.

Industry, simplicity, gayety, gentleness were the characteristics of these artists who rubbed elbows with the discrowned monarchs of "*Candide*," Casanova's nuns disguised as dashing cavaliers, Jean Jacque's little grisettes, Des Brosses's patricians and courtesans, the pampered prima donnas of St. Didier, the gamesters of the Ridotto, the spies and *bravi* of the Council of Ten, the masquerading beggars of Da Ponte, the dupes of Law, Marcello's threadbare poets and spoiled dancers, the free-living great ladies with their *casini* and *cicisbei*, the impoverished nobles who peddled their family pictures and plate to travelling *Milordi*, the *chevaliers d'industrie* with ragged shirts and cogged dice—the mimes of that marvellous theatre of intrigue and adventure—Venice. The sober, hard-working artists watched and painted the brilliant actors and their picturesque scenery, but were themselves more at home with Goldoni's "*Rusteghi*" and their womankind, prudent, amiable philosophers in farthingales like "*La Moglie Saggia.*"

A typical figure of her class and her profession was Rosalba, with its virtues and its limitations. Had she ever loved? Did she ever regret her marriage to Art? She herself does not answer this question which her biographers have asked in vain. Sensier, who adopted the national French attitude and advice in examining a woman's life and achievement: "*Cherchez l'homme*," found no lover for her. He tried conscientiously, loath to abandon a principle, to discover something more than meets the eye, in Rosalba's relations with Zanetti, but quite unsuccessfully. This old comrade of her student days was always a faithful friend, admiring, attentive, solicitous, careful even after Rosalba's death of her reputation as an artist, and of her fair fame. Rosalba in her Parisian journal mentions days of melancholy, and also records that on one occasion Zanetti also was sad. These are slender pegs on which to hang a romance; Rosalba's rare low spirits are amply accounted for by fatigue and eye-strain. A woman who constantly received and entertained visitors while at work, and who laid down her palette only to take up her pen, her violin, or a book, may naturally have paid for her constant activity by brief periods of depression. She evidently had her full share of the Italian birthright of cheerfulness, that blitheness of temper that when it was not a gift of nature was cultivated as a duty; there were few of her countrymen who pitied the gloomy folk in that particular hell-pit where Dante saw those who were sad in the sweet air punished by immersion in black mud.

Cheerfulness was made easy for Rosalba. She worked amid a chorus of bravas, she was well paid for her pains, she was able to maintain her independence, for hers was not the gilded slavery of the Court painter, and she enjoyed the most precious of all the rewards of toil, the happiness of benefiting those she loved. She was well repaid in tenderness, indeed few women have been so dear to those nearest to them. She possessed the absolute devotion of Giovanna as long as her life lasted, and died in

Angela's arms, who after her husband's death had taken Giovanna's place; Rosalba's pupils loved her, not as a mother or as a master, but as a sweet-tempered, clever comrade who had not forgotten her own youth. Indeed friendship, filial and fraternal affection so filled Rosalba's heart that in it passion found no place. Her art made large demands on her, and her life was so crowded with various interests that she literally had no time to entertain a tender flame, as her contemporaries would have called it. Her notions of love and marriage were clearly expressed in a letter addressed to a would-be suitor who had asked a friend to plead for him.

As I am obliged to leave the house and consequently to defer the honor of speaking with you, I have decided to write to you.
You surprised me very much. You could perfectly well have said to me what you entrusted to your friend, and spared me the embarrassment of seeing him inconvenienced for something that was not worth his while. He spoke so well for you that he would have persuaded me if I had been less far from any inclination to change my manner of life. My profession that occupies me so constantly, and a rather cold disposition, have hitherto kept me from thoughts of love and wedlock; I should certainly make everybody laugh heartily if now that my youth is past I should marry. Giovanna, who has always had the same intention of keeping herself free from any bond or engagement knows this [offer] but will not speak of it. I hope your friend will not either, and trust that you will believe without offence that I can never be anything but
     Your most devoted, obedient Servant,
       Rosalba Carriera.

If Rosalba had no time for love she devoted hours to the cultivation of friendship. She kept in constant touch with her friends; their joys and sorrows were never passed by in silence, and, like many diligent people, she found time for the small courtesies of life as well as the larger generosities. No artist was more munificent with his work. After every successful season gifts of pastels, miniatures, and sketches were sent to those who had obliged Rosalba in any way. Her open-handedness was sometimes exploited—by Rapparini, the agent of the Elector Palatine, for instance; but doubtless it increased her popularity. She was as generous of commendation as she was of her work, as prompt in thanks for a small kindness as in acknowledgments for important service. She was handsomely rewarded; few great artists have been so loved and esteemed. Collectors and savants like Mariette, Crozat, Caylus, Marulle, Cardinal Albani; painters, Coypel, Maratta, Vleughels, Rigaud, Watteau; men of letters, the Gozzis, Metastasio, Rossi; the musicians Marcello and Hasse were her friends and correspondents. Rosalba had, by force of character and sweetness of disposition quite as much as by her talent, made herself a place among the illustrious.

She was also singularly fortunate in her environment and in her choice of a profession. In Italy she did not defy public opinion by becoming a painter, and in earning her bread a woman broke with no tradition of her sex's proper sphere of activity; indeed, she followed an honored one. Her predecessors, Maria Robusti, Sophonisba Anguisciola, Elisabetta Sirani, painters of distinction, were examples which every ambitious girl student hoped to follow or surpass. Ages before Rosalba experimented with *gouache* and ivory, Italy had counted women not only among her artists and literati, but among her scientists and philosophers. It was not only the Bolognese Academy of Fine Arts that opened its doors to women sculptors and painters, the University boasted a long line of petticoated professors, who if their portraits were not flattered were as pleasant to contemplate as they were edifying to hear. In neighboring Florence the miniaturist, Giovanna Fratellini, was only second to Rosalba in popular estimation. As they violated no established rules, and were not in opposition to general usage, Rosalba and her sister workers were singularly free from the self-consciousness and aggressive attitude of women who are defying conventions. They had no prejudice to combat, no opposition to brave; they were not obliged to become martyrs or fighters, so that they took their tasks and their accomplishment as simply and naturally as professional men would have done. The wholesome action of enlightened opinion on the character and conduct of women workers can hardly be overestimated, and with few exceptions they were worthy of the esteem accorded them.

Rosalba's facile proficiency was not confined to

painting; she loved music and played the violin not only to accompany royalty, but well enough to take part with professional talent in the concert given by Crozat in Paris. She played the harpsichord, and one of her miniatures shows her at that instrument with an attentive and apparently appreciative parrot on the back of her chair. She tried her hand at sonnet-making also, as did most people of her acquaintance; she was deeply interested in pictures and a valiant sightseer in Paris and Vienna. Her greatest pleasure, she says, was conversation. "No one loves gayety more than I do; I try to have it at home, and to carry it wherever I go. Diversion and amusements are the best and universal remedy for our ills." Here speaks the daughter of Venice; then, fearful lest she should be misunderstood, Rosalba adds: "Nevertheless I think that pleasures should be enjoyed with great sobriety and moderation," and she shuns the society of libertines and disorderly folk. Probably for this reason the wise virgin avoided visiting the Court of her fervent admirers, Augustus II and III, and contented herself with painting Augustus II's daughter beautifully, and supplying him with a whole painted seraglio of Venetian beauties.

Like most generous and intelligent folk, Rosalba was quick-tempered and resented an imposition on her good nature. It was not always safe to ruffle this gentle creature, and on occasions she could peck as fiercely as an angry dove at an infringement of her dignity. A letter (of 1710) to Rapparini is an instance in point; Rapparini had tried vainly to induce Rosalba to visit the Court of the Elector Palatine, who greatly admired her work and who had bought several of her pictures. Rapparini had already profited largely by his handling of them, and had received several gifts from the open-handed painter. Rosalba declined the Elector's invitation, giving as an explanation, and perhaps as an admonition, that she was "too sincere to live in Courts."

Rapparini, rather piqued, replied that, he "pitied Signora Rosalba, obliged on her mother's account to stay in Venice without ever discovering that outside of the lagoons there were a world, men, and bread." To which Rosalba rejoined tartly: "You may be sure that I know that there are a world, men, and bread beyond the lagoons, but I submit to the will of heaven which has decreed that my journeys shall be only to my easel. I am contented with but little bread, while as to men, believe me there is nothing in the world that I think less of; I should not have received Signor Rapparini if I had not considered him as the husband of Signora Margarita (Rapparini's wife)." The *zitellona* was not to be trifled with, and Rapparini had some trouble to make his peace with her.

This was the painter who now sought the approval of Paris, the cap-sheaf of her successes. For in the early eighteenth century if the military glory of the great Louis was tarnished, his taste, or rather that of the artists he favored, was the *arbiter* of European elegance. The French language and literature, French architecture and gardens, French acting and manufactures, manners, and clothes were universally admired and adopted; every petty potentate aspired to a Versailles in miniature; every continental princess must have a peep at the latest French fashion-doll before ordering her new Court dress. A triumph in Paris was for a painter what a crown on the Roman Capitol was for a poet.

IV

Paris seen in historical perspective does not seem the abode of delight it appeared to Rosalba. Like all France, it was paying the costs of a half century of glory. The plague in the south was emptying towns and turning fruitful regions into desolate wastes. The bull *Unigenitus* had split the Gallican church asunder. Law's financial balloon was beginning to deflate, threatening wide-spread disaster. Present and future misery was, however, if not unknown to, at least ignored by Rosalba. What she saw was gay, brilliant, apparently prosperous, and often beautiful. She had neither time nor disposition to look below the surface; the surface only was her business. The warmth of her reception surpassed her hopes; Crozat was better than his word. The Carrieras were housed like princesses in his palace, which with its noble park and gardens occupied the site of many modern streets in the heart of Paris. Madame La Fosse, and the singer, Mademoiselle d'Argenon, who acted as hostesses in this widower's household, welcomed them warmly, and they enjoyed the comfort of a home with freedom from its cares.

Rosalba, hardly rested from the fatigues of a journey rendered unusually arduous by bad weather, began work soon after her arrival. The first entry in her journal (March, 1720) shows her busy with eleven portraits, several of the Crozat family and one of Mademoiselle d'Argenon. Her circle of sitters enlarged daily. Crozat's *protégée* was more than popular, she was fashionable; *the* fashion, like Law's *système* and the hoop-skirt. A less steady head than Rosalba's would have been turned by such rapid and universal success. She remained simple, and steadfast, apparently unaffected by her good fortune. Not a sentence in her correspondence or her journal would indicate that she was a petted, flattered artist with the great world of a great city for her eager clientèle.

In June (the 14th) the greatest gentleman of France gave her his first sitting. The solemn, rather stolid little King, then ten years old, was an excellent model, wearing his brocade coat, his ermine mantle, and his *Saint Esprit* with royal dignity. This was something of an achievement, for the rich and elaborate dress of noblemen often made plain children ridiculous. The little *émigré*, La Tour du Pin, brought up in America, on his return to Europe said of the first child he saw in gala costume: "Oh, mamma, is that a boy or a monkey?" The portrait of Louis XV was only the first of a series; one of them Rosalba carried back to Venice with her, where it hung in her own room; another, a miniature for a snuff-box lid, was a royal present to Madame de Ventadour, once head nurse to his Majesty, and still his lady in waiting.

Rosalba closely observed her shy, taciturn little sitter. She noted his sadness when on one fatal day he dropped his gun, killing his parrot and hurting his little dog. On a somewhat more cheerful occasion, Rosalba writes: "The King, knowing that the Duke de Noailles, Captain of the Royal Guard, was afraid of cats, touched him from behind with one of his cat's paws. The duke fell down in a faint and hurt himself. The King wept." The Duke de Noailles, fat and full-blooded, was often the victim of the young King's practical jokes. One of these was forcing the poor, puffy captain to run after his light-footed Majesty.

The King's governor, Maréchal de Villeroi, was also occasionally present at the royal sittings; he was as much of a courtier as a soldier and never failed to compliment the King or the painter. After the first sitting: "He took my hand, and said that '*il me devait savoir bon grai che le Roi se donat tant de pacience.*'" (The French is Rosalba's, not the maréchal's.) Again the amiable veteran remarked in Rosalba's presence to Madame de Veritadour: "*Com' ell' ha bone mine, toujours bien abiliée.*" Such praise from a Parisian "*qui s'y connaît*" in matters of dress was considered worthy of record. Villeroi showed his interest more practically in having Rosalba paid for her work in real money (*buona moneta*) not in the fairy gold of the bank. The Court had not waited for the King, but had from her arrival taken possession of Rosalba. The Regent, unannounced, with the *sans façon* of a brother artist, entered her studio one day and watched her work in pastel for half an hour, doubtless asking her many pertinent questions about processes, for he painted and engraved as well as collected. He could be as pleasing to a woman who respected herself as he was captivating to a woman who did not, and probably that half hour of informal chat counted among Rosalba's happy memories of Paris. With the Regent had come the Duke of Bouillon "*ed altri,*" for ducal and princely visits were usual occurrences, and duke was a generic name for noble with the Carrieras. There is an imposing list of them in the journal; a day without one was dull indeed.

The studio was also the habitat of duchesses. "While you were at the Academy," Mamma Alba told her daughters, "there came some duchesses and princesses." The old lace-maker's exactness was limited to her eyes and fingers; she wisely renounced the pronunciation of French names. Rosalba was more adventurous with them, and to thicken the plot added phonetic spelling. La Vrillière became Larsilier, Watteau Vatò, the Countess of Evreux Euré, Caylus Quellus and Chélus, De Revest Derverst, Lautrec Tré, then Otrek. The name of Vleughels, the painter, offered unlimited opportunity for variants. The current spelling was finally achieved after much experimentation, but was soon abandoned. Rosalba's renderings of foreign names are easy reading, however, compared to those of Italian chroniclers and annalists, as weary toilers through their archives in search of some English or German traveller, student, or artist, know. Where simple Hawkwood is disguised as Aguto, what hope remains for more complicated names?

Among Rosalba's noble patrons who wore the famous titles she miscalled were sorry rascals who should have been shipped off to Louisiana with Manon Lescaut and her card-sharping chevalier: the horrible, misbegotten dwarf, the Duc de la Vrillière, ruthless persecutor of Huguenots; the perverted, vicious young Villeroi and their brothers-in-law Harcourt and Boufflers, whom even the indulgent Regent banished from Versailles lest they should corrupt the little King. To the innocent painter, however, these wretches, who had they been plebeians would have been broken on the wheel *en Grève*, or chained to a galley-oar, were courteous gentlemen, admiring, complaisant, and excellent material for portraiture in their gleaming cuirasses and jewelled orders. The scandals and shames of the Regency found no harborage in Rosalba's record. She did not seek for the skeletons behind the carved and gilded panels, and she passed serenely beside dark abysses without a glance into their slimy depths. If the follies of the great people who thronged her studio were not entirely unknown to her, they were unnoticed. If a bit of current gossip finds its way into her journal it is purified by her interpretation. When Paris was shocked by the barbarous practical joke played on Madame de St. Sulpice at one of Monsieur le Duc's suppers, where the poor lady was burned by a petard placed beneath her chair, then rolled up in the tablecloths and napkins and sent home half dead, Rosalba's version of this horrible pleasantry is Bowdlerized *virginibus puerisque*. "While Madame de St. Sulpice was rouging herself for a ball before the chimney-piece mirror, her clothes caught fire, burned her stomach and she is dying."

From a few terse entries in Rosalba's journal one may suspect that a fierce little drama of sisterly envy was enacted under her nose, in which apparently she played the part of *ingénue*. Early in February (she was leaving for Italy in March) she promised to paint the portrait of Mademoiselle de Charolais and a certain Monsieur de Lacé. The next day the Duchesse of Bourbon, her mother, ordered the portrait of Mademoiselle de Clermont,

Mademoiselle de Charolais's younger sister. These princesses, granddaughters of Louis XIV and Madame de Montespan, were as imperious as their grandfather, and as lawless as the *belle* Athénaïs, though Mademoiselle de Clermont was gentler and far more discreet than her reckless elder, Mademoiselle de Charolais, who had already been painted for the irresistible Richelieu's gallery of lady-loves, costumed as nuns of different religious orders. The princess in a Franciscan's robe, girt with a heavy cord, holding a scrip under her arm, with a monastery at her back, may still be seen at Versailles, and almost justifies Voltaire's question:

> "*Frère Ange de Charolois,*
> *Dis nous par quelle aventure*
> *Le cordon de Saint François*
> *Sert à Vénus de ceinture?*"

Of Mademoiselle de Clermont the Baron de Pollnitz, a contemporary, wrote enthusiastically; her beauty, her grand air, her sweetness, her modesty, her *sagesse—le baron n'en tarissait pas*. His opinion of her good looks is more trustworthy than his praise of her virtue, and is confirmed by Raoux and Nattier, who painted the princess after Rosalba's portrait of her was destroyed. Mademoiselle de Clermont came to her sitting in Rosalba's studio under her mamma's wing, and followed by a brilliant *cortège* of courtiers. The portrait was almost finished and Rosalba's stay in Paris was nearly over when on February 21 "Monsieur Caylus came secretly, by order of Mademoiselle de Charolais, who would come at six o'clock in the morning if Rosalba could paint a portrait of her 'exactly like her sister's.'" A few days later the new portrait, the imitation of Mademoiselle de Clermont's was begun. It was progressing finely when in March Rosalba returned late from the opera to find the finished portrait of Mademoiselle de Clermont "ruined by an accident, which greatly annoyed the princess, her mother, and made Monsieur de Lacé, the person who was the cause of it, quite ill." The next day Mademoiselle de Charolais arrived triumphant in a magnificent gown of flowered silver brocade for her last pose. As Rosalba had no time to repaint Mademoiselle de Clermont, Mademoiselle de Charolais's picture remained unique, as she had wished, *coûte que coûte*. Let us hope that the service of the devoted Monsieur de Lacé was adequately rewarded, for though princes have always found some pliant instrument for their dirty work, they were not always grateful. The sisters had been rivals in beauty and gallantry. Was Monsieur de Lacé an agent of the elder's envy or jealousy? Who knows? Perhaps Rosalba suspected, but she gave no sign.

Not only the princesses of the blood royal, but the Queens of the left hand besieged Rosalba. Mesdames de Prie, and de Parabère, the Duchesse de Boufflers the typical *grande dame galante* of her century, Madame de la Vrillière, née Mailly, who first lured the exemplary young monarch, Louis XV, from the path of virtue and the side of Marie Leczinska; the Duchess of Richmond, granddaughter-in-law of Charles II and Louise de Kérouaille, all that was most blueblooded and most magnificently disreputable would be painted by La Carriera.

There were mysterious beauties, too, who came escorted by admirers eager to pay dear for a miniature or pastel portrait, but these prudent Rosalba "had no time to paint,' even when asked by her friend Caylus, but she *made* time for heads of Watteau and Pellegrini, of Oppenord and le Père Jacques. Pretty parvenues followed the fashion whose faces were not their fortunes, but who owed their titles and their lords to paternal ducats; the young Duchesse de Brissac, whose father, the miser, shutting himself into his treasure-chamber, was fastened in by a treacherous spring lock and starved to death among his money-bags—a prosaic pendant to the poetic figure of the Italian Ginevra—and the charming Comtesse d'Evreux, Crozat's daughter, whose noble husband after he had secured her dowry promptly deserted her. The Fleurys, husband and wife, the whole family of John Law, the clan of the Villeroi, the tribe of the Crozat, Mesdames de Lautrec, de Louvois, de Lorge, de la Carte, Mademoiselle de la Roche-sur-Yon filled every hour Rosalba could give.

During her sojourn in Paris Rosalba noted painting thirty-six portraits. Only one remains there, that of a young girl with a monkey in the Louvre, called Mademoiselle Law with some show of reason. The portrait of the little King in the Dresden Gallery is *probably* the one Rosalba carried away with her to Venice and kept in her own room. What has become of the others? Many of them were doubtless swept away with other fragile things by the torrent of the Revolution; many are perhaps in private collections; some of them, pale ghosts of their former selves, are still drifting about from one junk-shop to another, or passing from collector to *nouveau riche*, lighting up a dark corner in a scramblingly furnished "period" boudoir, or recently adopted as a family portrait, for "*ça fait toujours très bien comme ancêtre*," I was once assured by a bustling *bibelotière*.

Rosalba painted only part of the day, the rest of it and her evenings were devoted to sightseeing and amusement. She visited the royal palaces: Versailles lonely and deserted since the old King's death; the Luxembourg, Marly, St. Cloud, the Palais Royal. She was shown the Regent's fine collection of old masters, the Rubens of Queen Maria de' Medici, the Royal Academy of modern paintings, Mignard's ceiling in the church of Val-de-Grâce, her brother-in-law Pellegrini's model for his huge decorations in the Royal Bank. She was a welcome visitor at the studios of Largillière, Coypel, Rigaud, de Troy, l'Abbé Leblond, and Watteau. The exquisite painter of idyls and concerts, for which he often found his backgrounds on the stately terraces and velvet lawns of Crozat's gardens in the Rue Richelieu, or in the park at Montmorenci, had a decided penchant for Rosalba's work. Before he met her, he had commissioned his friend and studio companion to buy one of her miniatures or to exchange pictures with her, an offer which she gladly accepted. The saturnine, melancholy painter of Armida's gardens and operatic elysiums was an *habitué* of the Hôtel Crozat, and between him and the sprightly Venetians, who possessed "that gayety that God has put into the heart of woman to lighten the sadness of man," there sprang up a tender friendship that ended all too soon with Watteau's early death.

Of course church was regularly attended by the Carrieras, but they varied their devotional pleasures, and never lost a fine celebration at St. Roch, St. Merri, or St. Gervais, though the Petits Pères was Mamma Alba's favorite. They saw a dazzling review of the Mousquetaires, visited the Invalides, and were shown, curiously enough, the plans of all the fortresses and defenses of France. They went to the Gobelins, admired the tapestries, the state carriages, and especially the phaëtons, most graceful of modern vehicles appropriately designed for the *roi soleil*. The fair of St. Laurent was not forgotten, where everything in the world was for sale except those two dangerous articles, books and arms.

Evening brought no rest for tired eyes, for there was the opera for which noble friends sent boxes to the artist; the French and Italian comedy theatres, the Court balls where the grave little King "dances well." There were tickets for fireworks—always dear to Frenchmen—and, most enjoyable to our musical dilettante, concerts where, after the Italian fashion, great ladies and gentlemen took part *sans déroger*. In one of these, given for charity at the house of Crozat, the two sisters appeared as musicians, Rosalba playing the violin, Neneta singing with distinguished professional artists: Pacini the Royal chapelmaster, Rebel the future director of the opera, Antoine the famous lute-player, and Mademoiselle d'Argenon. Among the guests were the Regent, Law, though there was no loss of affection between him and the Crozats, rival financiers, the *fleur du pois* of Parisian aristocracy, the collectors and critics: Caylus, Mariette, de Julienne, Maroulle, President Hénin, the Comte de Morville, and a sad, weary-looking young man who amused himself during the performance by sketching the artists on a loose sheet of paper, which he gave to Mariette, and which to-day remains in the Louvre to show how Rosalba's clean-cut, energetic profile and Neneta singing looked to Watteau.

Perhaps the acquaintance of these critics and connoisseurs, house friends of the Crozats, counted for more in Rosalba's career than even her aristocratic patrons. Rarely since the Renaissance has such a group of enlightened amateurs of the arts been collected in one great centre. To their friendship and influence Rosalba owed more lasting fame than any caprice of fashion could have bestowed. One cannot help suspecting that her character and intelligence counted for much in her conquest of these *cognoscenti*, for they were not indulgent critics; Caylus never minced matters in expressing an artistic opinion; Mariette's appreciation of Rosalba's work in his "*Abécédario*" frankly defines her limitations, and the general moderation of her French admirers contrasts vividly with Zanetti's undiscriminating praise of Rosalba in his "Venetian Painting."

The sunshine of Rosalba's Parisian days were clouded only by the failure and flight of Law. Half a dozen obscure lines between lists of engagements and payments are devoted to the tragedy of the Rue Quincampoix. To read them aright one must refer to a larger page; Vianelli gave them up as impenetrably mysterious. On November 27 three words in Rosalba's journal, "*diminuzione della moneta*," stand for the collapse of the *système*, and the fatal run on the bank precipitated by the shameful rapacity of the princes, the weakness of the Regent, the robberies of the principal cashiers, the confiscation of the plate, jewels, gold and silver placed in the bank for safe-keeping, and the arrest of thousands of persons accused of dishonest dealings. Not far from where Rosalba sat tranquilly handling her chalks a Dante's hell-pit was seething, all the evil passions shrieking and whirling in a frenzy of greed. Robbers, murderers, suicides, honest folk driven mad by trust betrayed, weaklings transformed to furies by the loss of all they had in the world were howling, fighting, hurling themselves on barred doors, crushed and crushing to death against stone walls, while Rosalba laid aside her crayon-holder to jot down in her journal: "*Diminuzione della moneta.*"

On December 11 Rosalba again wrote: "I saw Law's daughter; her father . . . was disgraced this day." It was in effect on December 11 that Law resigned his offices, and in return the Regent, who had come out of the gigantic failure with clean hands, promised that Law's person and his property should be safe. Next day Rosalba "tried in vain to see Madame Law, who had gone to the opera" with her husband, to say farewell to the Parisian public. Four days later he left France, the three millions of francs he brought there, the riches he had acquired, his fourteen estates, and an unpaid painter, Pellegrini, Rosalba's brother-in-law, with his cosmic decoration on his hands. Rosalba, more fortunate, had received the money for her portraits and was able to lend it to Angela.

Just before Law's disgrace Rosalba finished the pastel of his daughter which is now in the Louvre, some critics believe. The portrait represents a very young girl, almost a child, with the awkward grace, the tender bloom of adolescence. Though the falling shoulders, the long slender neck, the dazzling white skin are those of English beauty, the brilliant dark eyes and the vivacity of the delicate face save the porcelain-like figure from insipidity. She seems a hothouse product, very far away indeed from nature, this gracile girl with her little monkey under her arm, a snapping patch of black, and is more like one of Kändler's Dresden china coquettes than a real flesh-and-blood creature.

On November 9 (1720) Rosalba was elected a member of the French Academy of Painting; her portrait of Louis XV was her letter of recommendation, and Coypel was her sponsor. As it was the custom for every new academician to give a picture to the academy, she promised a pastel for the next year. She was a woman of her word, and on January 31, 1722, the picture, a young girl with a laurel crown, was presented by Antoine Coypel. It was accompanied by a letter from Rosalba, written in that curious *lingua franca* which was the language of polite correspondence all over civilized Europe. After the usual compliments Rosalba apologizes for her picture:

"*J'envoie la pastelle à l'Académie et comment oserait-elle se présenter sans être protégée de vous. Je tâche donc de lui procurer par ces deux lignes cet avantage, et je croirois faire tort à la bonté que vous avez eue de porter tous ces illustres à m'accorder l'honneur bien grande d'être parmi eux, si je ne me flattais que vous leur persuaderez encore que j'ai fait tout mon possible pour leur témoigner ma reconnaissance, quoique*

cela ne paraîsse pas dans le tableau. J'a itâché de faire une jeune fille, sachant que l'un pardonne bien des fautes à la jeunesse. Elle représente aussi une nymphe à la suite d'Apollon, qui va faire présent de sa part à l'Académie de Paris d'une couronne de lauriers, la jugeant la seule digne de la porter, et de présider à tous les autres. Elle s'est determinée à s'arrêter dans cette ville, aimant mieux d'occuper la dernière place dans cette très-illustre académie que le sommet du Parnasse. C'est à vous donc à lui procurer cet avantage et à moi aussi de jouir de vos bonnes grâces et de tous les illustres de l'Académie, auxquels vous aurez la bonté de faire mes compliments et de me croire
"*Monsieur,*
"*Votre très-humble servante,*
"*Rosalba Carriera.*"

Though the fall of Law and the disappointment of poor Pellegrini were the sole thorns in Rosalba's garland of happy Parisian days, she felt the strain of constant activity. If it were not for the pleasures of life most artists would be equal to its work, but being a painter all day, and a lady of leisure every evening told on Rosalba's eyes and nerves. Mamma Alba too began to long for the more tranquil joys of Venice. True, one amused oneself there also but with calmness, and the pursuit of pleasure in the smoothly gliding gondola was very different from a mad chase in a jolting, swaying coach over the jagged Parisian pavements. So in spite of protestations, a press of orders, and the promise of many more, on March 15 the Carrieras turned their faces eastward. As Marseilles was pest-smitten they journeyed through Lorraine, returning to Venice by the Tyrol, and the first mild days of May found them in their house on the Grand Canal.

Rosalba was at home but not at rest. Her first care was to write to her dear friends in Paris; her next to paint and send *ricordi* to those she had not been able to oblige there: Rigaud, Julienne, the Abbé de La Porte, and Vleughels, from whom she learned of the death of Watteau. What has become of Rosalba's portrait of him to which Crozat alluded in his letter of August 11, 1721, and which he proposed to place in a memoir of the painter? The last news of it dates from the Remy de Juilly sale in 1770.

Mariette was the most constant and interesting of Rosalba's correspondents, for many years he kept her in touch with Paris and her old friends. She had promised him that when he married she would paint his bride as a wedding gift, and in January, 23, 1723, Mariette when announcing his betrothal to Rosalba referred to this promise, begged her to return to Paris in time for his marriage, and reminded her of the work waiting for her there. Rosalba, however, was suffering from a serious affection of the eyes, and was hardly recovered from it when she received an order from the Duke of Modena to paint his three daughters (July 29, 1723).

V

Duke Rinaldo had given much time to considering the project proposed by his resourceful agent two years before. He had not acted, however, hoping perhaps that merely putting his daughters on the market without the expense of advertising would be sufficient. No eligible suitor presenting himself meantime, and Rosalba's vogue and prices increasing, the duke was finally obliged to loosen his wallet-strings and see if an illustrated catalogue would hasten the sale of his goods. By the end of July Rosalba, accompanied by her mother and Neneta, was settled in Modena, and began what seemed to her the tedious task of painting one portrait after another of the three princesses. "Why so many of them?" she must have asked herself very often. Perhaps her question was soon answered, secrets are not well kept in palaces, and Rosalba was *fine mouche*, but the mystery was not referred to in the only letter written from Modena. Rosalba varied her labor by painting the duke and his duchess and studying the old masters of the palace gallery, then far richer than it is to-day.

Modena, the rosy little city set like a pink pearl in the green velvet of its smiling, fertile fields, was extremely dull. Nothing happened; there were no conversazioni, no music, no excursions; everything dozed in the long midsummer days. Rosalba painted princesses, Neneta copied Rosalba's pictures, and Mamma Alba nodded over her beads; even she must have grown restive, and desired a change. After a dozen portraits were finished and they began on the second series, probably princesses painted or in the flesh palled on the Carrieras. They may have understood why the bored Modenese had made such a fuss about a stolen bucket, and supposed that Ginevra's tragic little joke on her wedding-day was an attempt to relieve the monotony of Modena at any cost.

Modena was dull because in spite of the princesses' new gowns it was still a hundred years behind the times, still in the pompous, priest-ridden seventeenth century, mildewed and etiolated in the shadow of Austria. It was a Court largely composed of professionally religious persons, and of worldly persons who observed all the forms of piety, where you might possibly meet St. Francis de Sales, but where you were sure to encounter Tartuffe, where Madame Guyon could have been parched by spiritual dryness, but where Molière's Arsinoé would have flourished like a noisome weed. Duke Rinaldo had begun his career as a cardinal, and renounced the purple to succeed his nephew, Francesco II, who abdicated in order to enter a monastery. The later Estes were very devout; Francesco's sister, Beatrice d'Este, afterwards Queen of England, when a lovely, Juliet-like girl of fifteen, with floods of tears besought the Duke of York to abandon his suit to her and allow her to take the veil. She even offered him a substitute, her maiden aunt of thirty, as "a much more appropriate match for his Highness." In the Court of the ex-cardinal naturally the church was amply represented. Rosalba's princesses spent whole days in visits to convents, and in their secretary, Suor Beatrice Davia, an accomplished nun, Rosalba found a congenial companion. But to an intellectual woman fresh from free-thinking Venice, from the mental stimulus of Paris, the limitations, bigotry, and lack of large interests of the Court must have proved at once irritating and depressing. The supersubtle Venetian did not avow her boredom even to Angela, who had remained in Venice, but one learns to read between the lines of Rosalba's writing:

MODENA, October 22, 1723.

MY DEAREST SISTER,

Blessed be a thousand times these princesses and their father, who think of nothing but pleasing me, and therefore are letting us go home sooner than they wish. Everything that I do is going very well, one thing better than another, and it is always: "But you work too much! There is no one who works faster than you do!" Believe me, and laugh at my foolishness, but though it was to my disadvantage, after two months I wished to leave here. I have prejudiced many people against me on account of my haste as I will tell you by word of mouth soon, God willing. . . . *Amatemi e state allegra. Sono la vostra putella, Rosalba.* (Love me, and be cheerful, I am your girl.)

Putella! Rosalba, the man of the family, still was to her mother and sisters, and indeed always preserved, something of a girl's gay confidence and eager interest in life.

It is not from Rosalba's but from the letters of another woman, and a most frank and outspoken one, Mademoiselle de Valois, daughter of the Regent, Philippe d'Orléans, that a true notion of life in the palace of Modena may be found. The correspondence of this sister-in-law of the Modenese princesses and reluctant bride of their brother Francesco, with her father, and the minute reports of his agents Chavigny, Philibert, and Colibeaux, whom he sent to mediate between the princess and her father-in-law, Duke Rinaldo, leave little to be desired in exactness of detail and in copiousness of expression. These letters depict more forcibly than even Stendhal's *"Chartreuse de Parme"* the pettiness and artificiality of the small Italian Court, its three-ply intrigue, its tortuous ways, and microscopic aims.

Of course Charlotte Aglaé d'Orléans was a pampered and possibly a perverted person, who at fourteen went with her father to opera-balls, and "spoiled her nose with snuff," and who, following the fashion in sentiment, fell desperately in love with the conquistador of the Regency, the young Duc de Richelieu. It was an open secret that her passion for him was one of the reasons why the irresistible duke was removed from the scene of his conquests, and only allowed to contemplate them from the top of a tall tower of the Bastille. First lessons in love from so finished a *virtuoso* provided the princess with a dangerously high standard of comparison, and when Francesco d'Este, son and future successor of the Duke of Modena, was presented as a suitable match she would none of him. Cardinal Dubois, in view of the smallness of the duchy and his perquisites, at first sustained the princess in her refusal, but when Selvatico, the duke's emissary, advanced such irrefutable arguments in favor of the match as five fine old masters from Duke Rinaldo's famous collection, Dubois yielded to superior reasoning, and only Charlotte Aglaé remained in opposition to what the cardinal now considered the good of the state; but she had her price, too, and the Regent offered it: the liberation of Richelieu. The princess like a true lover accepted it, and the hand of Duke Francesco. She was desperately unhappy, "wept night and day," and tried to take the small-pox. Even the sixty dresses of the trousseau and the four million francs' worth of presents from the King could not dry her tears. They continued to flow at intervals during her royal and extremely slow, scandalously slow, progress towards Modena and nuptial bliss.

The way was made smooth for loiterers. Every city, Nevers, Lyons, Avignon, Vienne, Marseilles, where she and her suite of a hundred and thirty persons lodged was *en fête;* balls, plays and fireworks, banqueting and gaming marked each stage of the long journey. It would seem as though her countrymen were trying to sharpen the princess's regrets at leaving France, and she caught at every pleasure with the eagerness of one who was to die or to marry to-morrow. Various episodes further enlivened the travellers. Selvatico, the duke's envoy, fell in love with the princess, and his grotesque jealousy and fantastic compliments provided a farcical interlude between entertainments. Selvatico was a typical Court parasite. Something of a rascal, with a dash of the bully, and much of the buffoon, a kind of Scaramouch-Pulcinella, he was a distinctly Italian product, and an amusing curiosity to a French princess. Unfortunately she was not unworthy of her name and loved to laugh between tear-drops. Selvatico's fat sighs, rolling eyes, and languishing airs contributed amply to gayety which Aglaé took little pains to conceal. Mockery is the unpardonable sin in Italy, and if hell knows no fury like a woman scorned, it knows no hatred like an Italian ridiculed. Imagine Malvolio free to revenge himself on Olivia and Maria.

Thanks then to Selvatico's rancor, who encouraged Duke Rinaldo's parsimony, the princess was ill-received at Modena. She loved her sisters-in-law, Benedetta, Enrichetta, and Amalia; like everybody else, she took little notice of the effaced duchess; she despised Duke Rinaldo and laughed at her pious, gentle young husband. The home-bred youth was abashed by this precocious, experienced woman of the world; intimidated yet ready to do her bidding having the habit of obedience. The princess's letters cast a pitiless light on the unhandsome thrift of the ducal housekeeping. She was miserably lodged without fuel or light, in the half-ruinous palace of Reggio. She was "supplied with lame and one-eyed horses." Her pension was never paid. As to the Court at Modena it was sordid and dreary: "the marquises and counts that fill the antechambers here have only an old Parmesan gold louis a month for everything." The only pleasures were a musical high mass or a sermon by a Jesuit; the only amusements visits to convents, where at least there was sweet singing, delicious collations of toothsome dainties made by the good sisters, and pretty presents of pin-cushions and embroidered gloves. In truth the cloister seemed a gay and animated retreat after the tedium of the Court. There the princess could do nothing but wrong. She did not yield to dulness without a struggle, but her young rebelliousness was gradually quelled. She instituted private theatricals, and was accused of keeping the princesses up too late; her driving in her little phaëton was taboo because her pace was too hot. When she shut herself up in her rooms with her favorite lady in waiting, and spun industriously, that lady was dismissed from the palace. Finally, when Duke Rinaldo's second and favorite son fell in love with her, the situation grew impossible, and the desire to escape to France became almost a fixed idea with the princess. Francesco shared his wife's confidence and was as eager to struggle from under the duke's thumb. Under the pretext of a pilgrimage to Loretto, the young couple left Modena and tried to reach the French frontier. Caught and dragged back to Modena, Aglaé, as the instigator of the plan, was severely punished; the doors between her apartments and those of the sister princesses were walled up and she was forbidden to see them. These gentle, domesticated girls loved the strange wild kestrel who fluttered her notched wings and tore at her jesses; their petting and fostering was her one comfort in her captivity, and separation from them quenched her spirit, which paternal scoldings and director's admonitions had only quickened. The announcement of Richelieu's marriage and the agony of a day and night of tears that followed it completed her taming. She accepted with flat acquiescence the magnificent discomfort of the Reggio palace, the attentions of the scared little duke, and perhaps even the lame and one-eyed horses.

While Rosalba was painting there Princess Aglaé was not invited to Modena. It would have been too pleasant for her to meet the painter who knew her father and her friends, and with whom she could talk of France. Work alone kept Rosalba from echoing the princess's lament while she wandered through the spacious palace chambers: "*O, que je m'ennuie ici, O, que je m'ennuie*"; but diplomatic Rosalba managed to shorten her projected stay by promising to finish her copies of the portraits in her own studio. Her journal was discontinued during her visit to Modena, possibly from paucity of happenings, possibly from prudential motives.

What became of the portraits? Three of them are in the Uffizi in Florence, three in Dresden. Those sent to France are difficult to trace, and have momentarily disappeared. They were impatiently expected by that indefatigable match-maker the Duchess of Brunswick, who "wept with joy" when she learned they were en route, and declared that she should not enjoy a single night's sleep until they arrived. Prolonged insomnia must have followed, for the portraits found admirers by the way and never reached Paris. The Duke of Modena then sent three more from his stock by special courier, January 8, 1724. Alas! when they arrived, the Duchess of Bourbon was rather miffed that they had not been sent directly to her as a possible mother-in-law of one of the three princesses. Rangoni wrote regretfully to Duke Rinaldo that "though she praised them, it was with a certain reserve that marked her annoyance rather than her satisfaction." "The portrait of the Serenissima Benedetta is considered the most beautiful," Rangoni adds. Unfortunate man compelled to follow and note the mutations of a Bourbon, and of a she-Montespan Bourbon to boot. With such folk one is sure of nothing, and Rangoni must have seemed a very pinwheel of changing opinions to the anxious Court at Modena. For instance, Benedetta was leading in favor by several lengths when a little later Rangoni writes that just the other day when the Duchess of Bourbon was passing through the Duchess of Brunswick's room, where the three portraits were hanging, she remarked in a low voice but quite loud enough to be heard by the vigilant Rangoni, "Here is one that will suit us better than the others," and pointed to the pastel of Amalia! How confusing! And how sad it was that after all the expense and the carefully considered plans, the pretty portraits advertised Rosalba's talent rather than the princesses' charms. In the end partial fortune, passing over both Amalia and Benedetta, bestowed *two* husbands on Enrichetta, the Duke of Parma and the Prince of Hesse-Darmstadt.

VI

Rosalba on her return to Venice continued for some years to copy her portraits of the Modenese princesses, but only from time to time, slipping them in between more interesting orders. Joseph Smith, later English consul, an art dealer, discoverer of Canaletto and of the younger Venetian school, brought her many of his distinguished compatriots to paint. She counted some historic personages among her sitters: Augustus of Cologne Elector Palatine, and Faustina Bordone, a queen of song, of European reputation. Rosalba had known Faustina when she was the humble protégée of the Carriera's old friend, the patrician Alessandro Marcello, brother of the famous Benedetto. Alessandro was also a musician, a painter, and something of a poet; he had heard Faustina singing when she was a child, orphaned and destitute. He gave her a musical education such as only a dilettante of music could give in a Venice where music was in its glorious adolescence. Faustina bounteously rewarded her patron in many ways, gossip whispered. She had much in her favor: she was a very beautiful woman, which is unusual; she had a marvellous voice, which is rare; perfectly trained, which is rarer; directed with intelligence, which is rarest. No wonder that she, like several other ladies, was called the Tenth Muse. Had she acquired that extent and variety of emotional experience that is supposed to develop genius, or at least heighten dramatic expression, though Siddons and Jennie Lind got on very well without it? In any case, she possessed the temperament and caprices of the typical prima donna. One day while she was dressing for a ball a poor woman came to beg. Touched by her appeal, Faustina, whose purse was either empty or not at hand, unclasped a jewelled bracelet and pressed it into the beggar's palm. The first time Faustina heard the young golden-haired German composer Adolph

Hasse sing to the harpsichord at a little concert in a friend's house, the idolized diva vowed that he and none but he should be her lord; married him, sang his delicate, tender music for years, and lived to a green old age in Venice with her *caro Sassone*, as all Italy called the kindly musician. The gondoliers will still point out the house, once a nest of nightingales, in the Campo San Marcuola where folk used to gather to hear the Hasse children singing with their father at the harpsichord.

Faustina's is one of the most spirited of Rosalba's portraits, with head raised and lips parted, in the fervid *abandon* of a singing creature, as she looked doubtless "when she played with the music like a bird on a bough."

Paris did not forget Rosalba; orders came often for muses and nymphs. De Crozat and Mariette were constantly urging a return to France; de Morville promised Rosalba five thousand liras' worth of orders yearly. De Crozat was especially insistent, assuring Rosalba that her apartment was ready for her, and that she could occupy it at any time while waiting for the King to give her a lodging in the Louvre, and added what he knew would be more persuasive: "It would be a great consolation to me to enjoy your society before I die." Coypel the Younger sent a charming letter of congratulation on a pastel just received from her by de Morville, which was hung in a room Coypel himself was decorating.

Charles Coypel to Antonio Correggio, now called Rosalba:
I owe you felicitations which I offer with all my heart on the marvel you have just sent to Monsieur le comte de Morville. Many people might think you had played me a sorry trick by sending such a beautiful pastel for the library where I was beginning to show mine with some success. I will agree with them that the sight of yours at once makes my pictures lose their poor little reputation, but if your last work hurts those I did in the past I give you my word it will improve those I do in the future. Yes, Mademoiselle, the beauties of this charming picture have impressed me too deeply not to be helpful to me. . . . Your talent shall profit me in one way or another. If I cannot steal it, I shall have at least the glory of celebrating it more enthusiastically than any one, and that among brother artists is not an easy task. Permit me to send greetings to all the family.

Such generosity seems too good to be true. Charles Reade, an indefatigable collector of data, assures us that in the past painters praised and helped each other, and adds, feeling that such a statement needs a substantial prop, that "even Christians loved each other at the start."

In spite of kind letters and messages and proffered work, Rosalba deferred her return to Paris, excusing herself on account of her mother's ill health and dislike of travel. To short journeys and brief separations Siora Alba could be reconciled, and in the autumn of 1728 Rosalba went to Friuli for a holiday; while there she accepted an invitation to Gorizia for the fêtes given for the Emperor Charles VI. During her stay Rosalba painted several courtiers, and promised to visit Vienna, which she did in the following April; Pellegrini was already at work there, and a furnished house was hired for the summer.

On Rosalba's arrival Daniele Antonio Bertoli, the antiquarian, an Italian acclimated in Vienna, presented her to the Emperor, who, as already mentioned, remarked: "Bertoli, your painter-woman may be clever, but she's very homely!" Charles VI, Emperor of Austria, King of Hungary, Emperor of Germany, King of Naples and Sicily, Lord of Milanese, and Cæsar Augustus, was a solemn, pedantic, bigoted gnome; of a rare and finished hideousness himself, he was very sensitive to beauty in women, and though his Empress was plain, his mistresses were invariably handsome. Besides this pretty taste, he had one great passion—music.

His Court was clumsily frivolous, hypocritically devout, prudishly immoral. The Jesuits reigned there, and their bad taste and meretricious art pervaded everything except lovely, lately born Italian music. Tartuffe gave the tone to the Court, Tartuffism with mitigations. There was amusement for all except for those who diverted themselves with their minds. After mass in the morning you could do as you pleased provided you did not read French books or try to think for yourself; proper servility shown to the priests and proper homage paid to Cæsar, you were free to entertain the cardinal sins.

The Venetians, used to the easy manners of socially democratic Italy, the polish of a high civilization that had smoothed away social inequalities, were probably ill at ease in this Court of bedizened dwarfs and pettish male soprani, of meddling Jesuits and fussy majordomos, of mean squabbles over a place in a procession, a stool, or a ceremonial saucer to a coffee-cup; of petty honors: posts to hand the Emperor his shirt or his night-drink. Once in this artificial world the same nobles who came so simply to the little studio on the Grand Canal were transformed. *Then* they were incognito, had escaped from etiquette, had left it at home with their blazons; but here folk were rated by their quarterings; a coat of arms borne by the veriest ass was more honored than a fine talent or a great achievement. And these supercilious great lords with their loutish manners and guttural accents, these stall-fed, insolent ladies, stuck down behind their embroidery-frames, were arrogant or overfamiliar to a mere painter. It was only to a singer, of course a distinctly inferior being, but one whose place had been fixed outside the social hierarchy, and who could be petted and played with like a pug or a parrot, that these starched and contemptuous folk unbent. With few exceptions how dreary was this blue-blooded society! At the Countess of Althann's there was a tincture of Italian cultivation, and the same singers who were mere fatuous fops and mincing idiots while being flattered and caressed by condescending aristocrats became noble and conscientious artists when they sang. Did the sisters meet one of them, Farinello, for instance, whose life reads like an old tale of enchantment and a wonder-working talisman? Did Metastasio read his libretti to Rosalba when she painted him? There is no mention of such good fortune, and yet she has left us the portrait of the Court poet when he stood at the threshold of fame (1730).

He is a finished worldling, this dapper Abate Metastasio, in his neat black and fresh *rabato;* his curly hair is thinning, his pinched mouth betrays little of the quick wit and the cheerfulness that made him so popular in Italy. Newly created *poeta Cesareo* when Rosalba arrived, he was perhaps suffering from the same homesickness among the boorish, haughty Viennese, who regarded a poet very much as they would a writing-master, and whose Italian or French varnish cracked and split under the least friction, the slightest jar. But Metastasio was by temperament a courtier as well as by training, and the atmosphere that sickened Rosalba only desiccated him. Thanks to her, however, we can see what semblance of man was this strange anomaly who never gave his own and yet who won so many hearts; that of the crabbed, embittered old scholar who adopted and made him his heir; of the famous singer whose passion for him raised him to high fortune; of the great lady to whom he owed the dignity and comfort of his later life in an alien Court, among ignorant barbarians. He was a charmer, undoubtedly, this Metastasio; *homo duplex*, timid, prudent, a courtier, a valetudinarian, yet a poet to the core, in form as in feeling; romantic as Corneille, elevated as Racine, a writer of lofty and tender sentiments, of lovely and sonorous phrases worthy of their mating with the music of Jommelli and Paisiello, of Hasse and Handel.

Rosalba kept no diary in Vienna, no list of portraits painted there. The sisters' letters to their mother describe pleasant visits to convents, much like those of Lady Montague some years before, excursions to parks and palaces, and note the gayety of Viennese street life in spite of bad weather and worse pavements. There are allusions to difficulties in painting the great, notably the Empress, and one sentence is significant: "This is the age of music, not painting." They might well have thought so in the Court of the melomaniac Charles VI, but this was no complaint of personal neglect, for when the Carrieras left Vienna in the middle of October it was with heavy purses as well as light hearts.

VII

THE trip to Vienna was Rosalba's last journey; henceforth her "travels went no farther than her easel"; for sitters and orders sought her, and the pretty little house on the Grand Canal was too comfortable to leave. It still remains externally unaltered, opposite the ferry of San Maurizio, between the Da Mula and Venier palaces, a small two-storied house with balconies, and a pillared doorway on the Canale. The street entrance surmounted by a well-fed, sixteenth-century *putto* is in the Calle di Cà Centani a San Vio. The house had been extended on the land side and altered internally, especially in the lower stories, by the Biondetti to whom it has belonged for centuries. The Church of San Vio, where the Carrieras went to mass every morning, has been destroyed, but the pavement is still as rough as it was when Rosalba tottered over it in her high-heeled slippers; that pavement was one of the few things Rosalba hated.

For many years her modest house saw a press of gondolas before its sea-portal, a group of gallooned and gold-laced lackeys in its bare antechamber, and was a focus of interest to neighbors and passers. Less active ladies than the Carrieras, warming adjacent window-sills in shawl and petticoat, pushed back the heavy penthouses of hair from their brows to stare at the great who came to be painted, and felt a mild parochial pride in their local artist, while folk waiting at the ferry heard the pretty chatter in soft Venetian, the laughter of girls, sometimes the sound of violin and harpsichord and the voice of a famous singer floating out from the windows of *casa Carriera*.

A sitting at Rosalba's studio, when prince or *procuratessa* posed, should be painted in her own colors in their pristine brilliancy, in twinkling lights and tender tints. Black and white is as impotent to render the movement and picturesqueness of such a group as is pen and ink to present the color and glow of a flower-garden; for in the matchless spectacle that Venice offered to beauty-loving eyes the figures were no dark or sad-hued spots on the rich background, but a part and an essential part, of the whole color scheme.

So the *signoroni* who stepped from their gondolas at Rosalba's door were pictures even before they were painted, in peach and plum colored velvet coats, in gleaming satin gowns, in petticoats of striped and flowered brocade, in deep-toned jewels and dull-gold embroideries; and on the young faces with their flower-like bloom, the older, subtler faces delicately retouched and tinted, the dark or gold hair warm under the hoar-frost of powder, rose and fell the double illumination from sea and sky; flesh and hair, stuffs and metals were transfused, shot through, rendered pearly, silvery, almost iridescent, by the dual light, the magician's mirror of Venice.

Within, on festal occasions, Mamma Alba, in her finest lace cap and kerchief, kept a watchful eye on the maid, handing lemonade or chocolate in Dresden china cups, gifts of an old friend, the "King of Porcelain," as Frederick the Great called Augustus III; amateurs inspected portrait and sitter through gold quizzing glasses; Neneta glided from one group to another; compliments and suggestions were offered and accepted; fans fluttered in the cyprus-scented air; a local poet read a sonnet on the portrait, followed by a soft patter of applause; a trim *abatino* brought the last bit of gossip, and a periwigged *procuratore* told the latest anecdote (both purely local, for the Venetian's interest did not fly far afield) followed by gentle persiflage that flicked but did not lash; the give and take of amiable wits, light playful talk, and modulated laughter. The sitter preened herself, bit her lips, played with her fan; the visitors examined the pastel, watched the artist work, criticised and admired. Rosalba kept steadily at her task, and only the fixity of her smile and a slight contraction of the brows betrayed the effort that underlay her apparent facility.

It was effort as well that bound Fortune to Rosalba's easel; constant, intelligent effort to please, to satisfy, to retain old friends, to acquire new ones, to make each portrait so desirable that it was but the preliminary to another, to be generous with work, liberal with time, and to bestow substantial tokens of gratitude for favors done. The Venetian painters who envied La Carriera her "luck," who complained that she owed her vogue to dealers and the English, would have shrunk from the labor on which her success was based; it was easier to declaim against commercialism and denounce favoritism in vine-covered *trattorie* between draughts of *vino nostrano*, than to acquire her methods. Rosalba's would go far to prove that a successful career depends more on character than on talent.

Nine prosperous and happy years followed the return from Vienna, years rich in achievement, poor in adventures. Many pastels were sent to England: to Lord Rockingham, Lord Cornbury, and Robert Dingley. The Duchess Sforza and Cardinal Polignac were painted, a head was sent to Mariette, a picture to de Julienne, a miniature to Crozat, the Viennese orders were finished, among them Rosalba's own portrait as "Winter" in the set of Seasons, for Charles VI, and *ricordi* despatched to those who had furnished her with letters or introductions. For one of these *ricordi*, a miniature of the Saviour, sent to Suor Beatrice Davia, the painter received a letter of thanks which is so good an example of Italian urbanity and ecclesiastical unction as to justify citation.

✝

Viva Giesù

From our monastery of Modena, March 3, 1731.

MY DEAREST AND MOST ESTEEMED SIGNORA ROSALBA,

This day the 3d of March is a fortunate one for me as the most noble, most beautiful gift, sent me by your generosity, arrived safely. Blessed be the hand that so ably directed the brush that so perfectly delineated the Divine Saviour. It is so beautiful that it seems alive, and looks as though it were in Paradise. Tell me, have you in a flight of the spirit seen the Lord? You have found his aspect. But dear Signora Rosalba why am I worthy to own such a beautiful devotional picture? I thank you with all my heart, and I promise you that never, never shall I forget you in my poor prayers. May the Lord God repay you for your gift, preserve your health, and continually augment your goodness. . . . Embracing you tenderly a thousand times I leave you in the Sacred Heart of Jesus, whose portrait you have so admirably painted. May the Lord make you holy! I protest with all my heart my dear Signora Rosalba, that I am most devotedly yours.

Suor Maria Beatrice Davia.

P.S.—*I shall not show the beautiful gift that you sent me to the Most Serene Benedetta because Her Highness is such a lover of fine miniatures that I should be obliged to give it to her, and I am not generous enough to do so.*

With a greatly increased clientèle, Neneta's help could no longer suffice for finishing draperies, accessories, and copying her sister's work; so, after the Viennese journey, Rosalba took a pupil, one might say an apprentice, a young girl, Felicità Sartori, the niece of an old friend, Dell' Agata, who was himself a fair painter ("*pittore discreto*"). Felicità, half-servant, half-art-student, was kept at drawing and engraving for some years before beginning to paint. Following her uncle's advice, her prentice burin was exercised on religious subjects. "You can give away these devotional pictures, and ask those who accept them to say Ave Marias for you; and if they are of a size to place in a breviary, you may be able to get a mass or two from a priest, or some religious person, which will be a good investment. Thus, beginning your earnings by laying up treasure in heaven, you may hope that God will always give you interest, that is, temporal prosperity," counselled this other-worldly old gentleman. Felicità followed his advice, and in time received from the Conte di Collalto in exchange for an engraving of the Madonna an authentic bit of the True Cross. Dell' Agata bade her treasure it as a great rarity; "in all Gorizia, there were barely three other pieces." Thanks perhaps to her holy relic, Felicità, who possessed unusual facility, was soon capable of copying Rosalba's miniatures. These copies are carefully studied and conscientiously executed, cold in color, and lacking the transparency and limpidity of the originals, although by many collectors they are attributed to Rosalba.

A distinguished pupil of Rosalba was the poetess Irminda in Arcadia, in prose and life Luiza Bergalli. She loved pastel too well and not wisely, for in spite of patient study she never mastered the elusive material. She was far more fortunate with the pen; her translations of Racine were admired, and her tragedy of "*Agide di Sparta*" was played and enthusiastically applauded in Venice. The Court poet Apostolo Zeno begged her to accept the Emperor's invitation to Vienna, where a pension awaited her; but though poor she refused, unwilling to leave her parents who were old and ailing. To Rosalba she wrote several sonnets and supplied her with the verses for many songs. A third young girl, the daughter of an obscure Bolognese painter, was also working in the Carriera studio, so that the house lacked neither youth nor gayety.

Nine years flowed by as quietly as the ripples of the Canal under the windows; Rosalba always busy; Neneta coughing a little on damp mornings, looking after everybody and directing everything; Mamma Alba active and sound in spite of her weakness for Spanish biscuit and quince marmalade; Angela and her *burattino* coming and going, prosperous and cheerful, when suddenly a bolt fell on these happy people. Neneta sickened and died suddenly—of consumption the family doctor said. With this beloved sister, who had been her lifelong confidante and closest, dearest companion, Rosalba buried her heart. "I am beside myself," she wrote to a friend, "the prey of deepest melancholy, unalleviated by the fact that my mother and my other sister are in good health." This irreparable loss was soon followed by a minor one: the marriage of Luiza Bergalli with her poet-lover Gaspare Gozzi. He was ten years younger than his inamorata and though he had little to offer her but poverty, his noble family opposed the unequal match, and the Pindaric couple owed their happiness to Rosalba's mediation and good offices. A year after his wedding, rather tardily but all the more sincerely perhaps, Gozzi acknowledges his debt to Rosalba in a poem beginning:

". . . *donna cortese*
Anzi madre benigna, anzi sorella."

A better example of the editor-impresario-compiler-journalist-poet's Muse is a much later effusion on some cakes sent him by Rosalba. By this time in the Gozzi home-nest there were many tiny gaping beaks to be filled, so not one of Rosalba's tartlets reached the hungry bard. Rosalba kept the verses of the poetic couple among her MS., and continued her counsels to the indomitable idealist Luiza, who in dire straits, amid the clamors of her nursery and in the darkest recesses of the old rat-haunted pile at San Canziano, continued to write and paint. Carlo Gozzi, her critical brother-in-law who disliked learned ladies, preferring "the fierce little sultanas of Zara," draws a comical and pathetic picture of Luiza wrapped in her husband's cloak, with his huge buckled wig on her shoulders, dandling the annual baby with one hand, a pen in the other, shivering and scribbling in a huge frosty *sala* of the Gozzi palace. Luiza served as an awful example to grasping ladies who would be at once professional artists and patterns of domesticity, forgetting that the Muses were spinsters.

To fill Luiza's place, Rosalba sent for Angioletta Sartori, Felicità's younger sister, who had already studied under Dell' Agata. For some months after Neneta's death, Rosalba had been unable to work, but early in the following winter she was again at her easel, and probably found there the lethal draught that at least dulls when it cannot efface sorrowful memories. She was a woman of her word, so the Virtues, long since promised Cardinal Albani, were painted—Virtues of tender age and smoothly plump, for why should Vice monopolize dimples?

In August that observing traveller, the young President Des Brosses, visited Rosalba's studio, and though he thought his face was not worth the thirty *zecchini* she asked for a portrait, he "was foolish enough to offer her twenty-five gold louis for a Magdalen the size of my hand, that she had copied after Correggio, and fortunately for my twenty-five louis she did not wish to part with it."

Prince Frederick Christian, son of Rosalba's faithful friend, the King of Poland, arrived in Venice in December, to sit for his portrait, of course, but also with a royal order from his papa for forty of Rosalba's pastels, many of them from her own collection in her studio. Not content with these, he was an eager buyer from any one who had Rosalbas to sell. He heard fine things of the picture of a certain Maria Capitanio; discovered the owner, offered a hundred and fifty *zecchini* for it, was refused, repeated the offer, adding to it a dinner service in Dresden china worth as many more *zecchini*, and when his money and his porcelain were finally accepted, sent a special conveyance (*carro*) to carry off the precious portrait. Thus runs the legend, but where is the picture? and who was Maria Capitanio? Girolamo Zanetti answers neither of these questions, but simply repeats the story; it is not an improbable one, for Augustus III was lavish of tea-sets and avid of pastels.

Few patrons were as easily satisfied as his Majesty; pretty ladies especially were more difficult to please. There was the Princess Trivulzi, who had been painted by Rosalba in 1738 when all her friends pronounced the portrait a masterpiece, "an enchantment." The princess wrote from Lyons a year later asking for three copies of the picture, "exactly like the original," but with a difference; "the eyes brighter, the expression more joyous, and a little thinner, as I have grown extremely thin since I came to France." Rosalba rarely made copies, so Angioletta Sartori was accepted as a substitute; when the first of them was received, the princess not finding it sufficiently attenuated, returned it with a coaxing, courteous letter begging Rosalba to "diminish the contour of the face and to make the eyes larger and more lively," above all to make the face thinner, "as now that I am much more slender, every one thinks that I look better and younger than the portrait." Patient Rosalba bade Angioletta pare down the princess a little closer, but even then the result was not entirely gratifying, and La Trivulzi finally decided that no one save Rosalba's self could reduce her satisfactorily.

Besides her apprentices, Rosalba counted among her pupils a princess of Rocca Colonna who came to Venice to study with her, and the Empress of Austria, Elizabeth Christine of Wolfenbüttel-Blankenberg. "This sounds well in 'The Life of an Artist,'" remarked Marietta in his biography of Rosalba in the "*Abécédario*," "but in itself it amounts to very little." Rosalba's advice and instruction were constantly sought by beginners and experimenters in pastel and miniature painting, by ambitious dabblers in art who were persuaded that mastery lay in some "secret," in some particular kind of crayon, or the use of a special paper. Ladies were more imperative and categorical in their demands than the milder male practitioners. To all inquirers Rosalba replied with unfailing civility and seriousness. Pastel was a passion in the eighteenth century; everybody played with it as to-day every one experiments with photography. Each amateur had his theories and processes; de Morville even appealed to alchemy to furnish brighter and more durable tints. With dry pigment, easy to handle, to efface, and to retouch, scales of color already prepared, half-tones and gradations of color at one's hand, painting was made easy, and every tyro through this popularization of the facile medium fancied that he had art and nature at his command. So all the world essayed pastel from Frederick the Great to the professor's wife, who wrote to Rosalba for immediate and exact information. "Give me precise instructions as to how to prepare the ivory," demanded this would-be beneficiary, "with what kind of gum to mix the colors, in what sort of water to wet my brushes, and tell me if the gum should be mixed with the water; also I want a little brush, a medium-sized and a big brush, some dark colors, and some blacks and whites. I assure you that no living soul shall know of the favor you are doing me, as I have already some knowledge of this art, and therefore have no need of any one's assistance." To another lady with artistic yearnings who desired to know Rosalba's method of painting miniatures, she sent some materials with a word of advice: "These little brushes and colors are for miniature painting, but if one who desires to use them has not already worked with a master, it will be difficult to employ them."

These amiable replies to rather insistent seekers after knowledge added to Rosalba's correspondence, already extensive, and a tax on time and eyesight. From her answers we learn that the finest pastels came from France, that their color-scale was very limited, and that even the best of them were fragile, apt to break off, change color, and fade. Already, in 1710, Bötticher wrote to her that her pictures were paling, and advised her to strengthen the colors in her future work. Two years later the painter Lodovico Agricola told her: "I don't know how it happens" (I attribute it to the air) "that some of the colors have *vanished;* wherever there was carmine you see *nothing*, no one would believe it possible who had not seen it." The portrait of the Procuratessa Mocenigo, Rosalba's *capo d'opera*, thus faded away. Crozat begged Rosalba to try to find more permanent colors, and she replied to this advice: "I have asked several persons and they all agreed that [the fading] does not come from the pastels, which were carefully chosen, or excess of varnish, but from the place where they are kept and the difference in climate; for example, we see, and you too have observed, that the pictures on the mainland are better preserved than those in Venice. Their [fading] can come also from negligence and lack of care."

These letters are illuminating to modern art critics, whom visits to the Carriera rooms in the Dresden Gallery must have bewildered. The particular kind of encomium lavished upon Rosalba's work by contemporary painters who knew perfectly well what they were talking about, and were in some cases specially qualified judges of color and light, lead one to expect beauty of color of a subtile and sparkling character, not excluding force. This quality is present in the best of Watteau's work, and is perpetuated later in the finest Lancrets and Paters at Potsdam; of it Rosalba's pastels in Dresden possess almost nothing. They are not dirty, but while the darker colors are not absent there is a kind of blanched effect about them as though they had become anæmic in the shadow of Guido Reni. Her whites on whites, for instance, which to judge from contemporary admirers should anticipate Chardin's, are on the contrary sometimes suggestive of cold-cream and rice-powder. Yet Watteau greatly admired and coveted her work, famous artists praised her enthusiastically, and by ready election made her their peer. Evidently she deserved well at their hands. As evidently the color of her pastels, which constituted their charm and made the *cognoscenti* overlook her somewhat boneless draughtsmanship, has faded and in some cases vanished. Already in Rosalba's time the carmines disappeared and other tints paled. *We do not now see the same surfaces which charmed Watteau, the Flemish painters, and the members of the three great Art Academies.*

We are accustomed to-day to consider pastel permanent; some of it practically is, *vide* certain Latours and Chardins; but some of it evidently was not so; it is proved by contemporary complaints that the chemistry of the early manufacturers could not be trusted. Rosalba, it must not be forgotten, was an innovator, and the material she used was undoubtedly perfected later. Perhaps in gaining permanence pastel sacrificed something of its freshness. Mariette, after many praises (in the "*Abécédario*") of the master of the medium, Latour, added: "He has not in his color the freshness of Rosalba's." Modern art criticism is sceptical about changes in pigment, but there have been undoubted catastrophes even in the work of great colorists, and in the case of certain canvases we may count as a fellow victim with Tintoretto and Paolo, their humble fellow craftsman Rosalba.

Angioletta's assistance was hardly to be counted on when Rosalba lost Felicità; the manner of it would have served Goldoni for a gentle little comedy; "*La Putta Laboriosa,*" in which industry and virtue would be properly rewarded. With Prince Frederick Christian of Poland there came always to Rosalba's studio Councillor Hoffman, his governor, his manual of etiquette frivolous coffee-house folk called the punctilious, elderly courtier. His office was to keep the prince from tender entanglements and the Ridotto gambling-tables, and it was faithfully performed, but "*Quis custodiet custodes?*" Rosalba's pastels for the King were not to be hastily chosen, and in his long, frequent visits to the studio the rigorous guardian noticed the modest bearing of the pretty pupil Felicità. She was none of your trapesing Venetian minxes, but a demure, almost prim little person, at least in the presence of royalty. Councillor Hoffman looked, longed, and loved, but the nature of his mission forbade a declaration then and there. To be chosen as a mentor and to prove a Romeo was to invite laughter, and Hoffman was nothing if not dignified, so he covered his fire, or at least he fancied he did, and bore it smouldering back to Dresden with his intact charge, the prince. Once there he played not the lover but the prudent middle-aged suitor. He wrote Felicità condescendingly, paternally; she replied humbly and gratefully; then after eighteen months of a discreet correspondence, the position of miniature-painter to the Polish Court was offered to the astonished girl, to the delight of every one except the recipient of the honor. Rosalba was obliged to force her to accept, and no doubt the practically pious uncle, Dell' Agata, added his exhortations.

Thus admonished, Felicità wept, whimpered, and finally left Venice in May with her brother who was a priest, and in August, thanks to Faustina Hasse, who could not do enough for her dear Rosalba's *protégée*, Felicità was married to Councillor Hoffman with a dowry of a thousand ducats, and a casket of jewelry, the gift of the bridegroom, who generously left her the disposal of her pension, and sent a substantial sum of money to her family. Was Felicità's good fortune to be counted among the many miracles of the True Cross? Lacking Goldoni's dramatization, her adventure might serve at least for a moral tale of "The Industrious Apprentice."

Meantime the industry of another artist had been suddenly arrested; in 1742 Antonio Pellegrini had an apoplectic stroke followed by paralysis, and for ten months the poor *burattino* lay motionless, slowly dying. After his death Angela returned to her sister's house where her mother had died (1739) at an advanced age. A year later the sisters lost Crozat, who left his vast collections to be sold for the benefit of the poor.

Rosalba, in spite of her bereavements, in spite of her sixty years which she wore as if they were forty, valiantly kept at work; her vogue had lasted half a century, and still endured with no sign of abatement. The rise of a new school of pastel, the younger fame of the masters of the fragile medium, Mengs, Liotard, and the unique Latour, had left her popularity undiminished. Until 1746 orders were filled for Cardinal Albani, and the constant Augustus III, portraits of the Princess Trivulzi, Countesses Simoneta and Millini, and the English amateurs were painted, and another pastel sent to Mariette. Then the end came.

Twenty years before Rosalba had some grave trouble with her eyes; and the left one had never entirely recovered. Without warning, in 1744, it became blind; and the right eye was also threatened, but Rosalba, after consulting the celebrated oculist Righellini, promised the King of Poland to finish his series of "The Four Elements." These pastels, "Air" and "Water" were Rosalba's last work, for at the close of 1746 she became totally but not hopelessly blind. Righellini encouraged her to believe that when the two cataracts were mature an operation would restore the sight. For three years she was sustained by the hope of seeing, perhaps painting even, again.

In August, 1749, this hope was realized and her first impulse was to write to the devoted Mariette.

VENICE August 23, 1749.

Our mutual friend Zanetti has told you that for three years I have been deprived of my sight. I wish you to learn from my own hand that thanks to the Divine Goodness I have recovered it. I see but as one sees after an operation, that is to say very dimly. Even this is a blessing for one who has had the misfortune to become blind. When I was sightless I cared for nothing, now I want to see everything, and I am forbidden to do so until March when I am to undergo a second operation. So at present as I enjoy but little through my eyes, and I hope for but little in the future, let my ears at least give me the satisfaction of hearing your letters read, let me know the state of your health and that of the persons whom I had the honor of knowing in Paris. Assure them when you see them that in me they will always find a most devoted friend.

Will you present the assurance of my unalterable respect and esteem to M. le Comte de Caylus, and do you Monsieur please to accept the friendship and esteem of your very devoted, and very obliged servant,
ROSALBA CARRIERA.

The recovery of Rosalba's sight was only momentary, however, a last gleam of light before the eternal darkness fell, though she submitted to the further operation in March, and operations in 1750 exacted fortitude. Mariette, encouraged by Zanetti's hopes for her, sent her his book on engraved gems, begging her to turn over the leaves and glance at Bouchardon's engravings without tiring her eyes, and then to give the volume a place in her library. To this letter Rosalba replied with a kind of marmoreal calm.

VENICE January 2 1750.

Two months ago M. Zanetti sent me your letter of the 20th of August, through it I know how kind and gracious you are, and how much I owe you. Would to God that I were in a condition to see as you believe. I am entirely deprived of sight. I do not see any more than if I were plunged into the darkness of night. Imagine my regret at being unable to read your fine work. My sister, my family, and my friends are impatient to receive it, and I shall have only the pleasure of hearing it read. I can foresee the applause and praises that it will call forth.

I cannot then thank you enough. Nevertheless I am asking a new favor of you; it is to give me the means of corresponding at least in some way with you. Your fine talent honors your nation. . . .

ROSALBA CARRIERA.

P.S.—I have received your book and I pray God to grant you every happiness in the new year.

Rosalba, who had so loved light and color, spent the last seven years of her life in utter darkness. To possess a painter's vision, to live in Venice, and to become blind is to sound abysmal depths of misery. Her agony, her despair, the horror of the long hours of idleness naturally are unrecorded, for Rosalba's was a brave soul. She was also a true child of her century, with its distaste for heroics, its cheerful stoicism, its solid common sense, and its shrinking from violence and exaggeration. When like Joseph she retired into her chamber to weep, we may be sure she dried her eyes and washed her face before leaving it. One possessed of so much self-command and mental order surely soon found not only an endurable *modus vivendi*, but a sound philosophy to combat misfortune. Rosalba was a Christian and even to a rationalizing, Venetian Christian blindness was after all only a covered bridge leading from light to light; a few years of groping and stumbling and the Celestial Vision would be hers.

After Rosalba had abandoned all hope of ever seeing again, with Angela's assistance, she put her affairs in order and settled her business like one about to retire or to die. It was probably at this time that she collected and arranged the letters and journals now in the Laurentian Library at Florence, a wise way of living a happy past over again, and commemorating her own triumphs, for this bundle of old papers is her only monument. Meantime there were other consolations, pleasures even; repose with dignity in her own home surrounded by people who loved her. There was not only comfort but elegance in her little house; good books, several of them presents from their authors, on the walls a Watteau, a portrait of Maroulle by Coypel, Rosalba's own pastels: among them the Louis XV, the Isabella Pisani and her copy of Correggio's Magdalen. In its corner was the painted and gilded harpsichord and Rosalba's violin. There were luxuries: silver candelabra, part of the little store of plate mentioned in the painter's will; a snuff-box of lapis lazuli and gold; in its chiselled case a medal struck in Rosalba's honor, a gift of the Elector Palatine, and from generous Augustus III some bewitching little "Crinoline" groups in Meissen porcelain, dainty, artificial, and brilliant in color as Rosalba's own pastels. On fête-days came the Pedrottis and Pensos, the young cousins from Chioggia with bouquets and good wishes, and some little offering of snuff or chocolate to their illustrious kinswoman. They and her old friends were Rosalba's only visitors. Was it pride, the pride of a strong man who dreaded to be seen helpless and dependent that made her close her door to the travellers and sightseers who once crowded her studio? The poor fallen star would not be a gazing stock to curious tourists, to boys and their bear-leaders.

Would she have been happier if she had kept in closer touch with the great world she once painted? We know she welcomed her old friends to her hermitage; Zanetti came almost daily with news and books and letters, the Princesses Benedetta and Amalia of Modena were among her visitors during their exile, but to Venice she was known no more. Perhaps she was tired: she had seen so much frivolity, she had ministered to so much vanity, she had heard so much futile chatter; fundamentally serious-minded, with solid intellectual interests, preferring the society and conversation of cultivated people to any other social pleasure, she had spent a large part of her life in listening to gossip and personalities, to prattle about clothes and cosmetics. Were not her hours of silence grateful to her, interspersed as they were with music, with reading, and good talk?

Owing, however, to her seclusion and to the popular love of the tragic, a lugubrious legend grew up about the memory of Rosalba. It is still believed in Venice that she passed her old age in poverty, blind, mad, and neglected by those she had enriched. Unfortunately, her best friend Zanetti had given some color to the accepted story of her madness. Some few weeks before her death, Rosalba then eighty-two years old, became childish and lost her memory from an attack of what is known to-day as senile insanity. Zanetti was so horrified at the overthrow of a well-balanced, cultivated mind, which had been truly a kingdom to its possessor, that in his biography of Rosalba he gave undue importance to this short mental malady, which was a symptom of approaching dissolution, and should have had no part in any record of Rosalba's life. Her last will, made four months only before her death, is the best refutation of the melancholy tradition. This will is characterized by good sense and a judicious and loving care for the well-being of the family and friends she is so soon to leave; Rosalba began it by thanking God "who has made her rich through her painting," and then proceeds to the division of her property, some fifty thousand dollars. At a time when the purchasing power of money was far greater than to-day this was considered a handsome fortune.

Angela of course was her sister's heir; after Angela's death the property was to pass to the nearest relatives, the families of the Pedrotti and the Penso of Chioggia. Rosalba's plate and jewelry were divided among her friends, for she had always loved to give; even Felicità, whom she had not seen for many years, was left a legacy. Two thousand five hundred ducats were devoted to annual masses for Rosalba and her dead, to be celebrated by the priests of her family, and if it should become extinct, by the clergy of San Vio. Poor Rosalba took many precautions—are masses still said for that *anima gentile* and those she loved?

On April 15, 1757, Rosalba ceased to be blind. She was buried in San Vio beside her beloved Neneta. In more than fifty years afterwards the church was destroyed, the sisters' tomb profaned, and their ashes scattered. When, in 1865, Gaspare Biondetti bought the ruins of the little church and on its site built a small chapel which he dedicated to the saints Vito and Modesto, he set in its walls several stones bearing the names of those who had been buried in old San Vio. On a disk of colored marble under a cross the words "Rosalba Carriera, Pittrice," and the date 1757 may be read to-day.

The bloom of Rosalba's pastels like her own ashes has vanished, and it is largely a matter of history that it once existed. Something is left of her art: pose, arrangement, suavity of lines and types, but a rose pressed in a book is the wan spectre of a rose, and the Carriera collection in Dresden is only a *hortus siccus*. "*Pulvis et umbra sumus*," quoted Diderot apropos of pastel-portraits, and of Rosalba it may be said, "Here lies one whose name is writ in dust," but the dust was the down of the peach, the iridescence of the butterfly's wing, as lovely and as fugitive. If then Rosalba's painting has only

> ". . . vécu comme vivent les roses
> L'espace d'un matin,"

what remains of her pure and laborious life, of her hard-won triumphs? The rebirth of the miniature and the revival of pastel, for Augustin and Latour followed the way she frayed; a few delicate miniatures, a score of portraits, a sheaf of manuscripts, and a name that honors her native city and the art she practised.